TEENAGE MUTANT NINJA TURTLES

ENEMIES OLD, ENEMIES NEW · VOL. 2

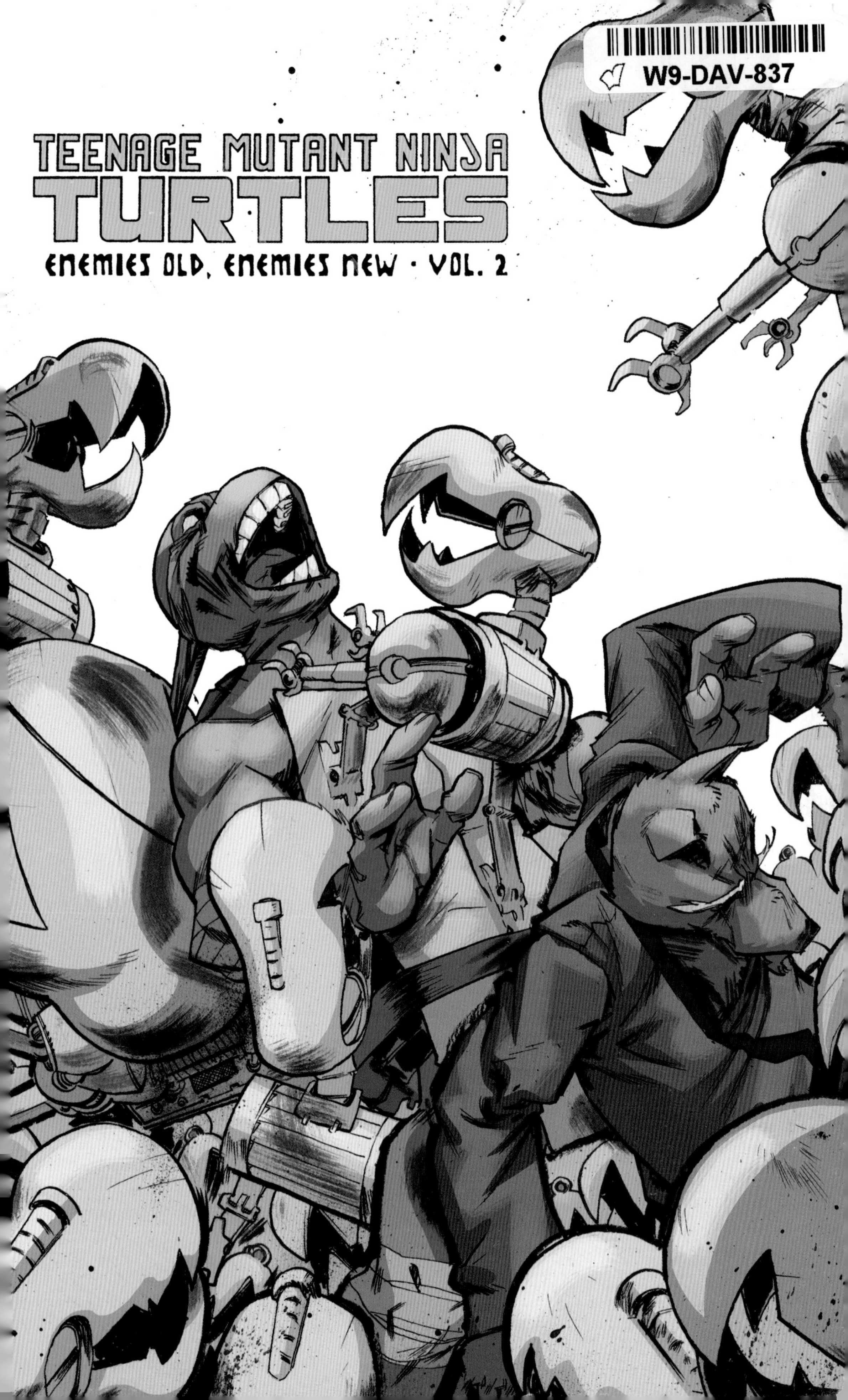

Story by Kevin Eastman & Tom Waltz · Script by Tom Waltz

Art by Dan Duncan & Mateus Santolouco (Issue #5 Feudal Japan)

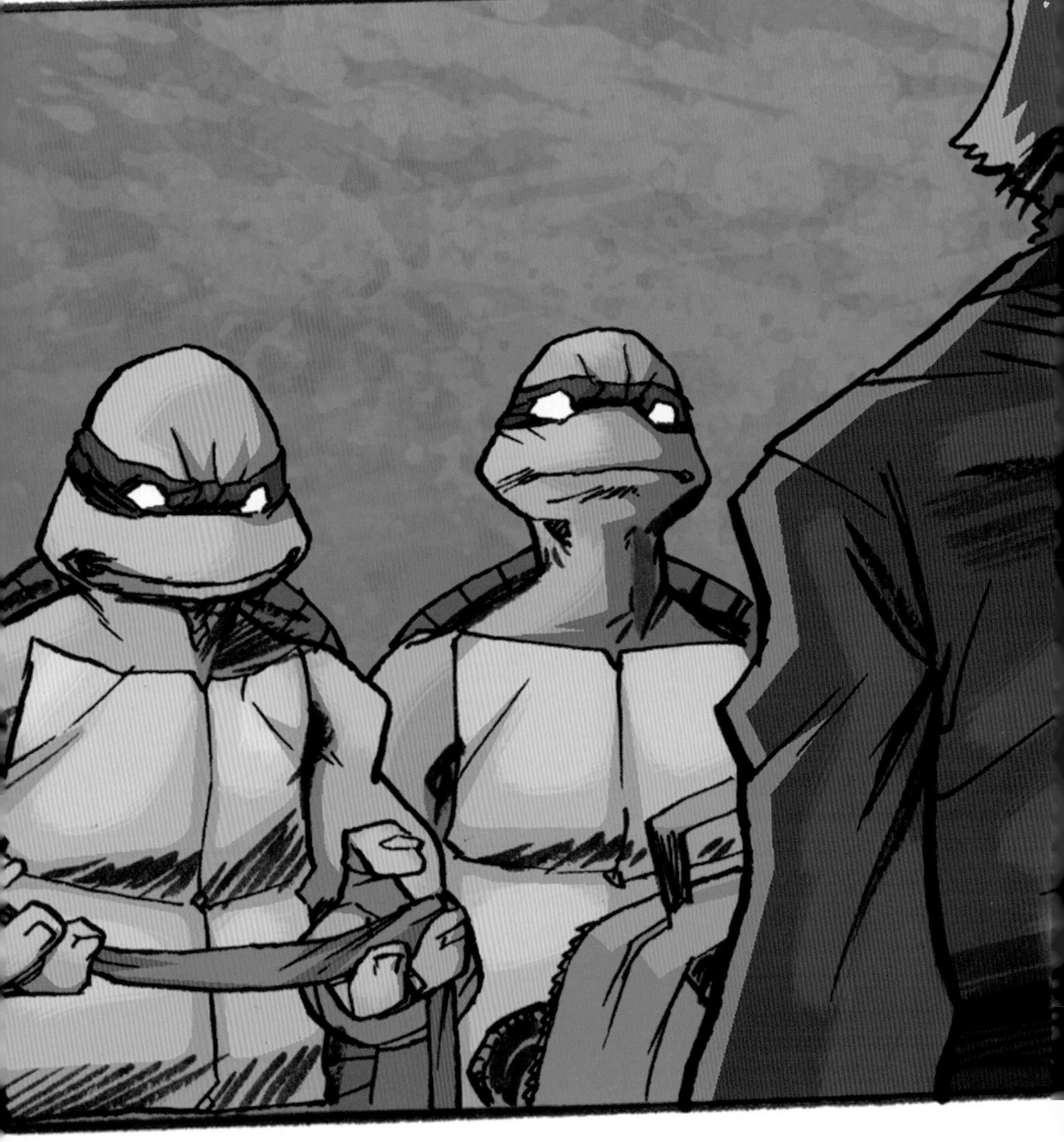

Special thanks to Joan Hilty, Linda Lee, and Kat van Dam for their invaluable assistance.

IDW founded by Ted Adams, Alex Garner, Kris Oprisko, and Robbie Robbins

ISBN: 978-1-61377-288-1

16 15 14 13 3 4 5 6

Ted Adams, CEO & Publisher
Greg Goldstein, President & COO
Robbie Robbins, EVP/Sr. Graphic Artist
Chris Ryall, Chief Creative Officer/Editor-in-Chief
Matthew Ruzicka, CPA, Chief Financial Officer
Alan Payne, VP of Sales

Become our fan on Facebook **facebook.com/idwpublishing**
Follow us on Twitter **@idwpublishing**
Check us out on YouTube **youtube.com/idwpublishing**
www.IDWPUBLISHING.com

Originally published as TEENAGE MUTANT NINJA TURTLES Issues #5–8.

Colors by Ronda Pattison • Letters by Shawn Lee
Series Edits by Bobby Curnow

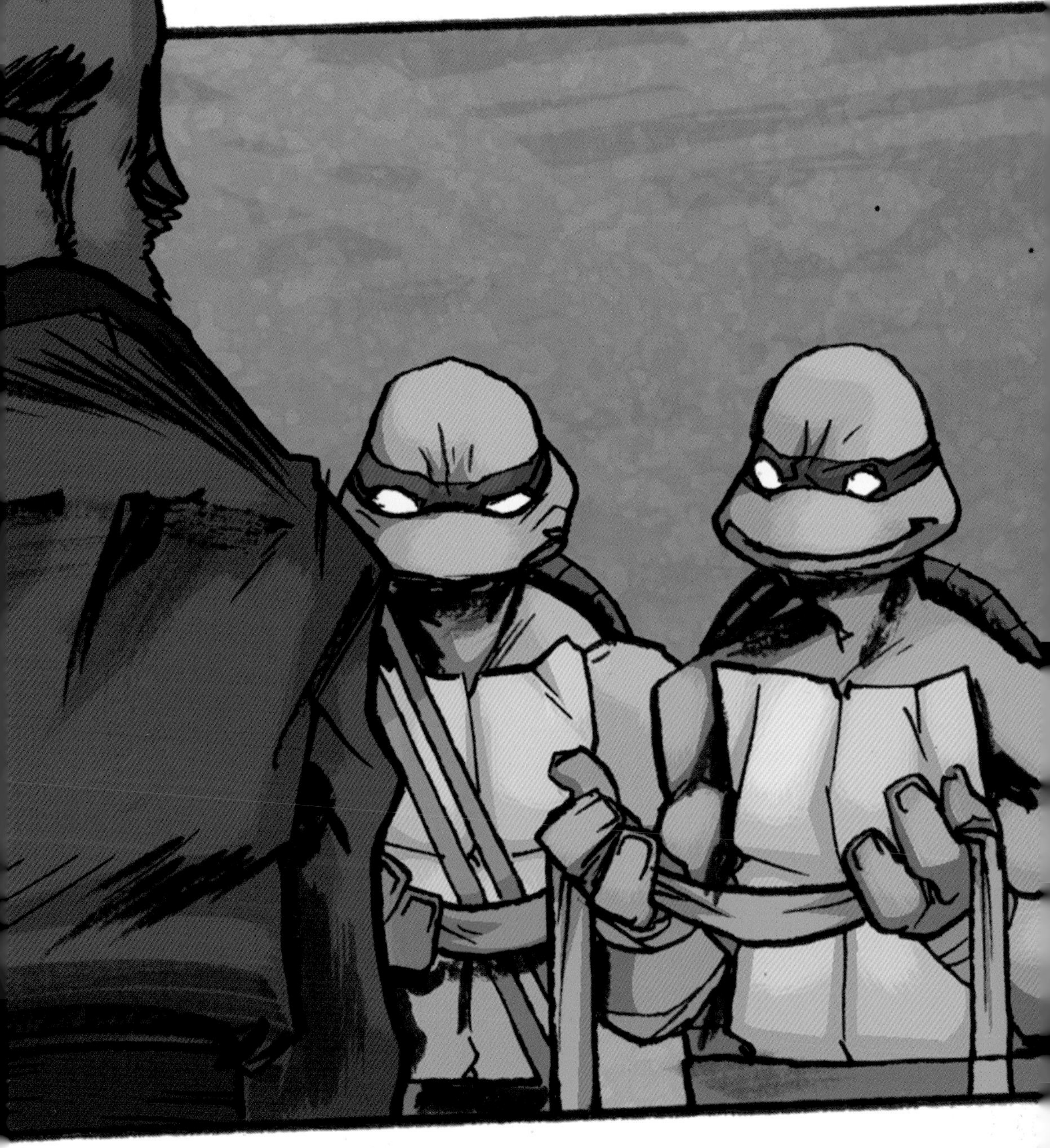

Collection Edits by Justin Eisinger & Alonzo Simon

Collection Design by Shawn Lee • Cover by Dan Duncan • Cover Colors by Ronda Pattison

Based on characters created by Peter Laird and Kevin Eastman

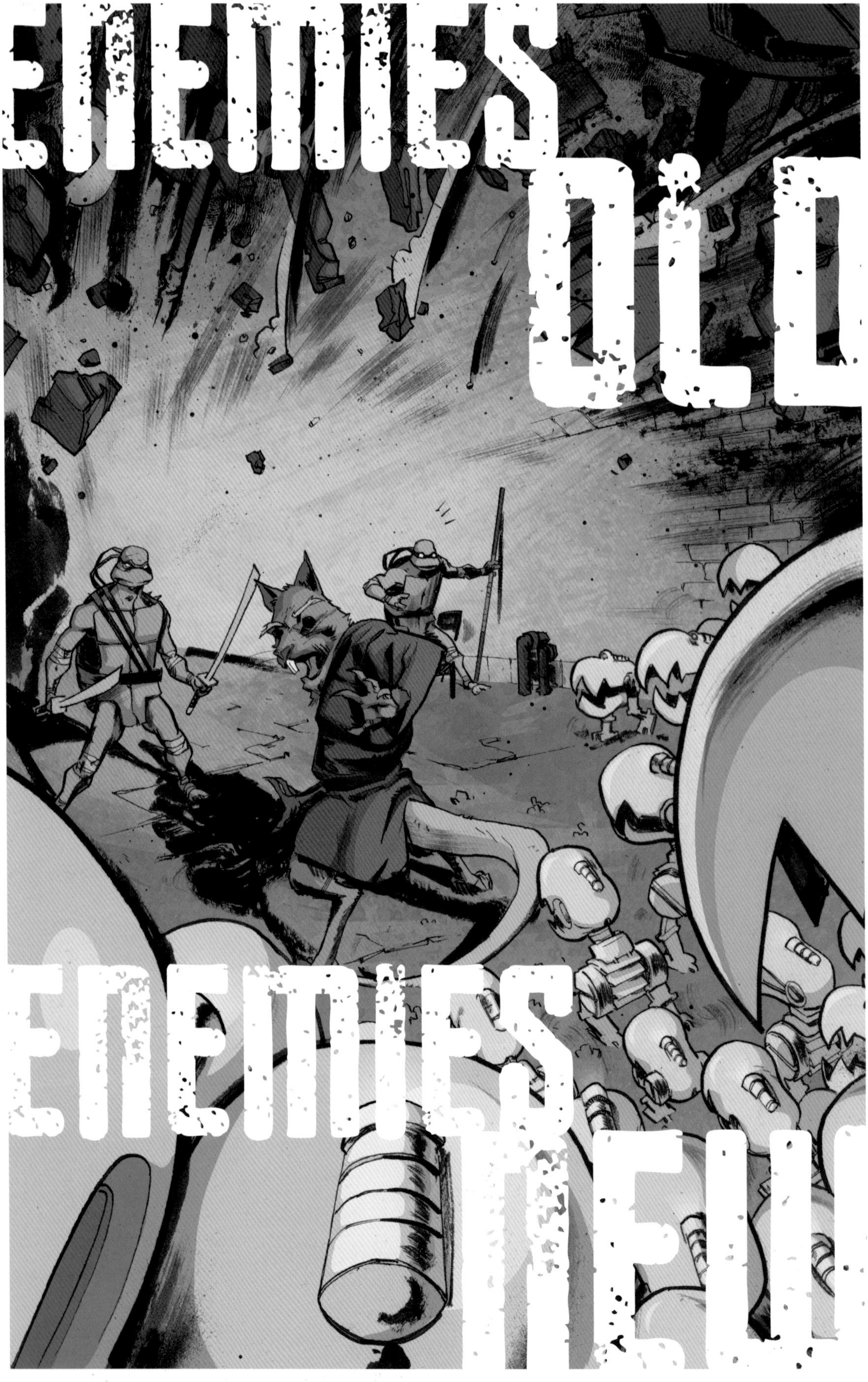
ENEMIES
OLD
ENEMIES

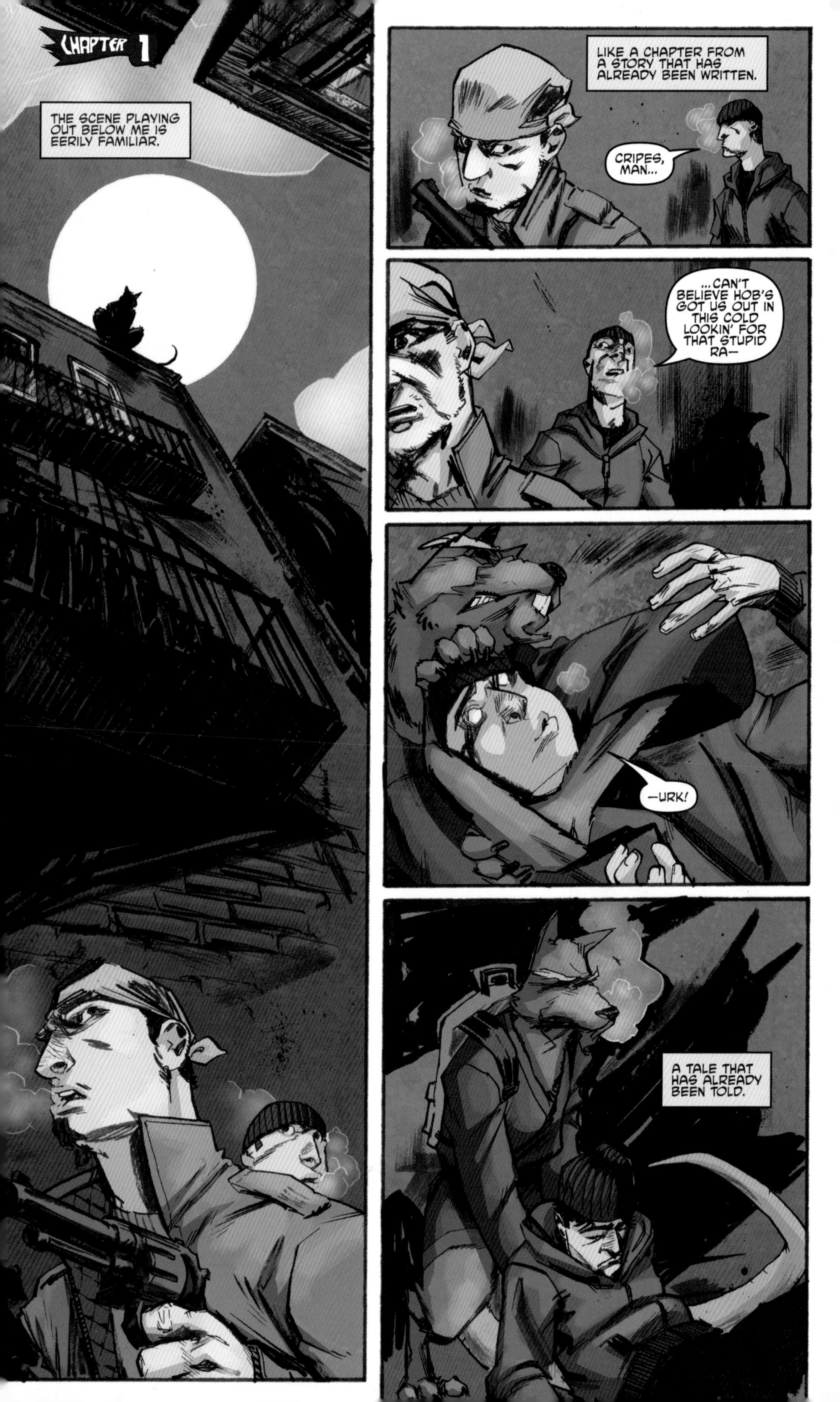
CHAPTER 1
THE SCENE PLAYING OUT BELOW ME IS EERILY FAMILIAR.
LIKE A CHAPTER FROM A STORY THAT HAS ALREADY BEEN WRITTEN.
CRIPES, MAN...
...CAN'T BELIEVE HOB'S GOT US OUT IN THIS COLD LOOKIN' FOR THAT STUPID RA—
—URK!
A TALE THAT HAS ALREADY BEEN TOLD.

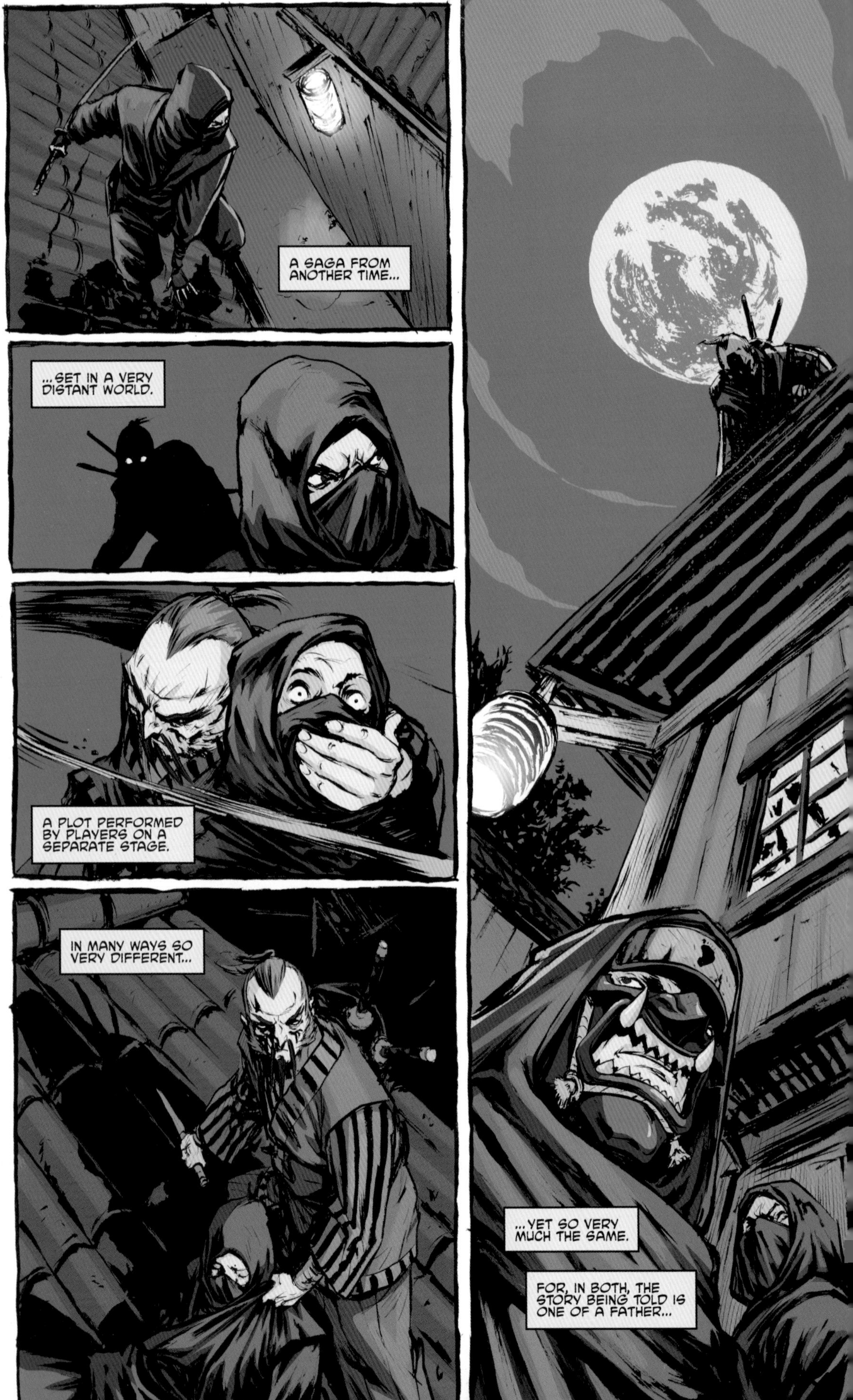
A SAGA FROM ANOTHER TIME...
...SET IN A VERY DISTANT WORLD.
A PLOT PERFORMED BY PLAYERS ON A SEPARATE STAGE.
IN MANY WAYS SO VERY DIFFERENT...
...YET SO VERY MUCH THE SAME.
FOR, IN BOTH, THE STORY BEING TOLD IS ONE OF A FATHER...

...AND HIS FOUR SONS.

WELL.... WHATCHA CHUMPS WAITIN' FOR?

RYAH!

GOT YA, BRO!

NOT TODAY, MIKEY!

WATCH YOUR BACK, RAPH!

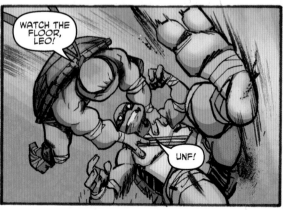

WATCH THE FLOOR, LEO!

UNF!

YOU READY TO MISS AGAIN, DONNIE?

HEH. COLOR ME IMPRESSED.

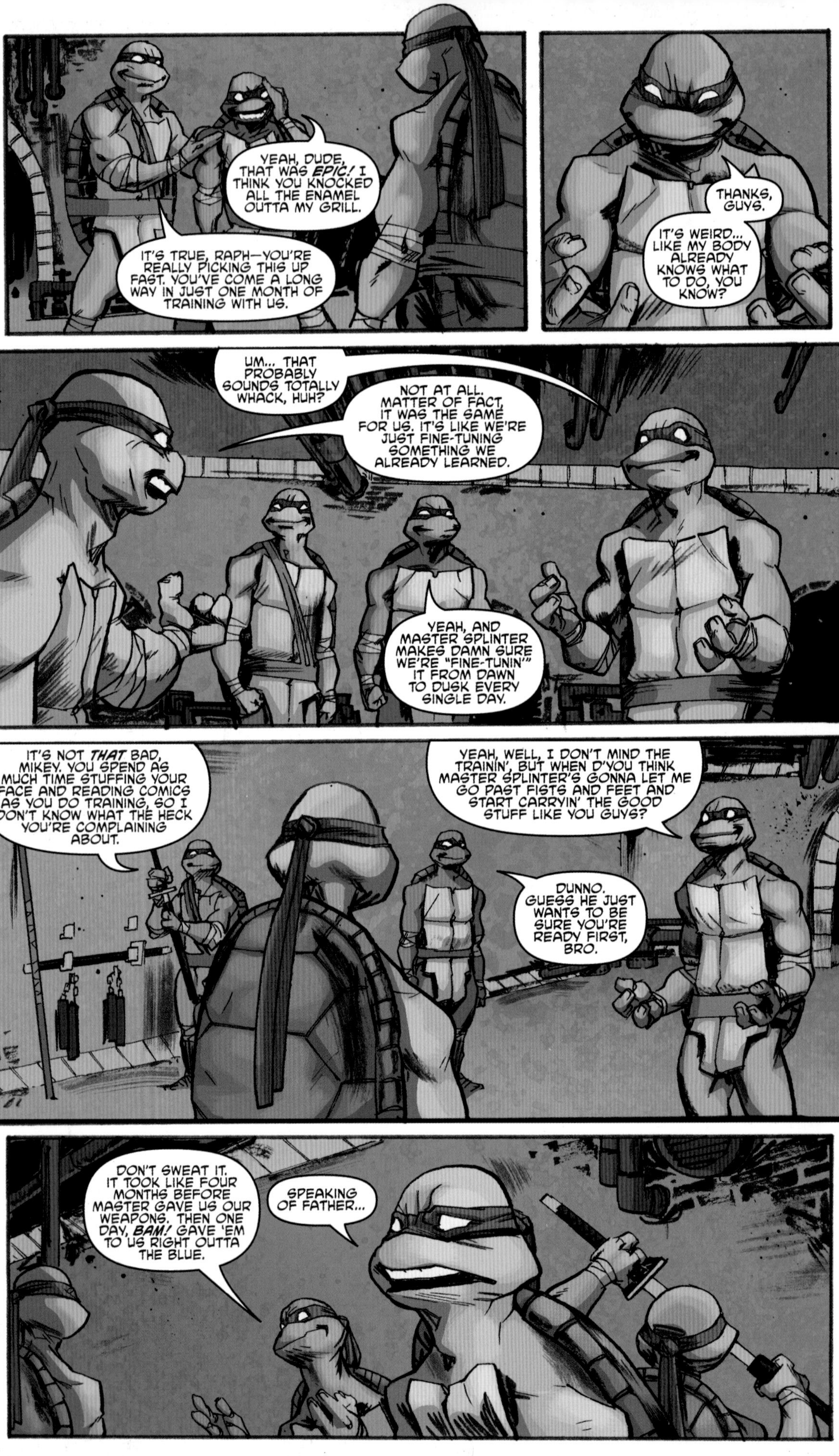
YEAH, DUDE, THAT WAS *EPIC!* I THINK YOU KNOCKED ALL THE ENAMEL OUTTA MY GRILL.
IT'S TRUE, RAPH—YOU'RE REALLY PICKING THIS UP FAST. YOU'VE COME A LONG WAY IN JUST ONE MONTH OF TRAINING WITH US.
THANKS, GUYS.
IT'S WEIRD... LIKE MY BODY ALREADY KNOWS WHAT TO DO, YOU KNOW?
UM... THAT PROBABLY SOUNDS TOTALLY WHACK, HUH?
NOT AT ALL. MATTER OF FACT, IT WAS THE SAME FOR US. IT'S LIKE WE'RE JUST FINE-TUNING SOMETHING WE ALREADY LEARNED.
YEAH, AND MASTER SPLINTER MAKES DAMN SURE WE'RE "FINE-TUNIN'" IT FROM DAWN TO DUSK EVERY SINGLE DAY.
IT'S NOT *THAT* BAD, MIKEY. YOU SPEND AS MUCH TIME STUFFING YOUR FACE AND READING COMICS AS YOU DO TRAINING, SO I DON'T KNOW WHAT THE HECK YOU'RE COMPLAINING ABOUT.
YEAH, WELL, I DON'T MIND THE TRAININ', BUT WHEN D'YOU THINK MASTER SPLINTER'S GONNA LET ME GO PAST FISTS AND FEET AND START CARRYIN' THE GOOD STUFF LIKE YOU GUYS?
DUNNO. GUESS HE JUST WANTS TO BE SURE YOU'RE READY FIRST, BRO.
DON'T SWEAT IT. IT TOOK LIKE FOUR MONTHS BEFORE MASTER GAVE US OUR WEAPONS. THEN ONE DAY, *BAM!* GAVE 'EM TO US RIGHT OUTTA THE BLUE.
SPEAKING OF FATHER...

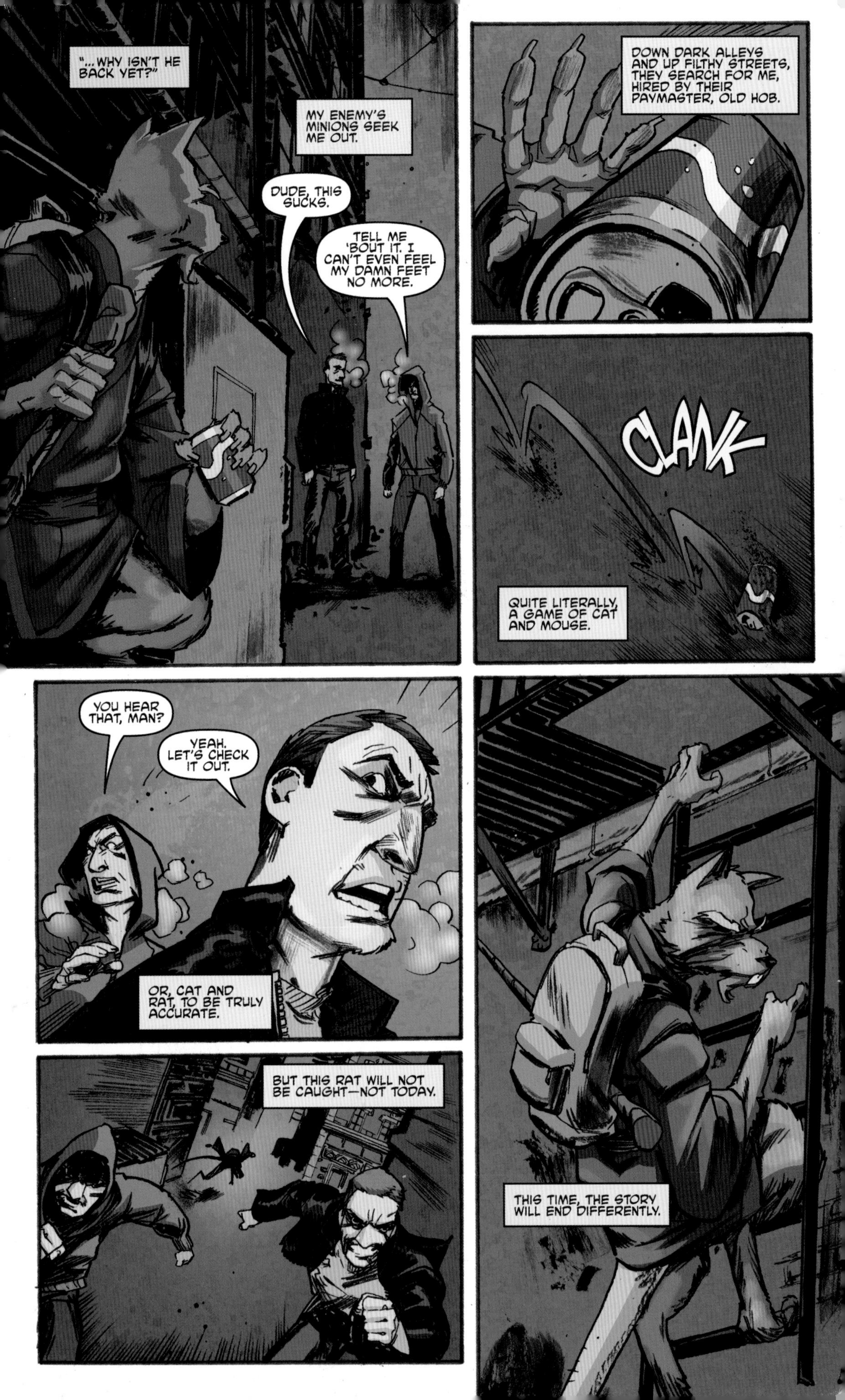
"...WHY ISN'T HE BACK YET?"
MY ENEMY'S MINIONS SEEK ME OUT.
DUDE, THIS SUCKS.
TELL ME 'BOUT IT. I CAN'T EVEN FEEL MY DAMN FEET NO MORE.
DOWN DARK ALLEYS AND UP FILTHY STREETS, THEY SEARCH FOR ME, HIRED BY THEIR PAYMASTER, OLD HOB.
CLANK
QUITE LITERALLY, A GAME OF CAT AND MOUSE.
YOU HEAR THAT, MAN?
YEAH. LET'S CHECK IT OUT.
OR, CAT AND RAT, TO BE TRULY ACCURATE.
BUT THIS RAT WILL NOT BE CAUGHT—NOT TODAY.
THIS TIME, THE STORY WILL END DIFFERENTLY.

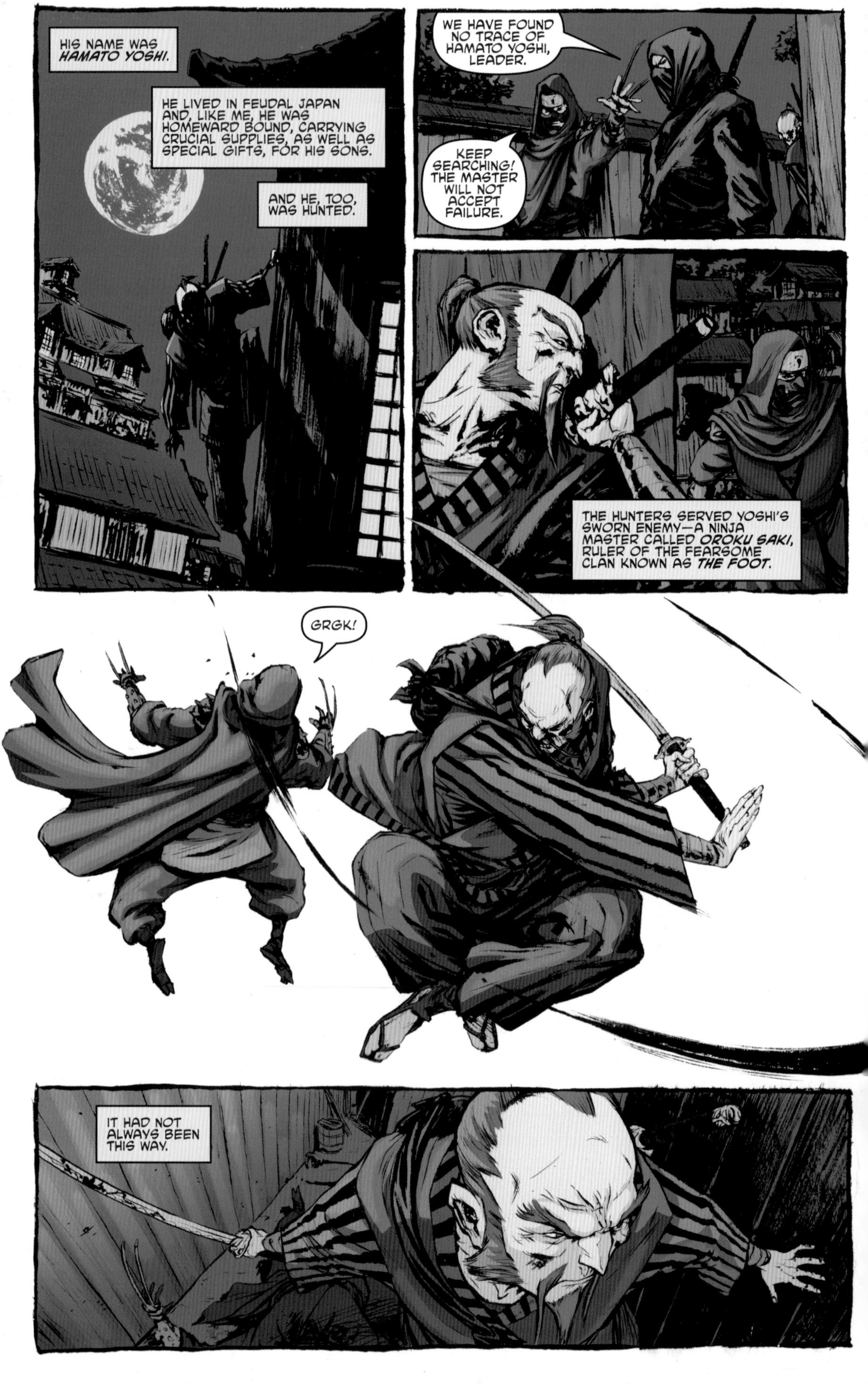

HIS NAME WAS *HAMATO YOSHI*.
HE LIVED IN FEUDAL JAPAN AND, LIKE ME, HE WAS HOMEWARD BOUND, CARRYING CRUCIAL SUPPLIES, AS WELL AS SPECIAL GIFTS, FOR HIS SONS.
AND HE, TOO, WAS HUNTED.
WE HAVE FOUND NO TRACE OF HAMATO YOSHI, LEADER.
KEEP SEARCHING! THE MASTER WILL NOT ACCEPT FAILURE.
THE HUNTERS SERVED YOSHI'S SWORN ENEMY—A NINJA MASTER CALLED *OROKU SAKI*, RULER OF THE FEARSOME CLAN KNOWN AS ***THE FOOT***.
GRGK!
IT HAD NOT ALWAYS BEEN THIS WAY.

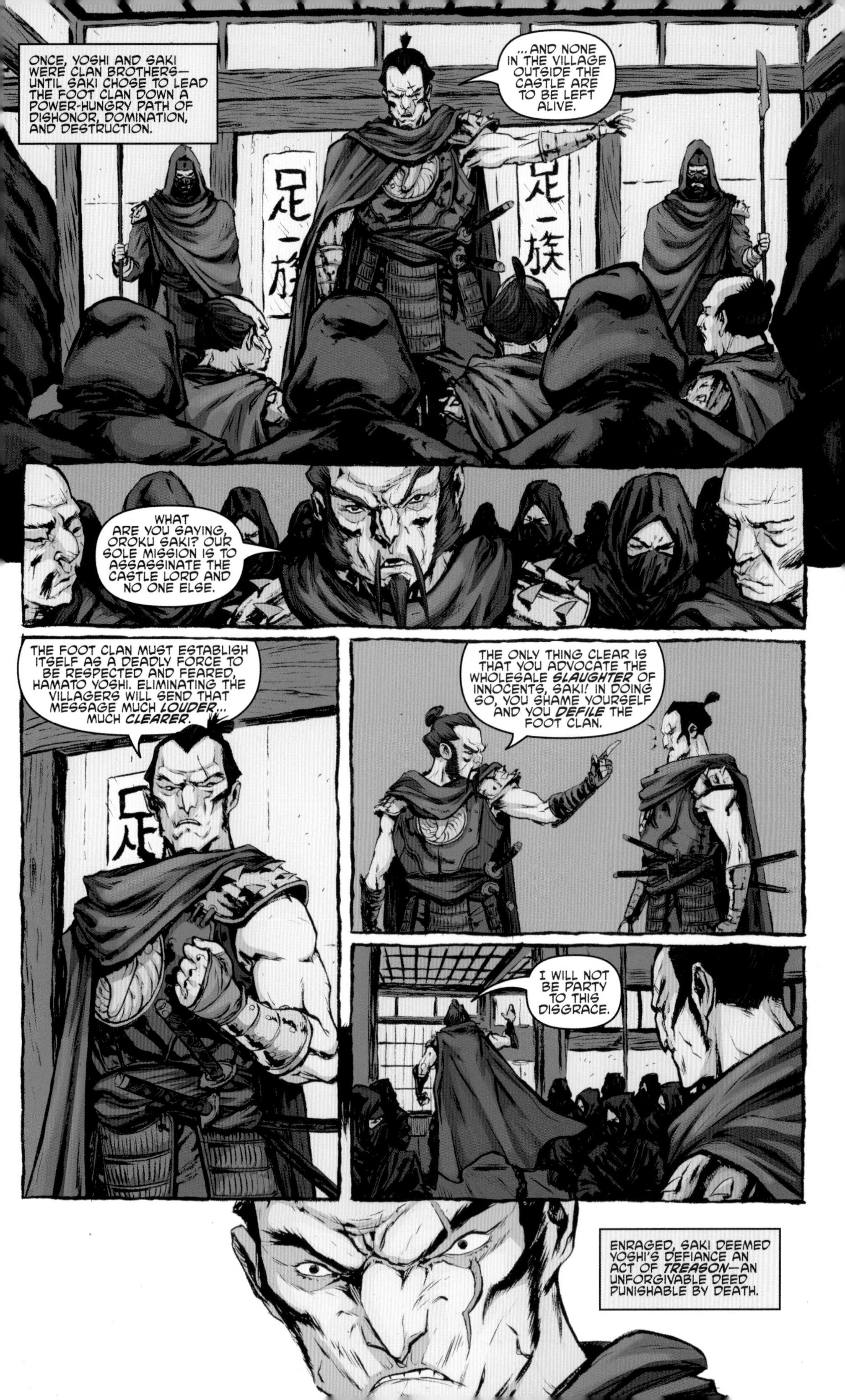
ONCE, YOSHI AND SAKI WERE CLAN BROTHERS—UNTIL SAKI CHOSE TO LEAD THE FOOT CLAN DOWN A POWER-HUNGRY PATH OF DISHONOR, DOMINATION, AND DESTRUCTION.
...AND NONE IN THE VILLAGE OUTSIDE THE CASTLE ARE TO BE LEFT ALIVE.
足一族
足一族
WHAT ARE YOU SAYING, OROKU SAKI? OUR SOLE MISSION IS TO ASSASSINATE THE CASTLE LORD AND NO ONE ELSE.
THE FOOT CLAN MUST ESTABLISH ITSELF AS A DEADLY FORCE TO BE RESPECTED AND FEARED, HAMATO YOSHI. ELIMINATING THE VILLAGERS WILL SEND THAT MESSAGE MUCH LOUDER... MUCH CLEARER.
THE ONLY THING CLEAR IS THAT YOU ADVOCATE THE WHOLESALE SLAUGHTER OF INNOCENTS, SAKI! IN DOING SO, YOU SHAME YOURSELF AND YOU DEFILE THE FOOT CLAN.
I WILL NOT BE PARTY TO THIS DISGRACE.
ENRAGED, SAKI DEEMED YOSHI'S DEFIANCE AN ACT OF TREASON—AN UNFORGIVABLE DEED PUNISHABLE BY DEATH.

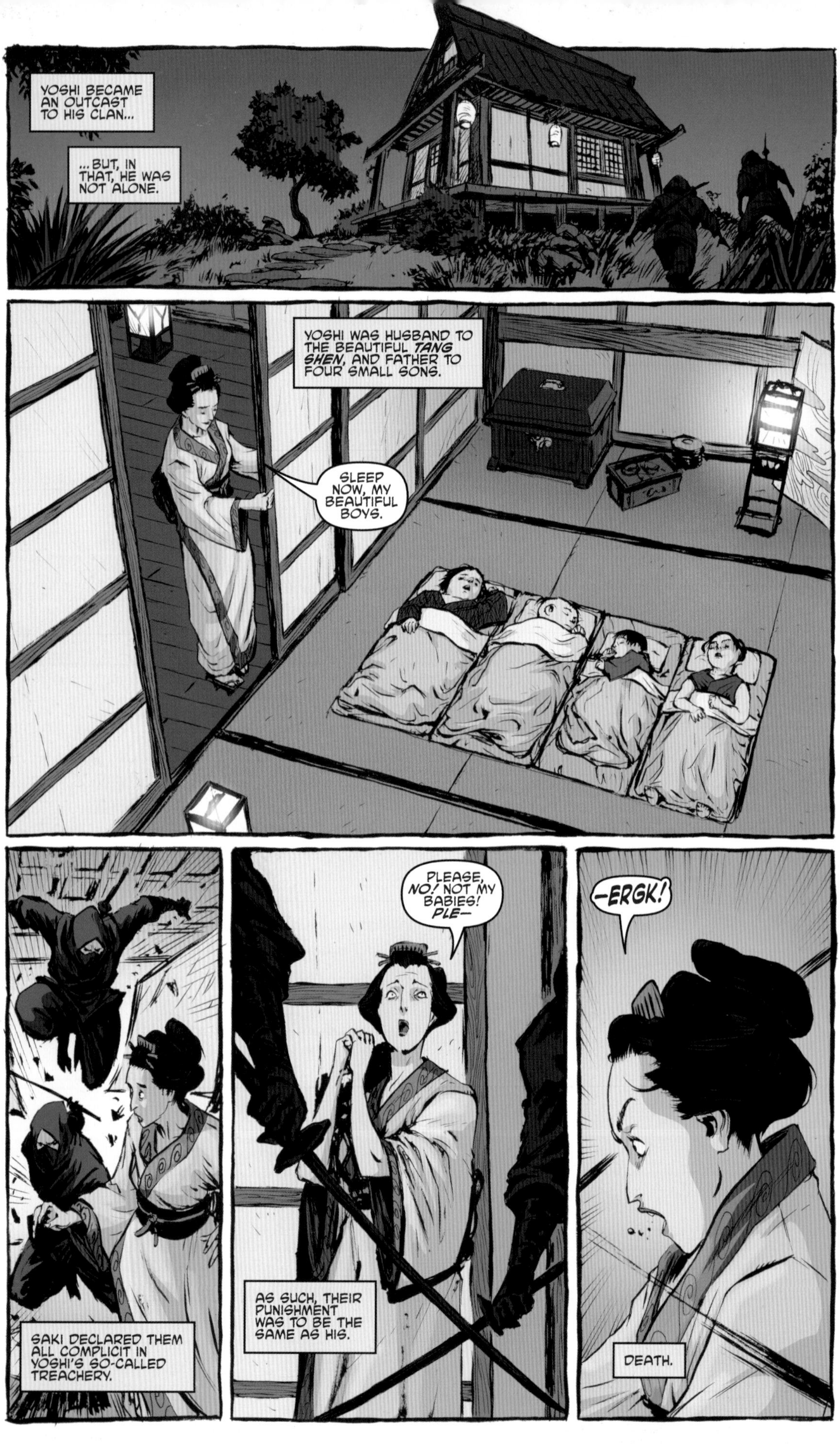
YOSHI BECAME AN OUTCAST TO HIS CLAN...
...BUT, IN THAT, HE WAS NOT ALONE.
YOSHI WAS HUSBAND TO THE BEAUTIFUL *TANG SHEN*, AND FATHER TO FOUR SMALL SONS.
SLEEP NOW, MY BEAUTIFUL BOYS.
SAKI DECLARED THEM ALL COMPLICIT IN YOSHI'S SO-CALLED TREACHERY.
PLEASE, *NO!* NOT MY BABIES! *PLE—*
AS SUCH, THEIR PUNISHMENT WAS TO BE THE SAME AS HIS.
—ERGK!
DEATH.

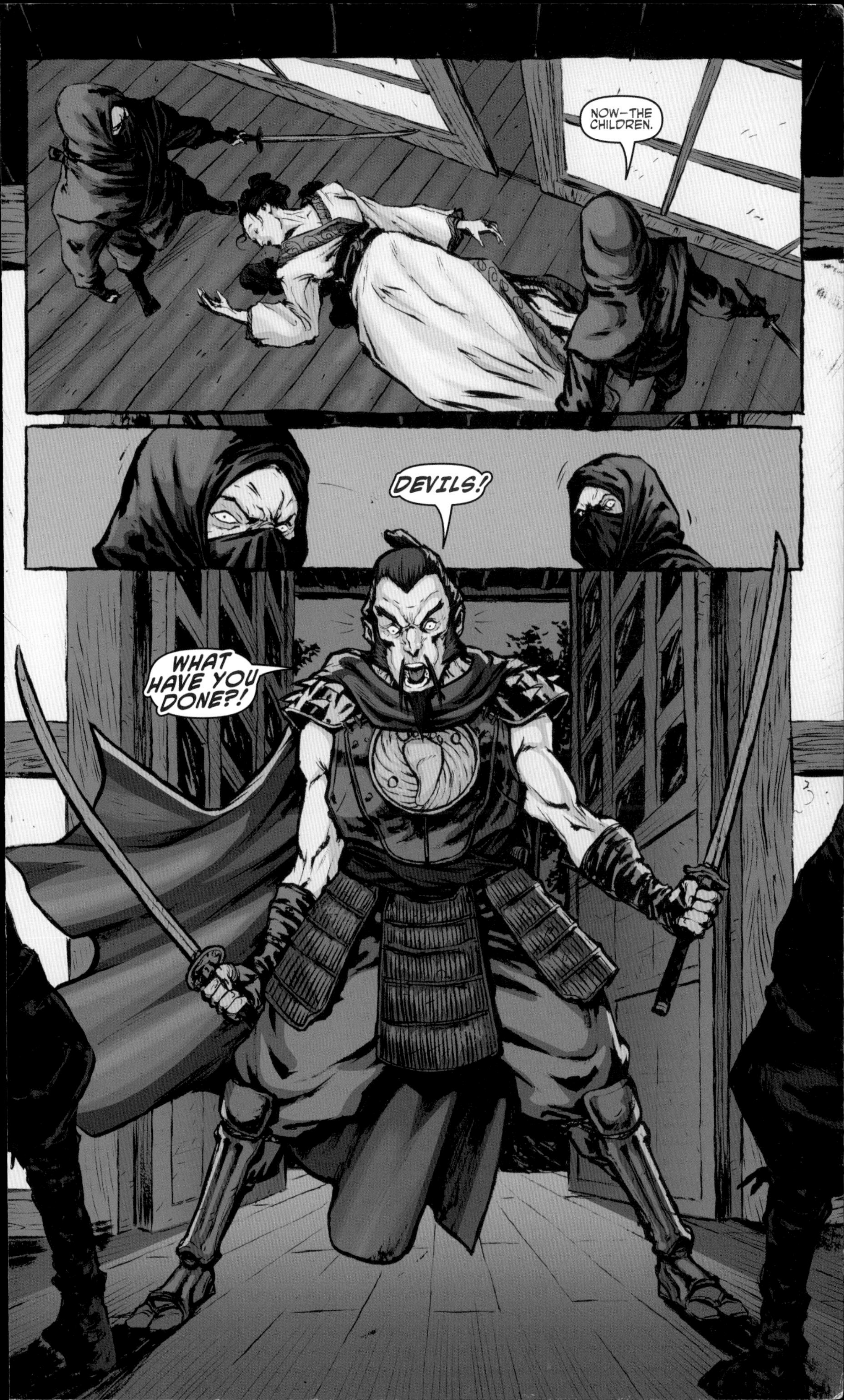
NOW—THE CHILDREN.
DEVILS!
WHAT HAVE YOU DONE?!

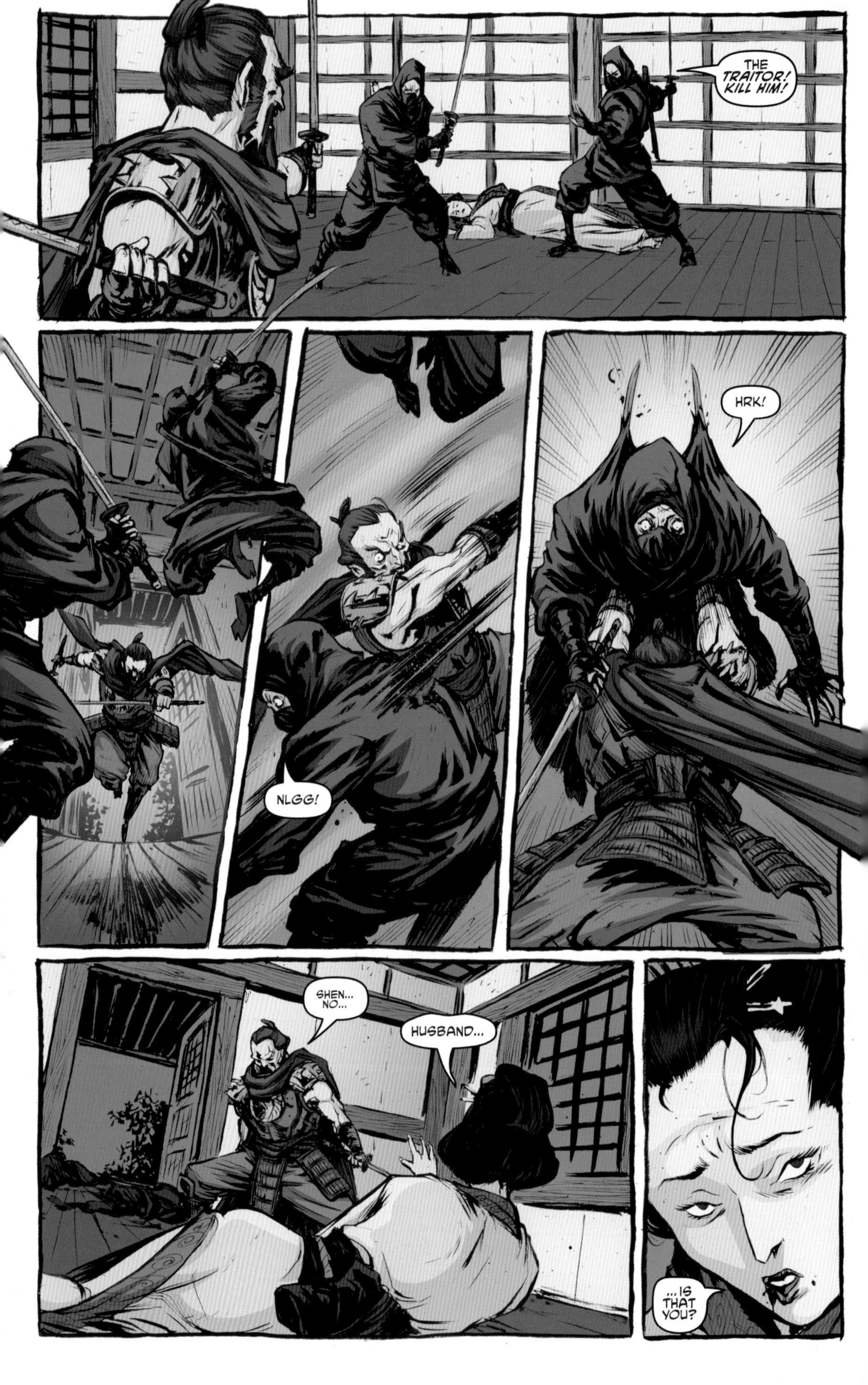
THE TRAITOR! KILL HIM!
NLGG!
HRK!
SHEN... NO...
HUSBAND...
...IS THAT YOU?

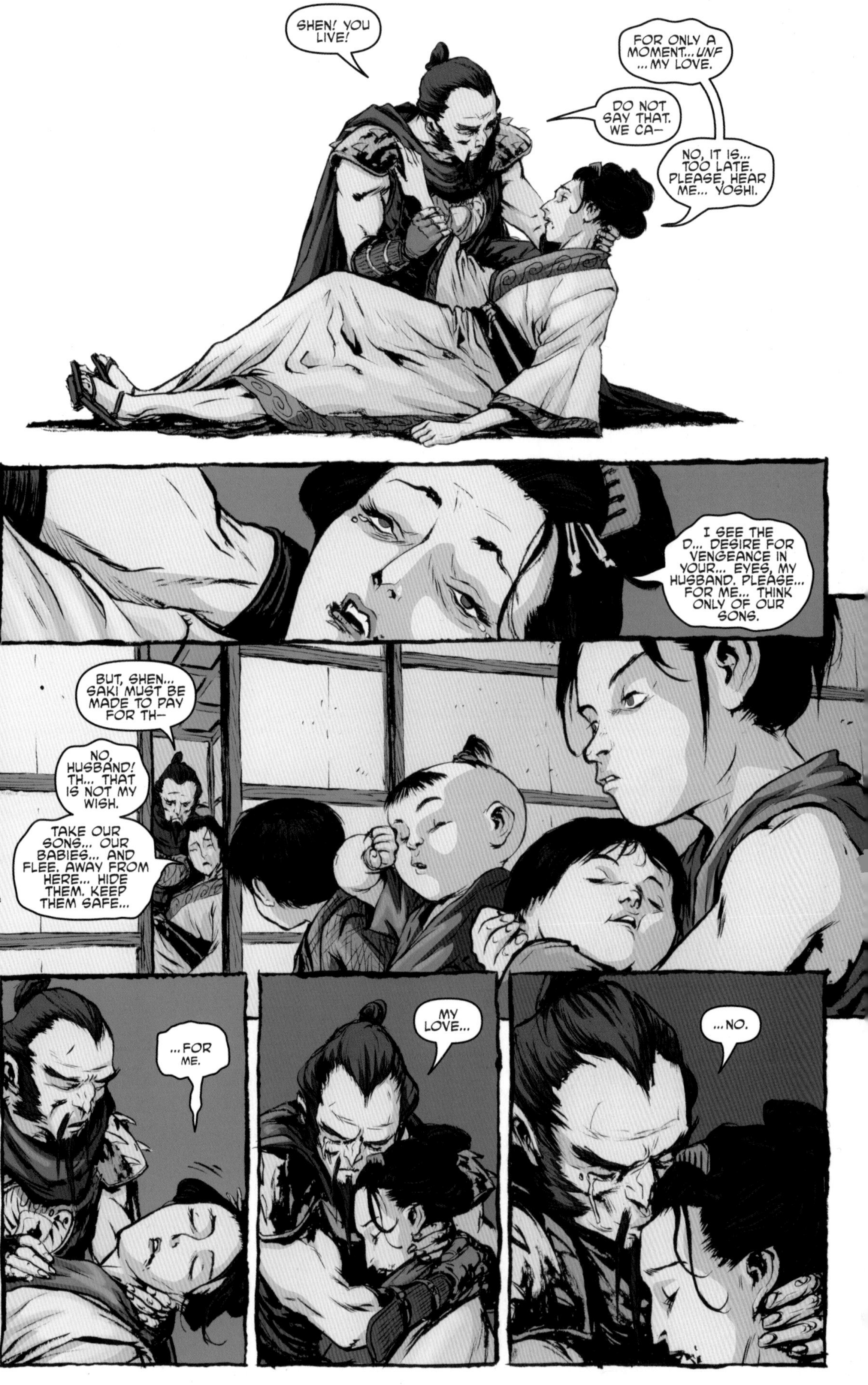
SHEN! YOU LIVE!
FOR ONLY A MOMENT...UNF ...MY LOVE.
DO NOT SAY THAT. WE CA—
NO, IT IS... TOO LATE. PLEASE, HEAR ME... YOSHI.
I SEE THE D... DESIRE FOR VENGEANCE IN YOUR... EYES, MY HUSBAND. PLEASE... FOR ME... THINK ONLY OF OUR SONS.
BUT, SHEN... SAKI MUST BE MADE TO PAY FOR TH—
NO, HUSBAND! TH... THAT IS NOT MY WISH.
TAKE OUR SONS... OUR BABIES... AND FLEE. AWAY FROM HERE... HIDE THEM. KEEP THEM SAFE...
...FOR ME.
MY LOVE...
...NO.

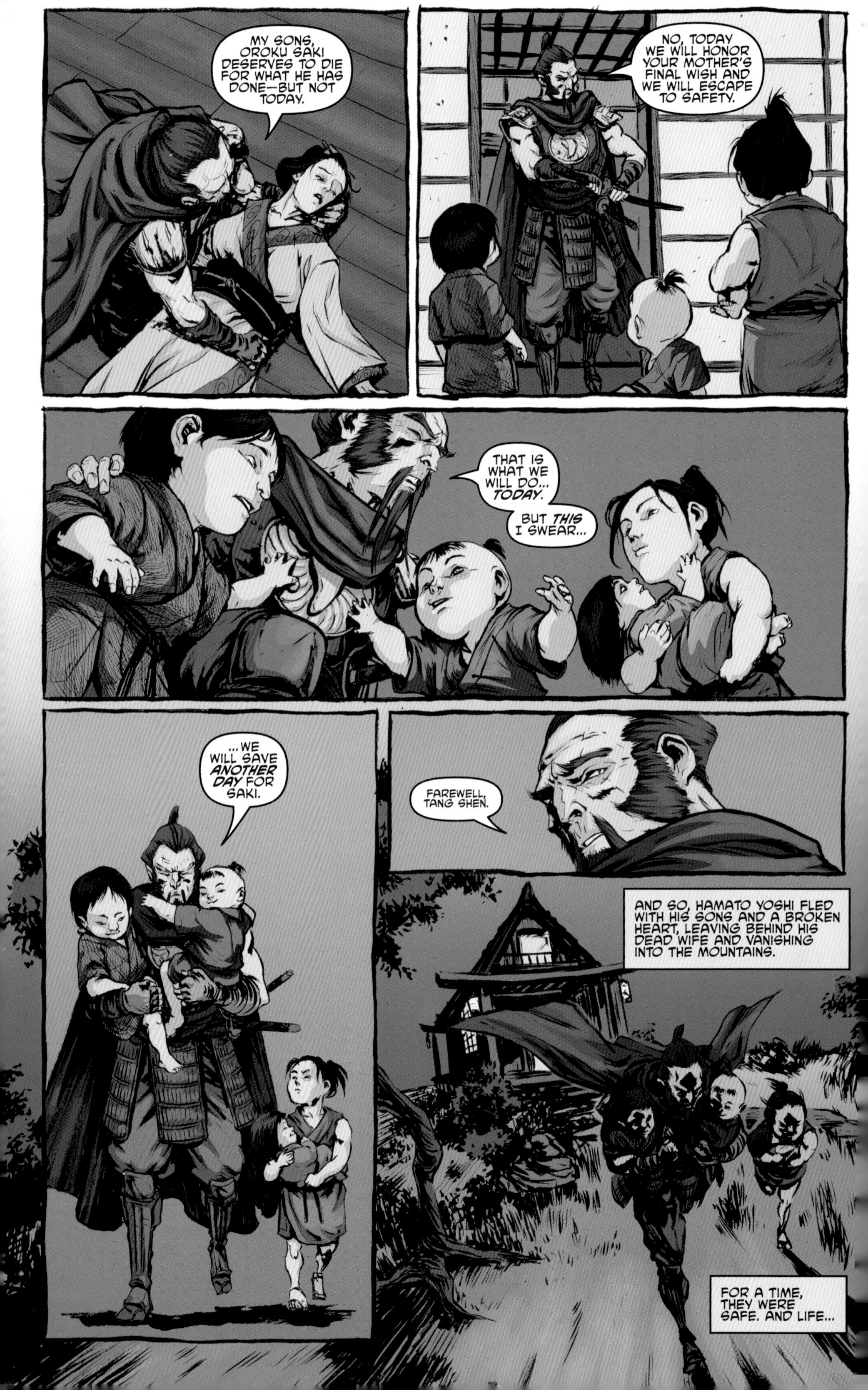

MY SONS, OROKU SAKI DESERVES TO DIE FOR WHAT HE HAS DONE—BUT NOT TODAY.
NO, TODAY WE WILL HONOR YOUR MOTHER'S FINAL WISH AND WE WILL ESCAPE TO SAFETY.
THAT IS WHAT WE WILL DO... TODAY.
BUT THIS I SWEAR...
...WE WILL SAVE ANOTHER DAY FOR SAKI.
FAREWELL, TANG SHEN.
AND SO, HAMATO YOSHI FLED WITH HIS SONS AND A BROKEN HEART, LEAVING BEHIND HIS DEAD WIFE AND VANISHING INTO THE MOUNTAINS.
FOR A TIME, THEY WERE SAFE. AND LIFE...

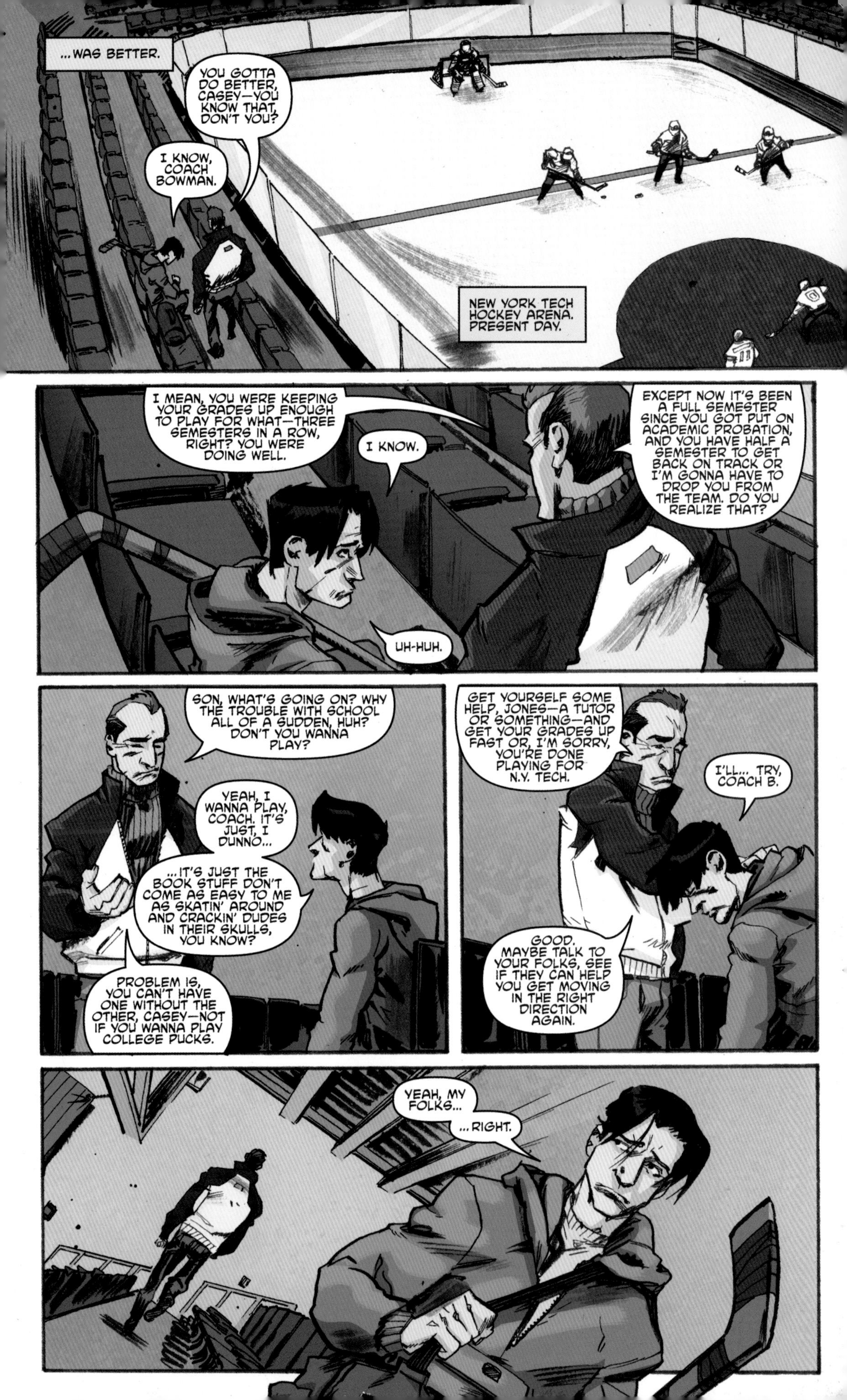
...WAS BETTER.
YOU GOTTA DO BETTER, CASEY—YOU KNOW THAT, DON'T YOU?
I KNOW, COACH BOWMAN.
NEW YORK TECH HOCKEY ARENA. PRESENT DAY.
I MEAN, YOU WERE KEEPING YOUR GRADES UP ENOUGH TO PLAY FOR WHAT—THREE SEMESTERS IN A ROW, RIGHT? YOU WERE DOING WELL.
I KNOW.
EXCEPT NOW IT'S BEEN A FULL SEMESTER SINCE YOU GOT PUT ON ACADEMIC PROBATION, AND YOU HAVE HALF A SEMESTER TO GET BACK ON TRACK OR I'M GONNA HAVE TO DROP YOU FROM THE TEAM. DO YOU REALIZE THAT?
UH-HUH.
SON, WHAT'S GOING ON? WHY THE TROUBLE WITH SCHOOL ALL OF A SUDDEN, HUH? DON'T YOU WANNA PLAY?
YEAH, I WANNA PLAY, COACH. IT'S JUST, I DUNNO...
...IT'S JUST THE BOOK STUFF DON'T COME AS EASY TO ME AS SKATIN' AROUND AND CRACKIN' DUDES IN THEIR SKULLS, YOU KNOW?
PROBLEM IS, YOU CAN'T HAVE ONE WITHOUT THE OTHER, CASEY—NOT IF YOU WANNA PLAY COLLEGE PUCKS.
GET YOURSELF SOME HELP, JONES—A TUTOR OR SOMETHING—AND GET YOUR GRADES UP FAST OR, I'M SORRY, YOU'RE DONE PLAYING FOR N.Y. TECH.
I'LL... TRY, COACH B.
GOOD. MAYBE TALK TO YOUR FOLKS, SEE IF THEY CAN HELP YOU GET MOVING IN THE RIGHT DIRECTION AGAIN.
YEAH, MY FOLKS...
...RIGHT.

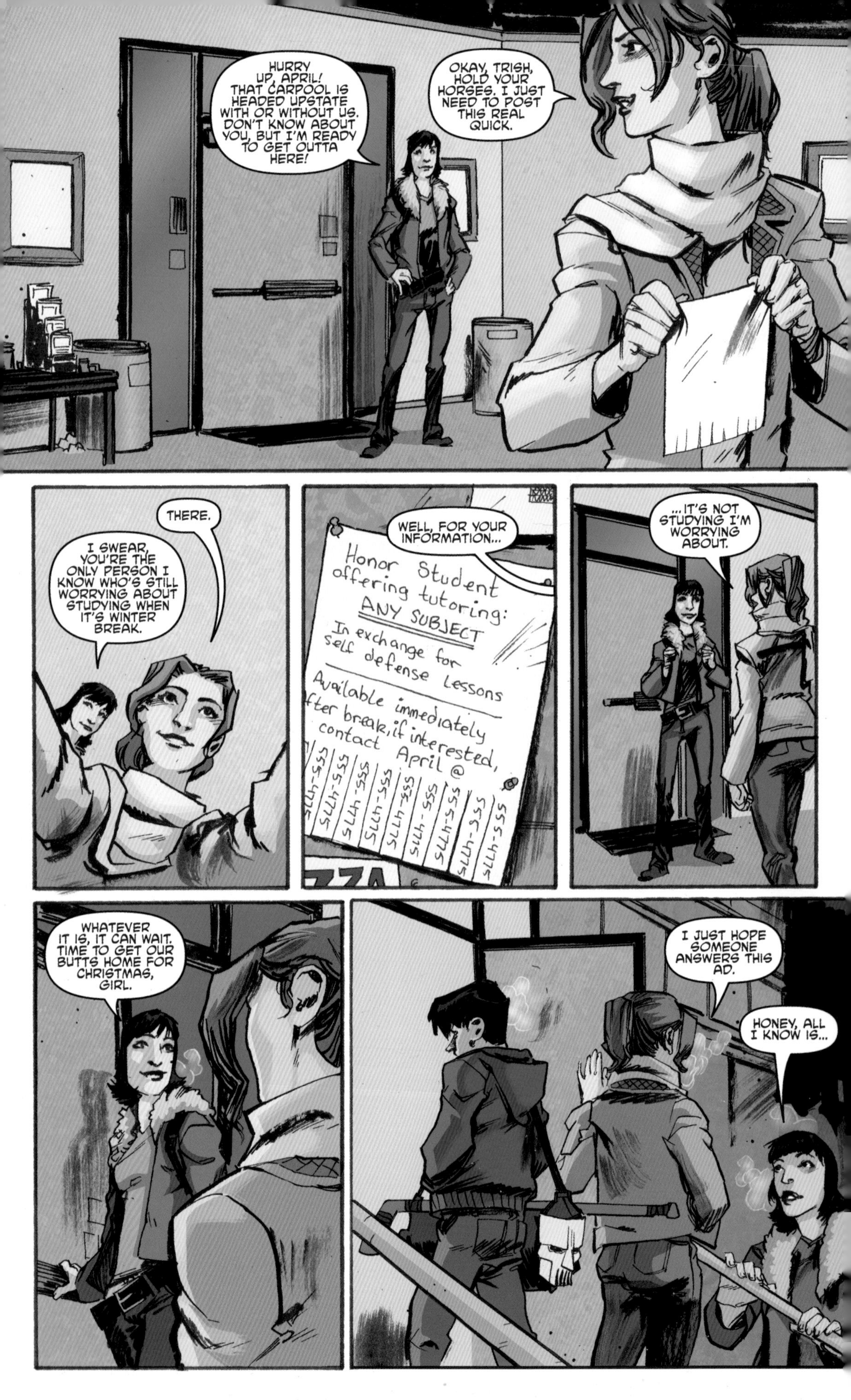
HURRY UP, APRIL! THAT CARPOOL IS HEADED UPSTATE WITH OR WITHOUT US. DON'T KNOW ABOUT YOU, BUT I'M READY TO GET OUTTA HERE!
OKAY, TRISH, HOLD YOUR HORSES. I JUST NEED TO POST THIS REAL QUICK.
THERE.
I SWEAR, YOU'RE THE ONLY PERSON I KNOW WHO'S STILL WORRYING ABOUT STUDYING WHEN IT'S WINTER BREAK.
WELL, FOR YOUR INFORMATION...
Honor Student offering tutoring: ANY SUBJECT
In exchange for self defense Lessons
Available immediately after break, if interested, contact April @
555-4775
...IT'S NOT STUDYING I'M WORRYING ABOUT.
WHATEVER IT IS, IT CAN WAIT. TIME TO GET OUR BUTTS HOME FOR CHRISTMAS, GIRL.
I JUST HOPE SOMEONE ANSWERS THIS AD.
HONEY, ALL I KNOW IS...

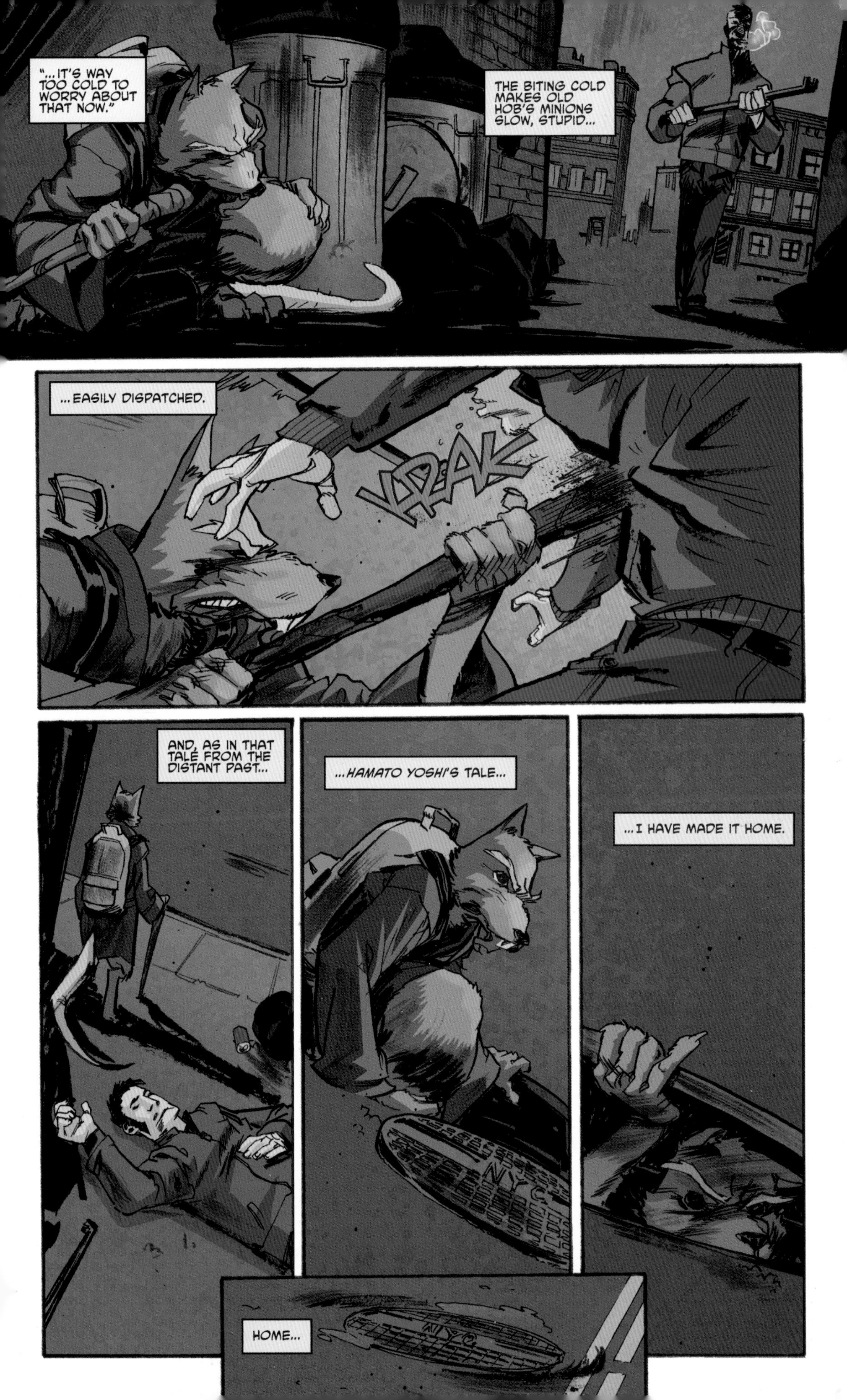
"...IT'S WAY TOO COLD TO WORRY ABOUT THAT NOW."
THE BITING COLD MAKES OLD HOB'S MINIONS SLOW, STUPID...
...EASILY DISPATCHED.
KRAK
AND, AS IN THAT TALE FROM THE DISTANT PAST...
...HAMATO YOSHI'S TALE...
...I HAVE MADE IT HOME.
HOME...

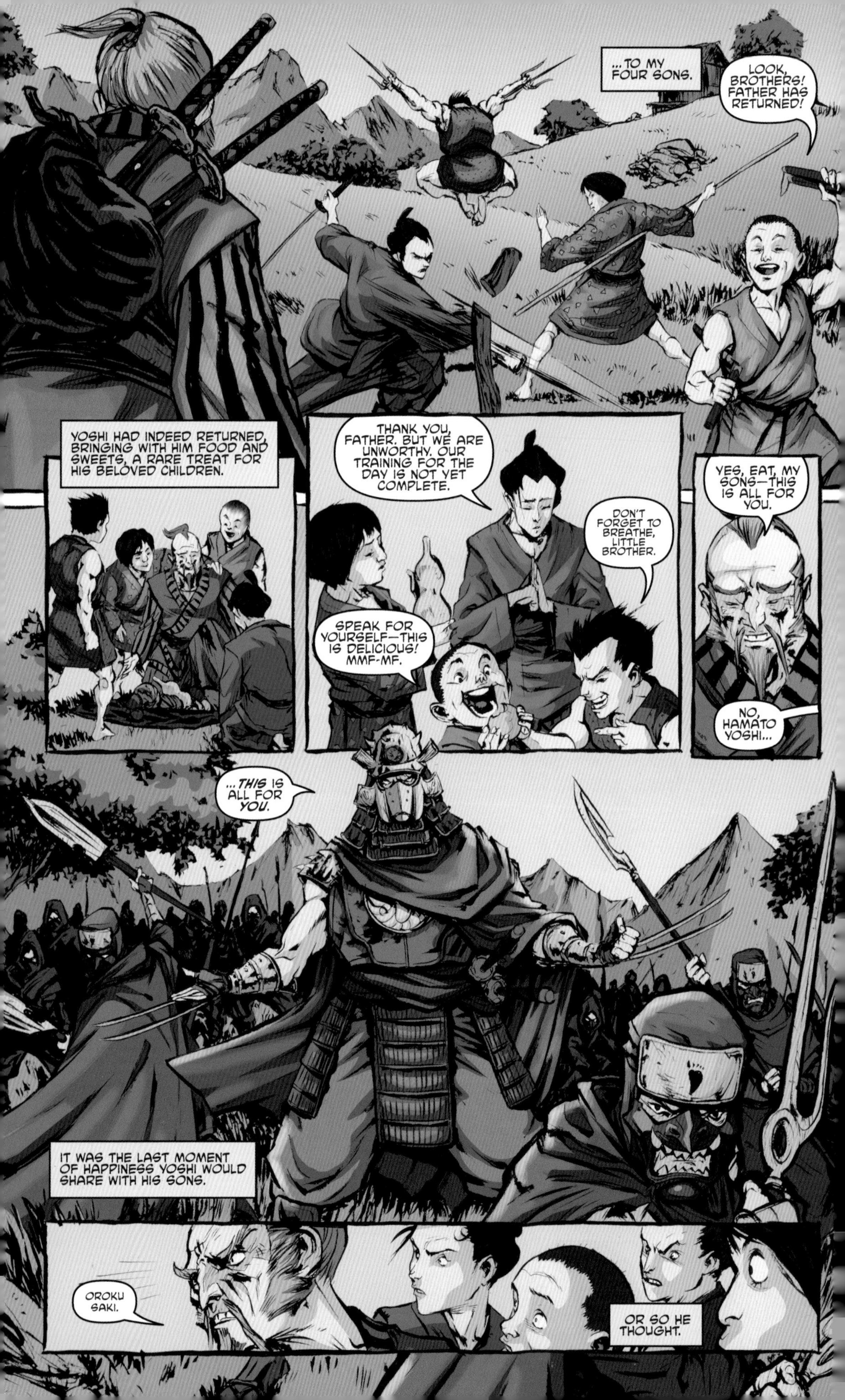
...TO MY FOUR SONS.
LOOK, BROTHERS! FATHER HAS RETURNED!
YOSHI HAD INDEED RETURNED, BRINGING WITH HIM FOOD AND SWEETS, A RARE TREAT FOR HIS BELOVED CHILDREN.
THANK YOU, FATHER. BUT WE ARE UNWORTHY. OUR TRAINING FOR THE DAY IS NOT YET COMPLETE.
DON'T FORGET TO BREATHE, LITTLE BROTHER.
SPEAK FOR YOURSELF—THIS IS DELICIOUS! MMF-MF.
YES, EAT, MY SONS—THIS IS ALL FOR YOU.
NO, HAMATO YOSHI...
...THIS IS ALL FOR YOU.
IT WAS THE LAST MOMENT OF HAPPINESS YOSHI WOULD SHARE WITH HIS SONS.
OROKU SAKI.
OR SO HE THOUGHT.

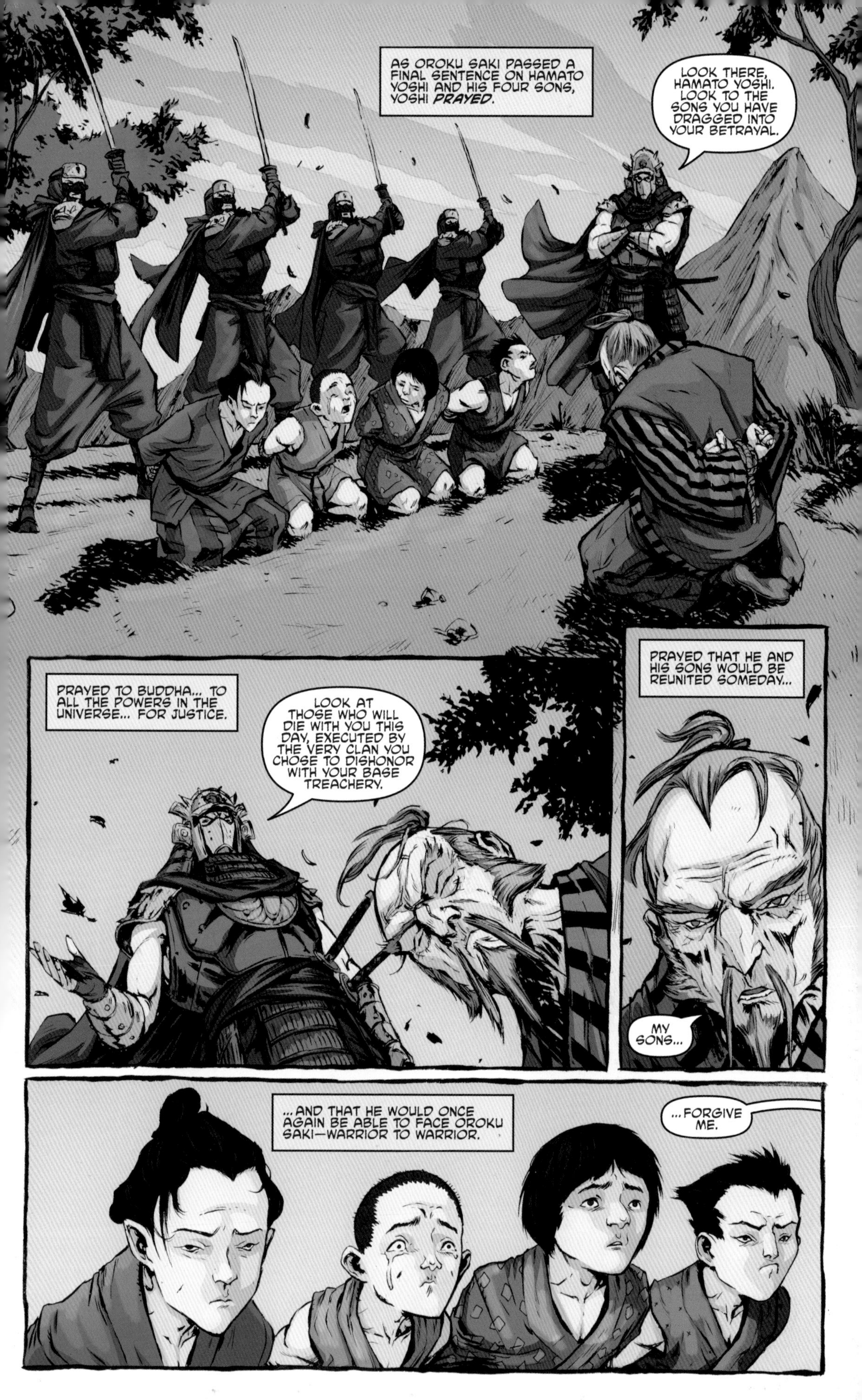
AS OROKU SAKI PASSED A FINAL SENTENCE ON HAMATO YOSHI AND HIS FOUR SONS, YOSHI *PRAYED*.
LOOK THERE, HAMATO YOSHI. LOOK TO THE SONS YOU HAVE DRAGGED INTO YOUR BETRAYAL.
PRAYED TO BUDDHA... TO ALL THE POWERS IN THE UNIVERSE... FOR JUSTICE.
LOOK AT THOSE WHO WILL DIE WITH YOU THIS DAY, EXECUTED BY THE VERY CLAN YOU CHOSE TO DISHONOR WITH YOUR BASE TREACHERY.
PRAYED THAT HE AND HIS SONS WOULD BE REUNITED SOMEDAY...
MY SONS...
...AND THAT HE WOULD ONCE AGAIN BE ABLE TO FACE OROKU SAKI—WARRIOR TO WARRIOR.
...FORGIVE ME.

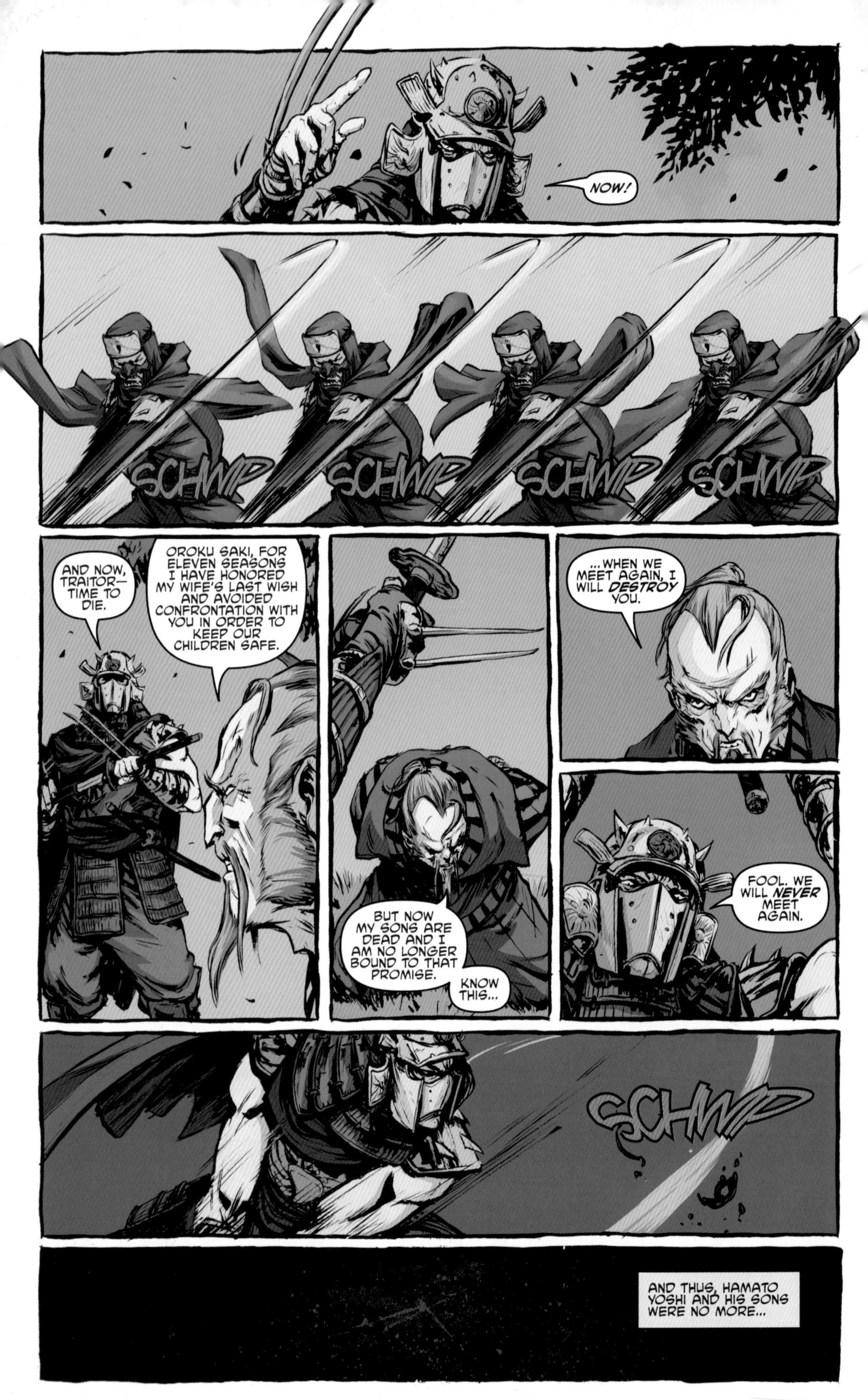
NOW!
SCHWIP
SCHWIP
SCHWIP
SCHWIP
AND NOW, TRAITOR— TIME TO DIE.
OROKU SAKI, FOR ELEVEN SEASONS I HAVE HONORED MY WIFE'S LAST WISH AND AVOIDED CONFRONTATION WITH YOU IN ORDER TO KEEP OUR CHILDREN SAFE.
BUT NOW MY SONS ARE DEAD AND I AM NO LONGER BOUND TO THAT PROMISE.
KNOW THIS...
...WHEN WE MEET AGAIN, I WILL DESTROY YOU.
FOOL. WE WILL NEVER MEET AGAIN.
SCHWIP
AND THUS, HAMATO YOSHI AND HIS SONS WERE NO MORE...

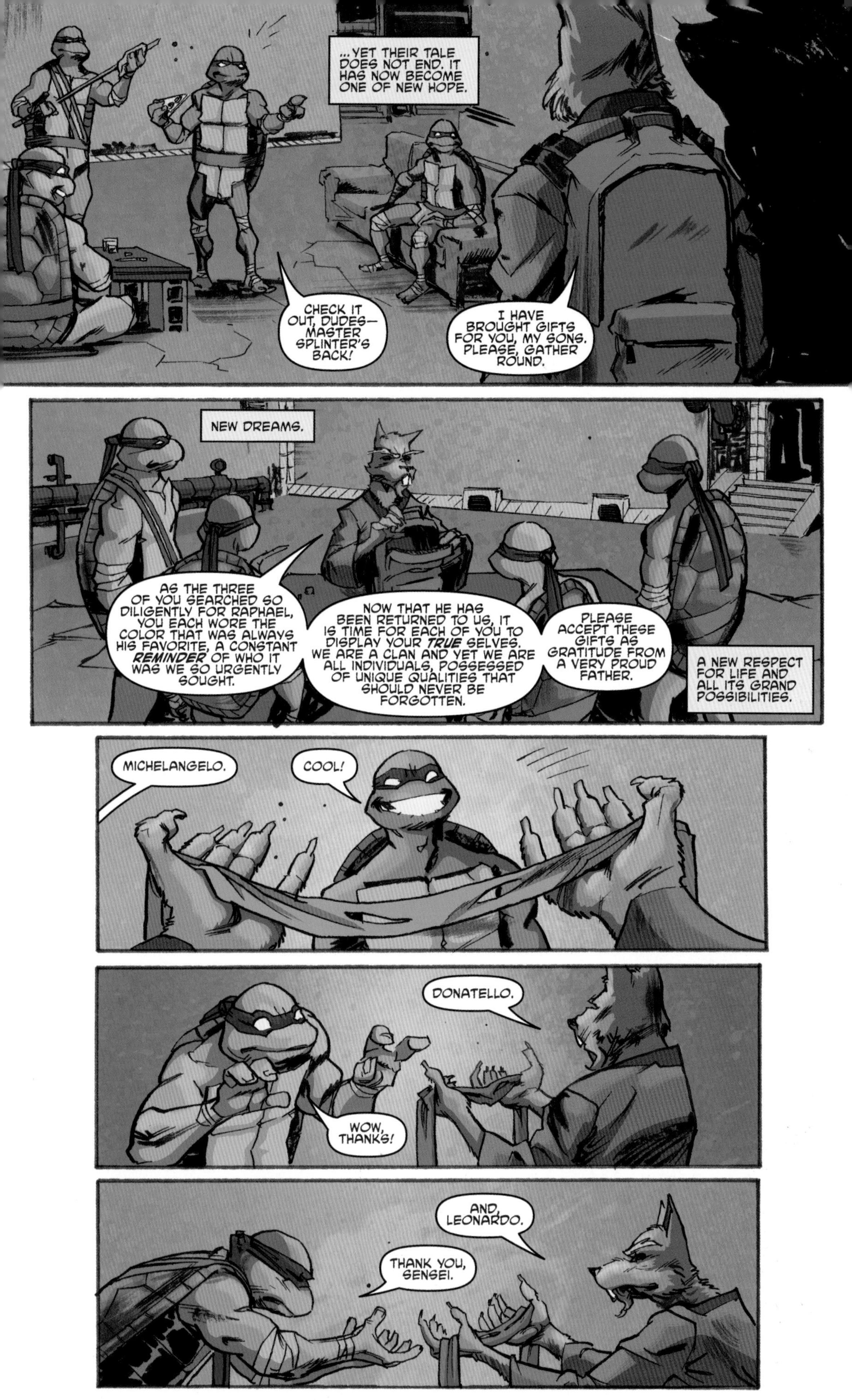
...YET THEIR TALE DOES NOT END. IT HAS NOW BECOME ONE OF NEW HOPE.
CHECK IT OUT, DUDES— MASTER SPLINTER'S BACK!
I HAVE BROUGHT GIFTS FOR YOU, MY SONS. PLEASE, GATHER ROUND.
NEW DREAMS.
AS THE THREE OF YOU SEARCHED SO DILIGENTLY FOR RAPHAEL, YOU EACH WORE THE COLOR THAT WAS ALWAYS HIS FAVORITE, A CONSTANT *REMINDER* OF WHO IT WAS WE SO URGENTLY SOUGHT.
NOW THAT HE HAS BEEN RETURNED TO US, IT IS TIME FOR EACH OF YOU TO DISPLAY YOUR *TRUE* SELVES. WE ARE A CLAN AND YET WE ARE ALL INDIVIDUALS, POSSESSED OF UNIQUE QUALITIES THAT SHOULD NEVER BE FORGOTTEN.
PLEASE ACCEPT THESE GIFTS AS GRATITUDE FROM A VERY PROUD FATHER.
A NEW RESPECT FOR LIFE AND ALL ITS GRAND POSSIBILITIES.
MICHELANGELO.
COOL!
DONATELLO.
WOW, THANKS!
AND, LEONARDO.
THANK YOU, SENSEI.

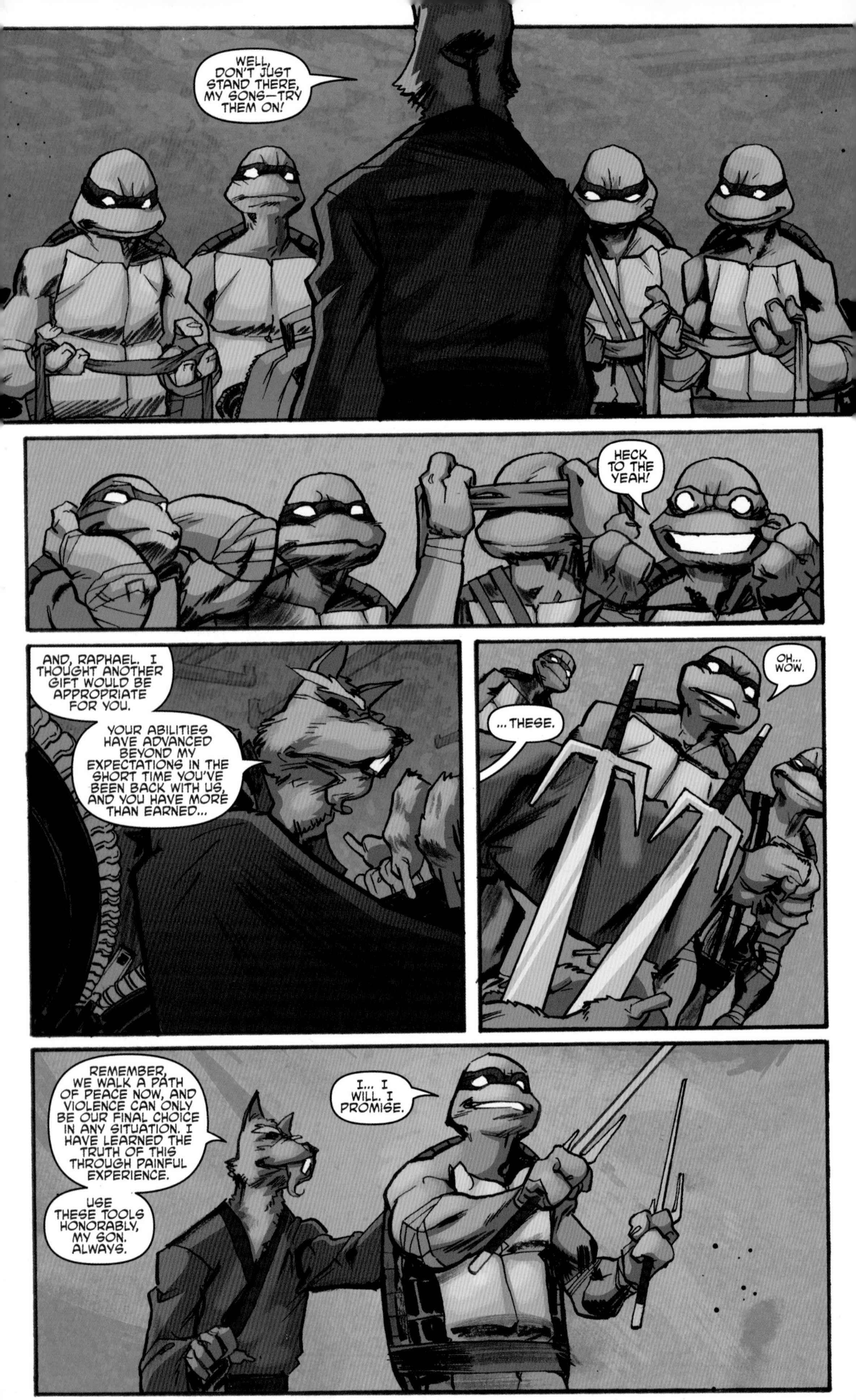
WELL, DON'T JUST STAND THERE, MY SONS—TRY THEM ON!
HECK TO THE YEAH!
AND, RAPHAEL. I THOUGHT ANOTHER GIFT WOULD BE APPROPRIATE FOR YOU.
YOUR ABILITIES HAVE ADVANCED BEYOND MY EXPECTATIONS IN THE SHORT TIME YOU'VE BEEN BACK WITH US, AND YOU HAVE MORE THAN EARNED...
...THESE.
OH... WOW.
REMEMBER, WE WALK A PATH OF PEACE NOW, AND VIOLENCE CAN ONLY BE OUR FINAL CHOICE IN ANY SITUATION. I HAVE LEARNED THE TRUTH OF THIS THROUGH PAINFUL EXPERIENCE.
USE THESE TOOLS HONORABLY, MY SON. ALWAYS.
I... I WILL. I PROMISE.

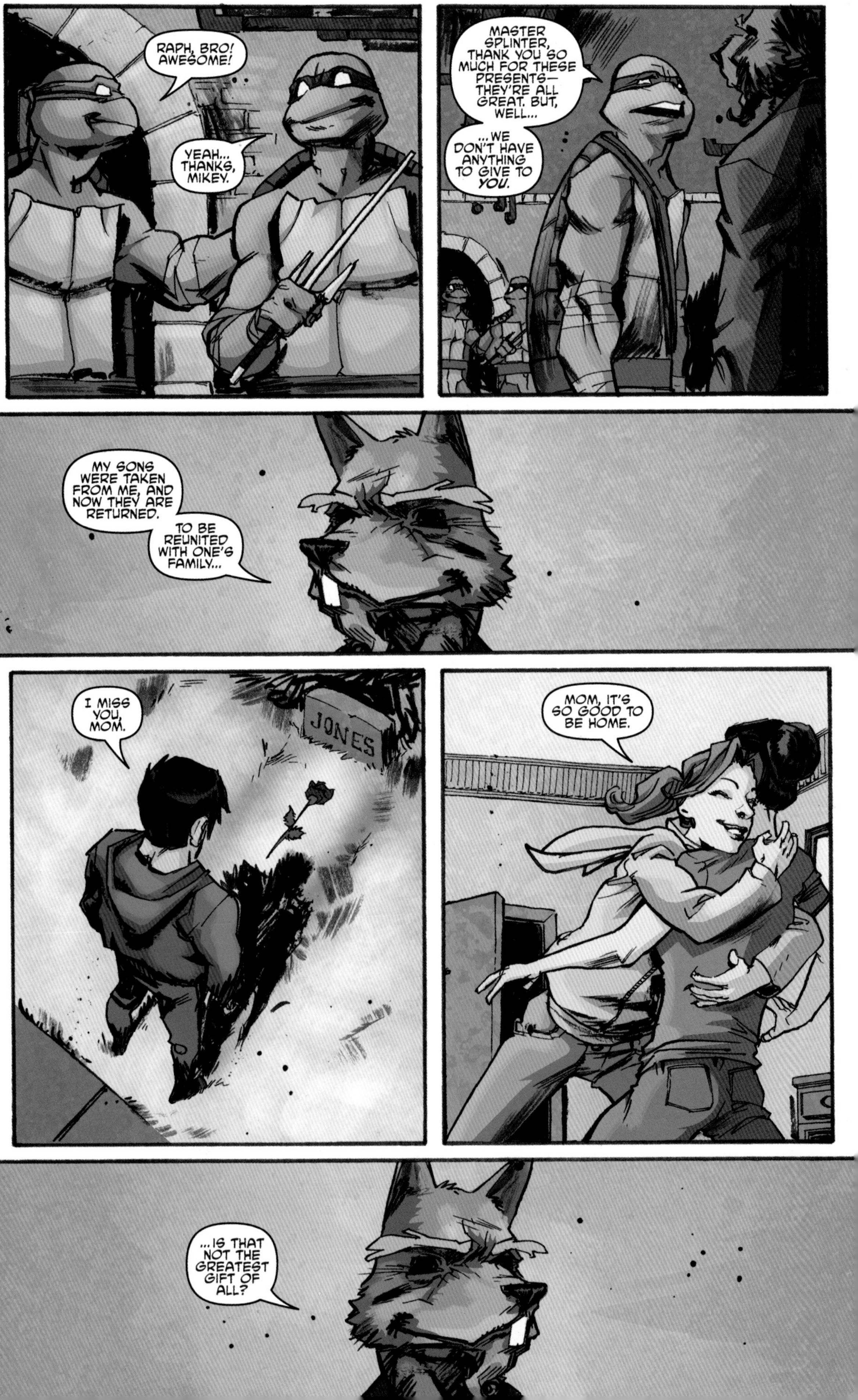
RAPH, BRO! AWESOME!
YEAH... THANKS, MIKEY.
MASTER SPLINTER, THANK YOU SO MUCH FOR THESE PRESENTS— THEY'RE ALL GREAT. BUT, WELL...
...WE DON'T HAVE ANYTHING TO GIVE TO *YOU*.
MY SONS WERE TAKEN FROM ME, AND NOW THEY ARE RETURNED.
TO BE REUNITED WITH ONE'S FAMILY...
I MISS YOU, MOM.
JONES
MOM, IT'S SO GOOD TO BE HOME.
...IS THAT NOT THE GREATEST GIFT OF ALL?

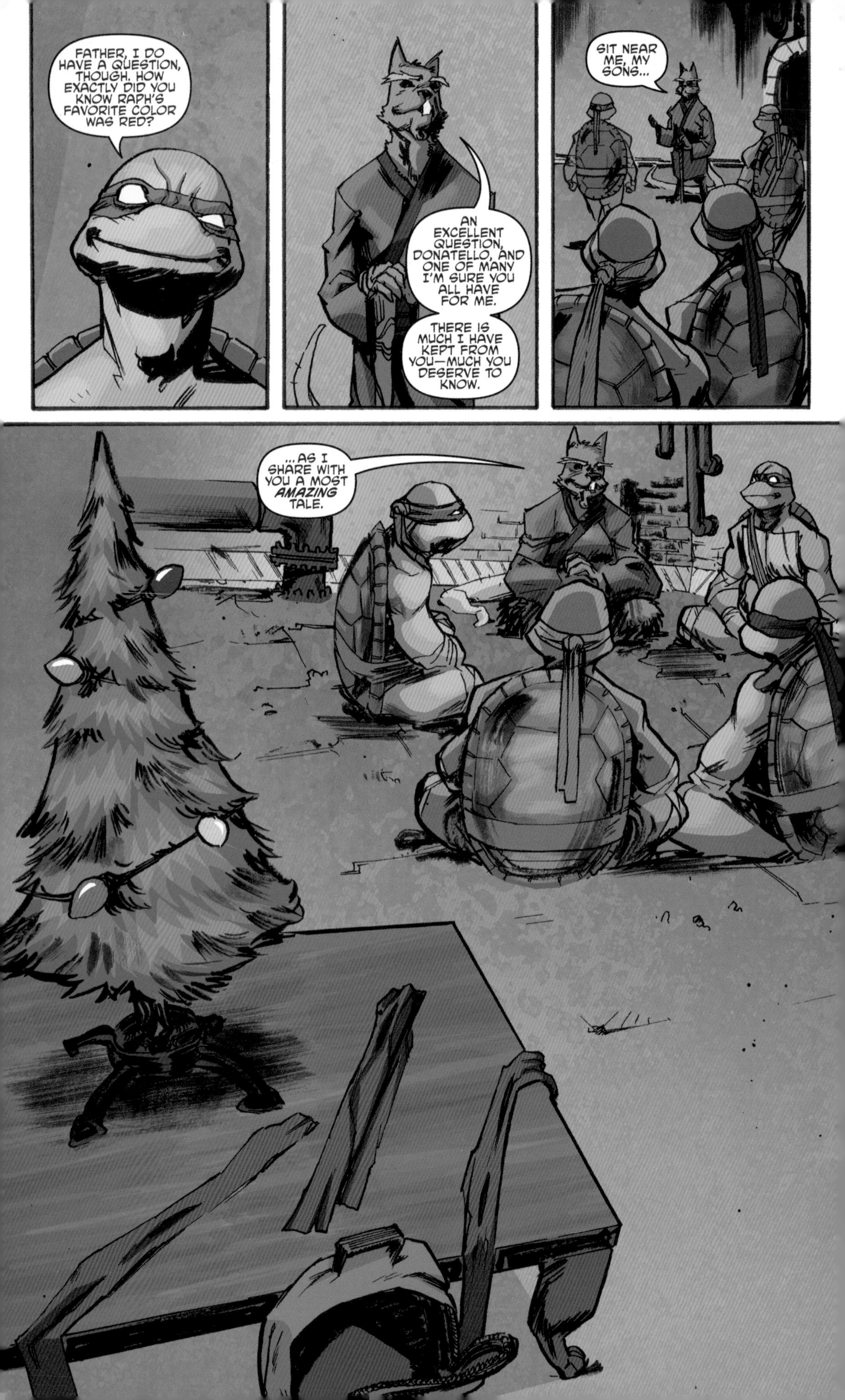
FATHER, I DO HAVE A QUESTION, THOUGH. HOW EXACTLY DID YOU KNOW RAPH'S FAVORITE COLOR WAS RED?
AN EXCELLENT QUESTION, DONATELLO, AND ONE OF MANY I'M SURE YOU ALL HAVE FOR ME.
THERE IS MUCH I HAVE KEPT FROM YOU—MUCH YOU DESERVE TO KNOW.
SIT NEAR ME, MY SONS...
...AS I SHARE WITH YOU A MOST *AMAZING* TALE.

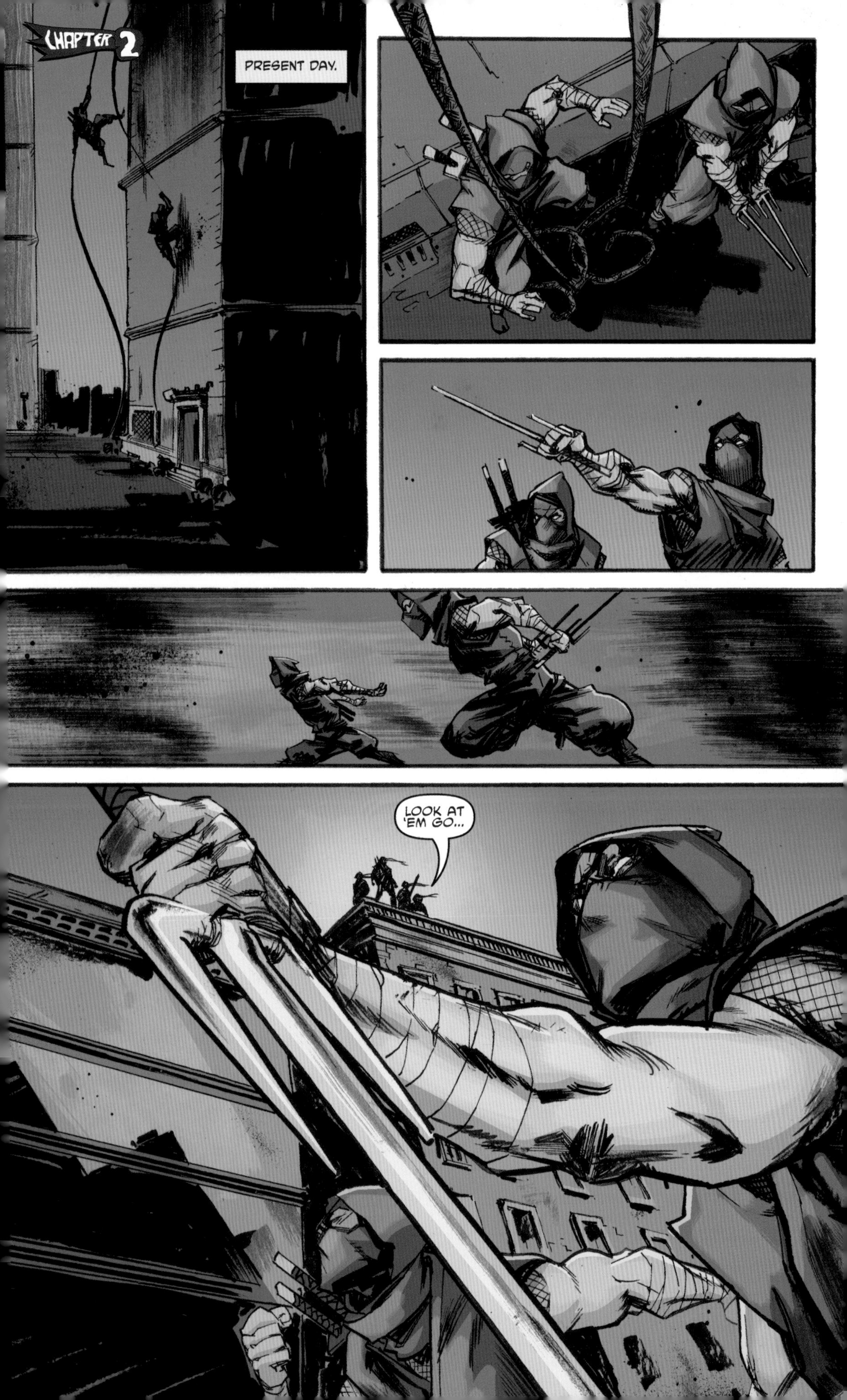
CHAPTER 2
PRESENT DAY.
LOOK AT 'EM GO...

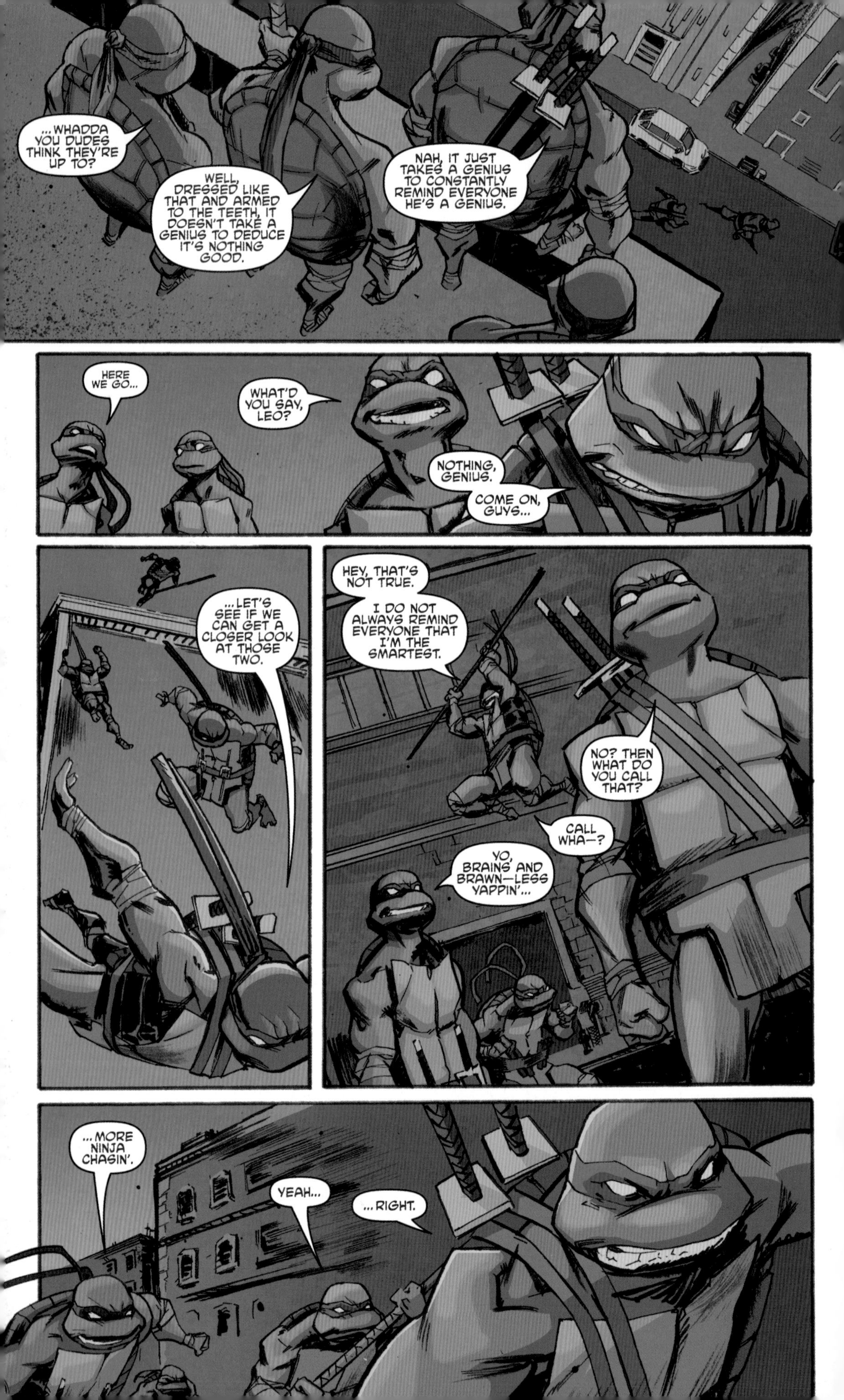
...WHADDA YOU DUDES THINK THEY'RE UP TO?
WELL, DRESSED LIKE THAT AND ARMED TO THE TEETH, IT DOESN'T TAKE A GENIUS TO DEDUCE IT'S NOTHING GOOD.
NAH, IT JUST TAKES A GENIUS TO CONSTANTLY REMIND EVERYONE HE'S A GENIUS.
HERE WE GO...
WHAT'D YOU SAY, LEO?
NOTHING, GENIUS.
COME ON, GUYS...
...LET'S SEE IF WE CAN GET A CLOSER LOOK AT THOSE TWO.
HEY, THAT'S NOT TRUE.
I DO NOT ALWAYS REMIND EVERYONE THAT I'M THE SMARTEST.
NO? THEN WHAT DO YOU CALL THAT?
CALL WHA—?
YO, BRAINS AND BRAWN—LESS YAPPIN'...
...MORE NINJA CHASIN'.
YEAH...
...RIGHT.

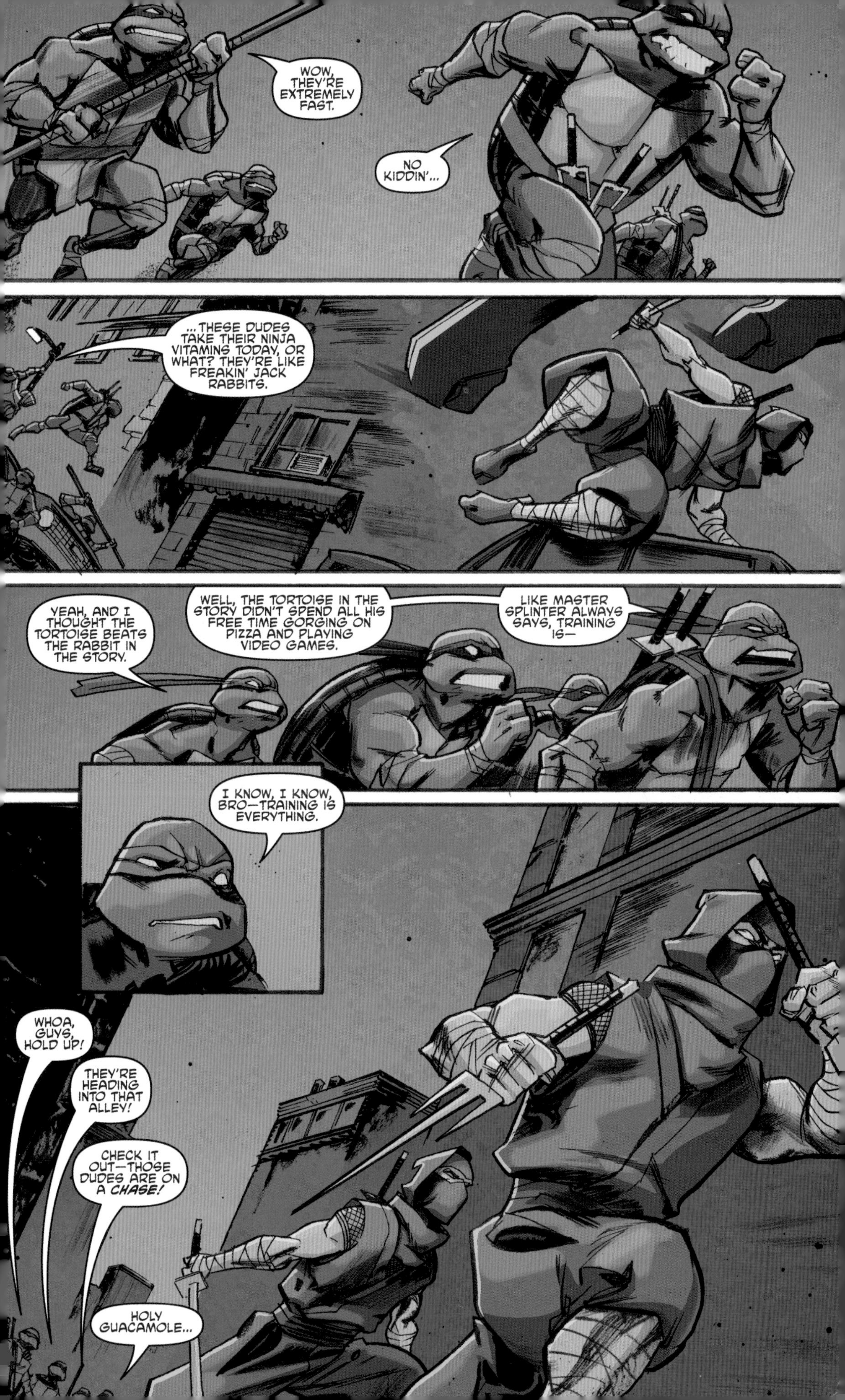
WOW, THEY'RE EXTREMELY FAST.
NO KIDDIN'...
...THESE DUDES TAKE THEIR NINJA VITAMINS TODAY, OR WHAT? THEY'RE LIKE FREAKIN' JACK RABBITS.
YEAH, AND I THOUGHT THE TORTOISE BEATS THE RABBIT IN THE STORY.
WELL, THE TORTOISE IN THE STORY DIDN'T SPEND ALL HIS FREE TIME GORGING ON PIZZA AND PLAYING VIDEO GAMES.
LIKE MASTER SPLINTER ALWAYS SAYS, TRAINING IS—
I KNOW, I KNOW, BRO—TRAINING IS EVERYTHING.
WHOA, GUYS, HOLD UP!
THEY'RE HEADING INTO THAT ALLEY!
CHECK IT OUT—THOSE DUDES ARE ON A *CHASE!*
HOLY GUACAMOLE...

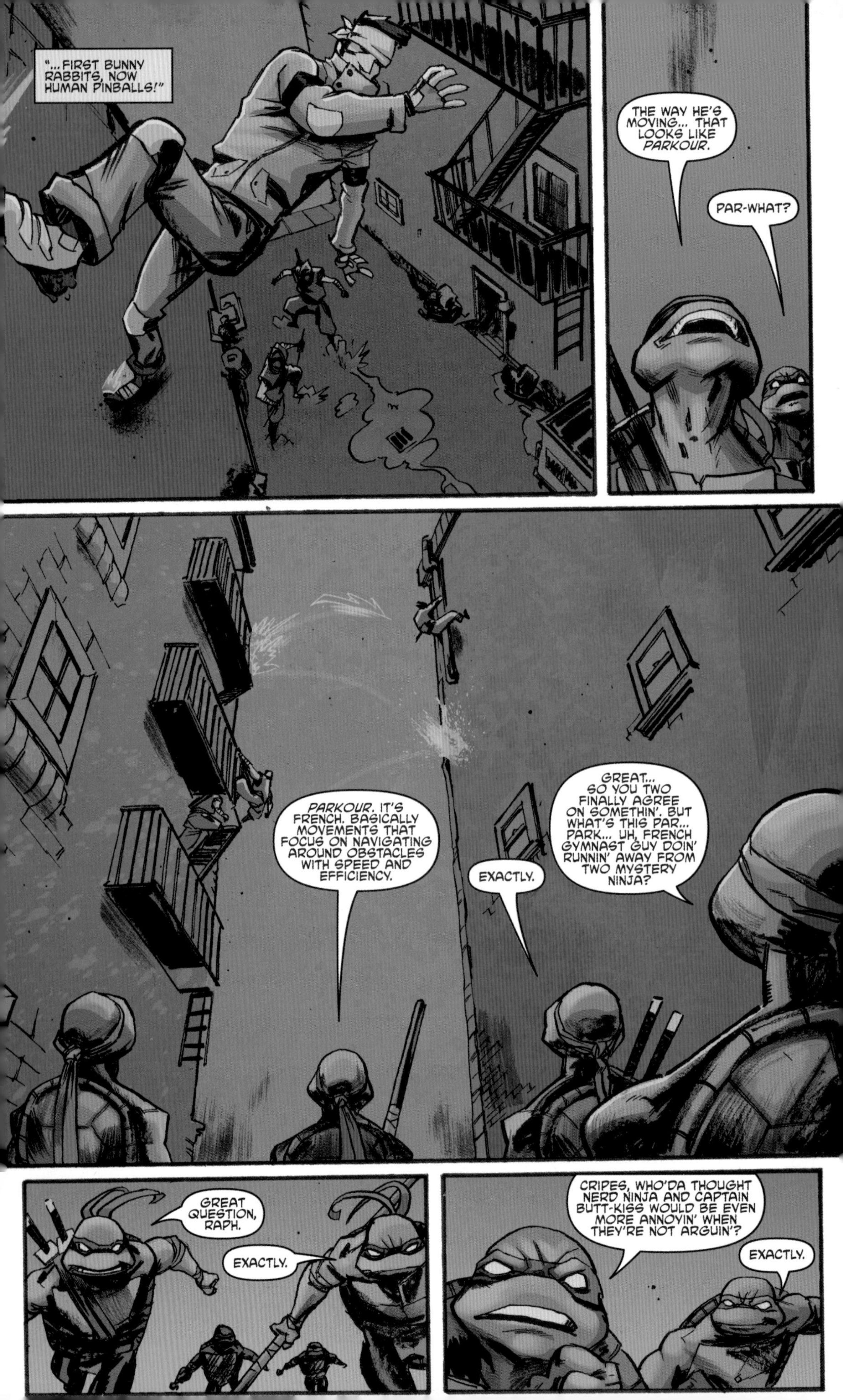
"...FIRST BUNNY RABBITS, NOW HUMAN PINBALLS!"
THE WAY HE'S MOVING... THAT LOOKS LIKE *PARKOUR*.
PAR-WHAT?
PARKOUR. IT'S FRENCH. BASICALLY MOVEMENTS THAT FOCUS ON NAVIGATING AROUND OBSTACLES WITH SPEED AND EFFICIENCY.
EXACTLY.
GREAT... SO YOU TWO FINALLY AGREE ON SOMETHIN'. BUT WHAT'S THIS PAR... PARK... UH, FRENCH GYMNAST GUY DOIN' RUNNIN' AWAY FROM TWO MYSTERY NINJA?
GREAT QUESTION, RAPH.
EXACTLY.
CRIPES, WHO'DA THOUGHT NERD NINJA AND CAPTAIN BUTT-KISS WOULD BE EVEN MORE ANNOYIN' WHEN THEY'RE NOT ARGUIN'?
EXACTLY.

SHH, GUYS... LISTEN.

ALLEZ...

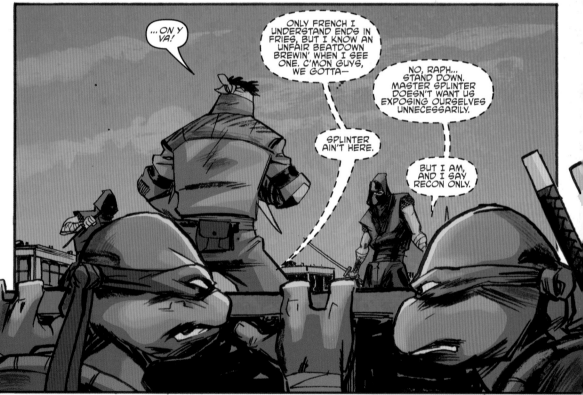

...ON Y VA!

ONLY FRENCH I UNDERSTAND ENDS IN FRIES, BUT I KNOW AN UNFAIR BEATDOWN BREWIN' WHEN I SEE ONE. C'MON GUYS, WE GOTTA—

NO, RAPH... STAND DOWN. MASTER SPLINTER DOESN'T WANT US EXPOSING OURSELVES UNNECESSARILY.

SPLINTER AIN'T HERE.

BUT I AM, AND I SAY RECON ONLY.

BUT, LEO, TWO AGAINST ONE, MAN—THAT AIN'T COOL.

MAYBE NOT...

"...BUT THIS ISN'T OUR DANCE."

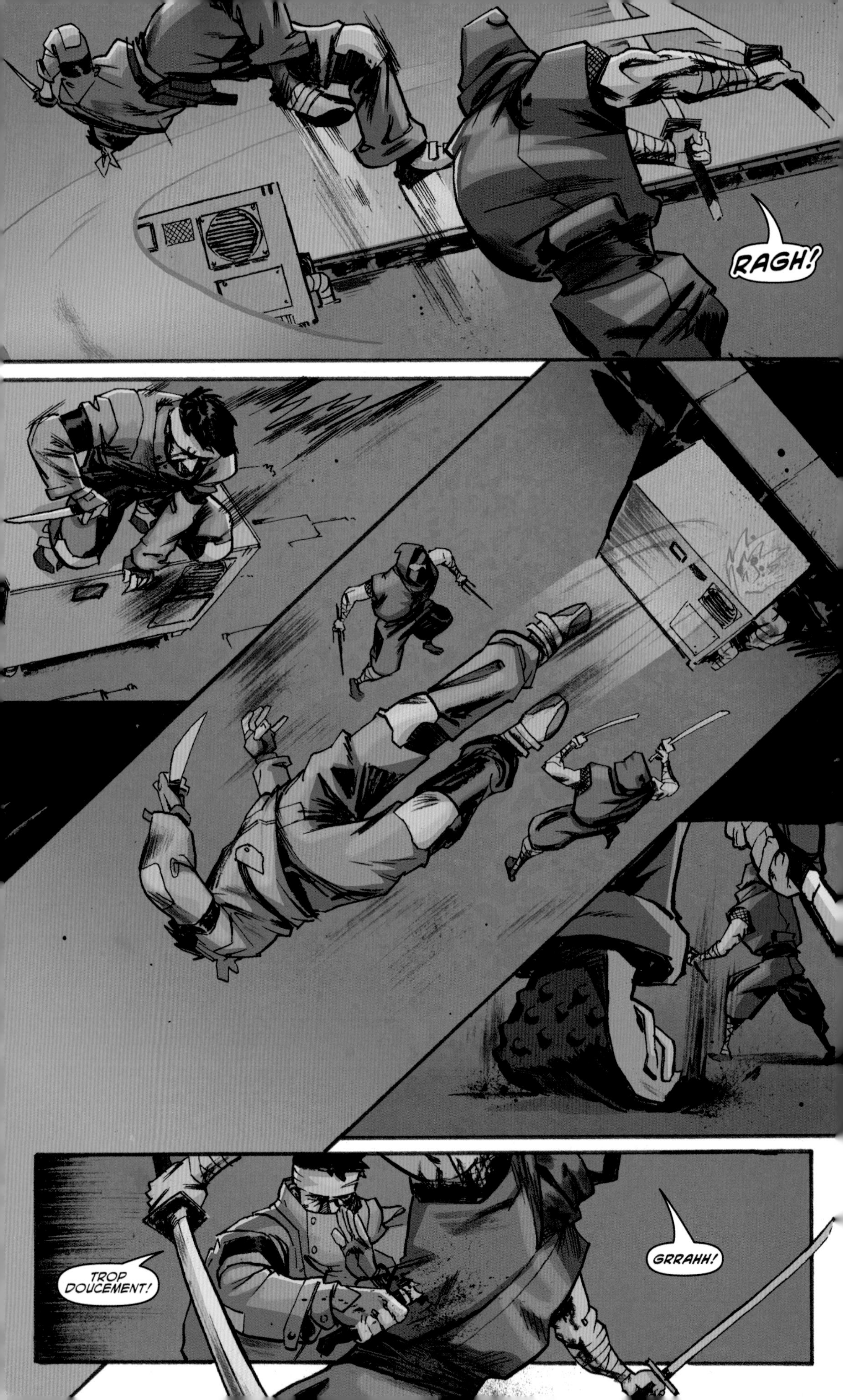
RAGH!
TROP DOUCEMENT!
GRRAHH!

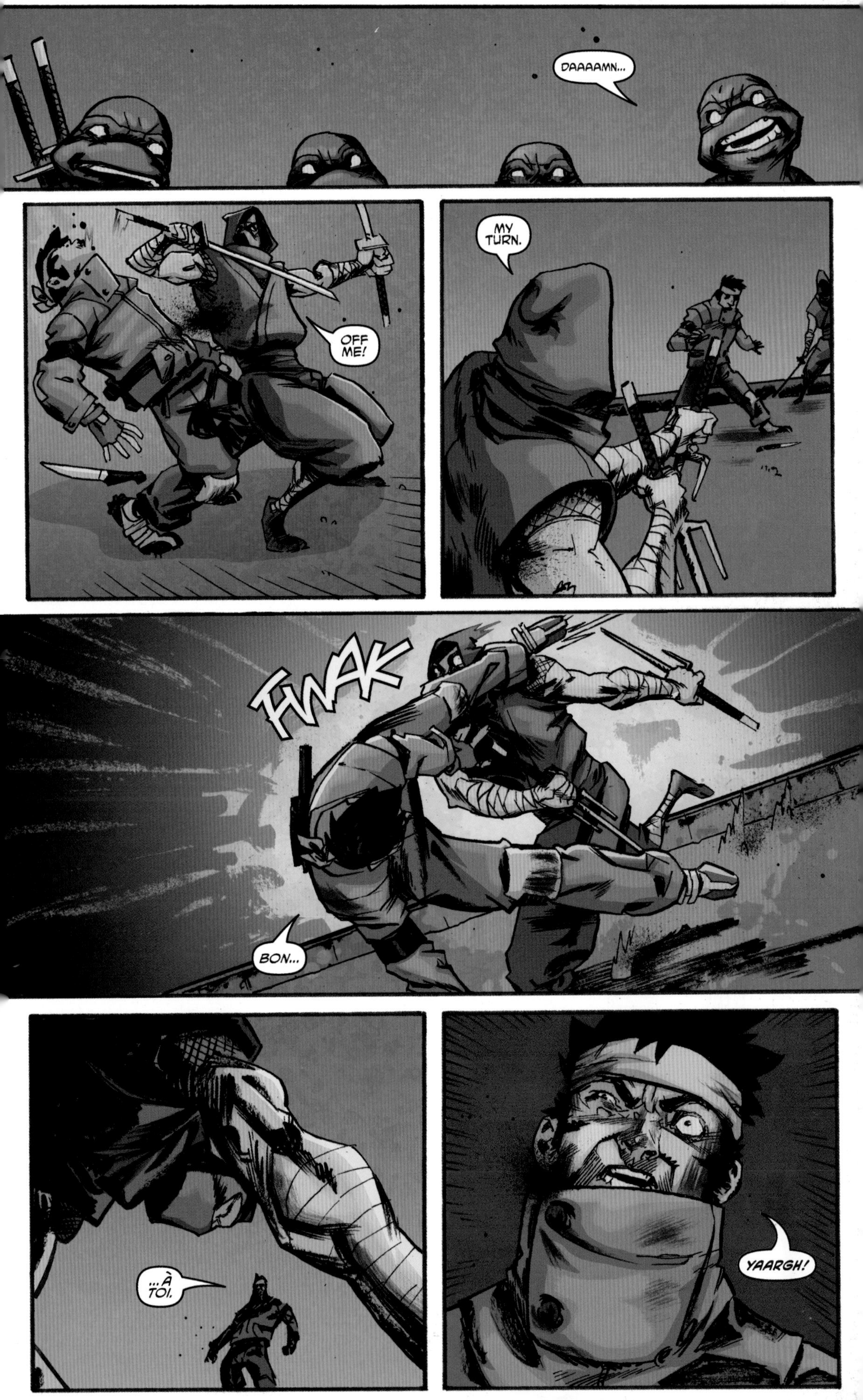
DAAAAMN...
OFF ME!
MY TURN.
FWAK
BON...
...À TOI.
YAARGH!

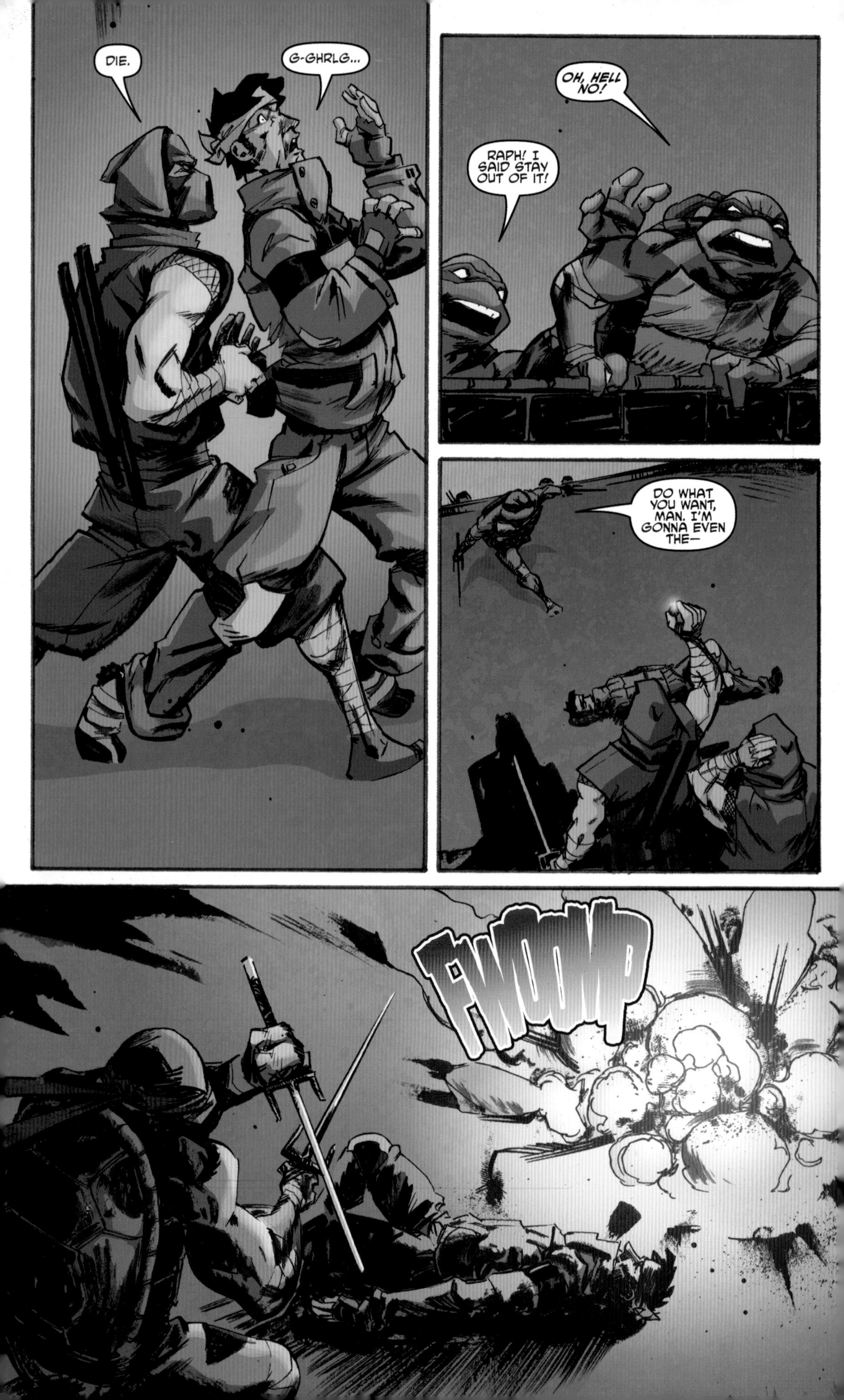
DIE.
G-GHRLG...
OH, HELL NO!
RAPH! I SAID STAY OUT OF IT!
DO WHAT YOU WANT, MAN. I'M GONNA EVEN THE—
FWOOMP

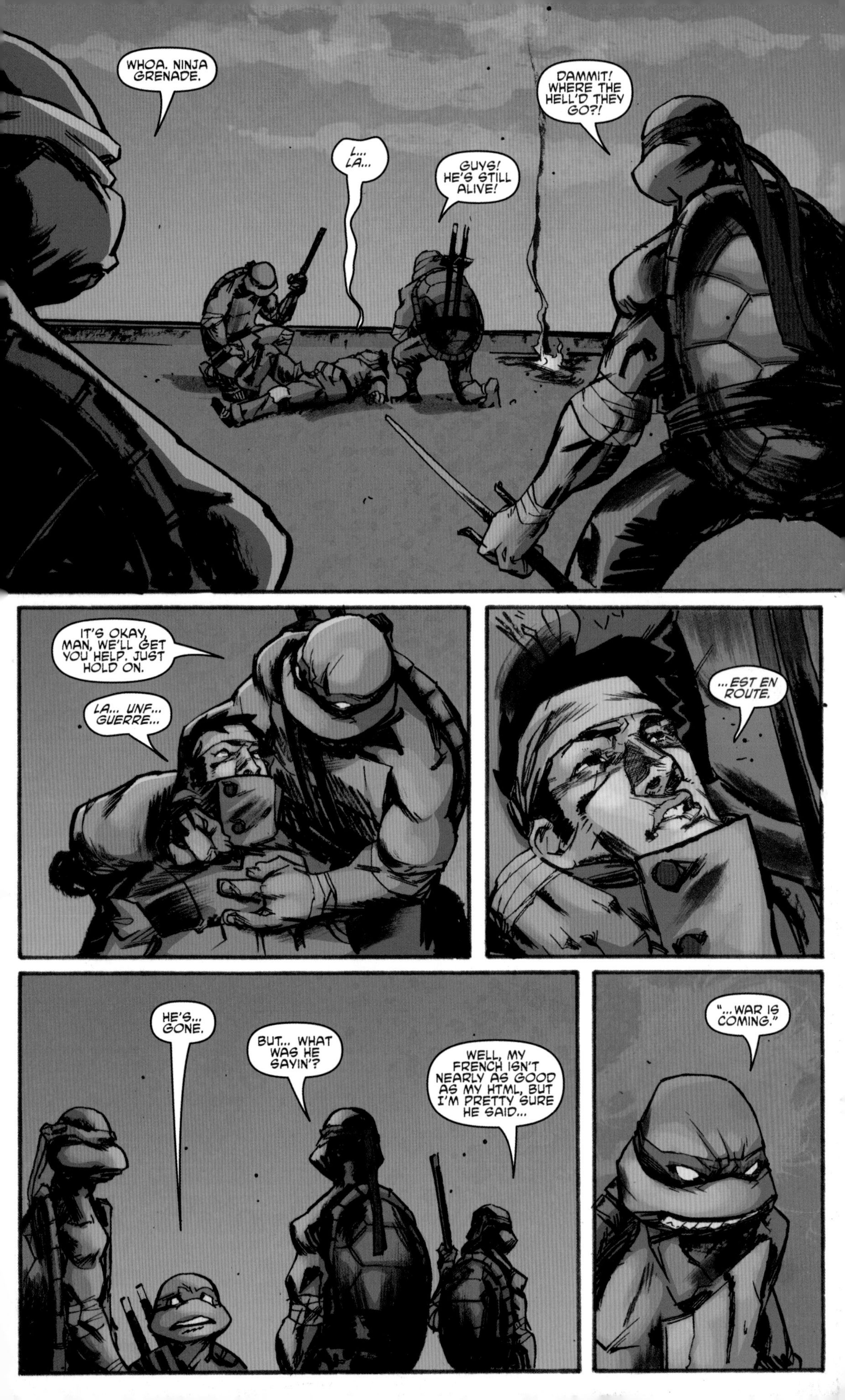
WHOA. NINJA GRENADE.
L... LA...
GUYS! HE'S STILL ALIVE!
DAMMIT! WHERE THE HELL'D THEY GO?!
IT'S OKAY, MAN, WE'LL GET YOU HELP. JUST HOLD ON.
LA... UNF... GUERRE...
...EST EN ROUTE.
HE'S... GONE.
BUT... WHAT WAS HE SAYIN'?
WELL, MY FRENCH ISN'T NEARLY AS GOOD AS MY HTML, BUT I'M PRETTY SURE HE SAID...
"...WAR IS COMING."

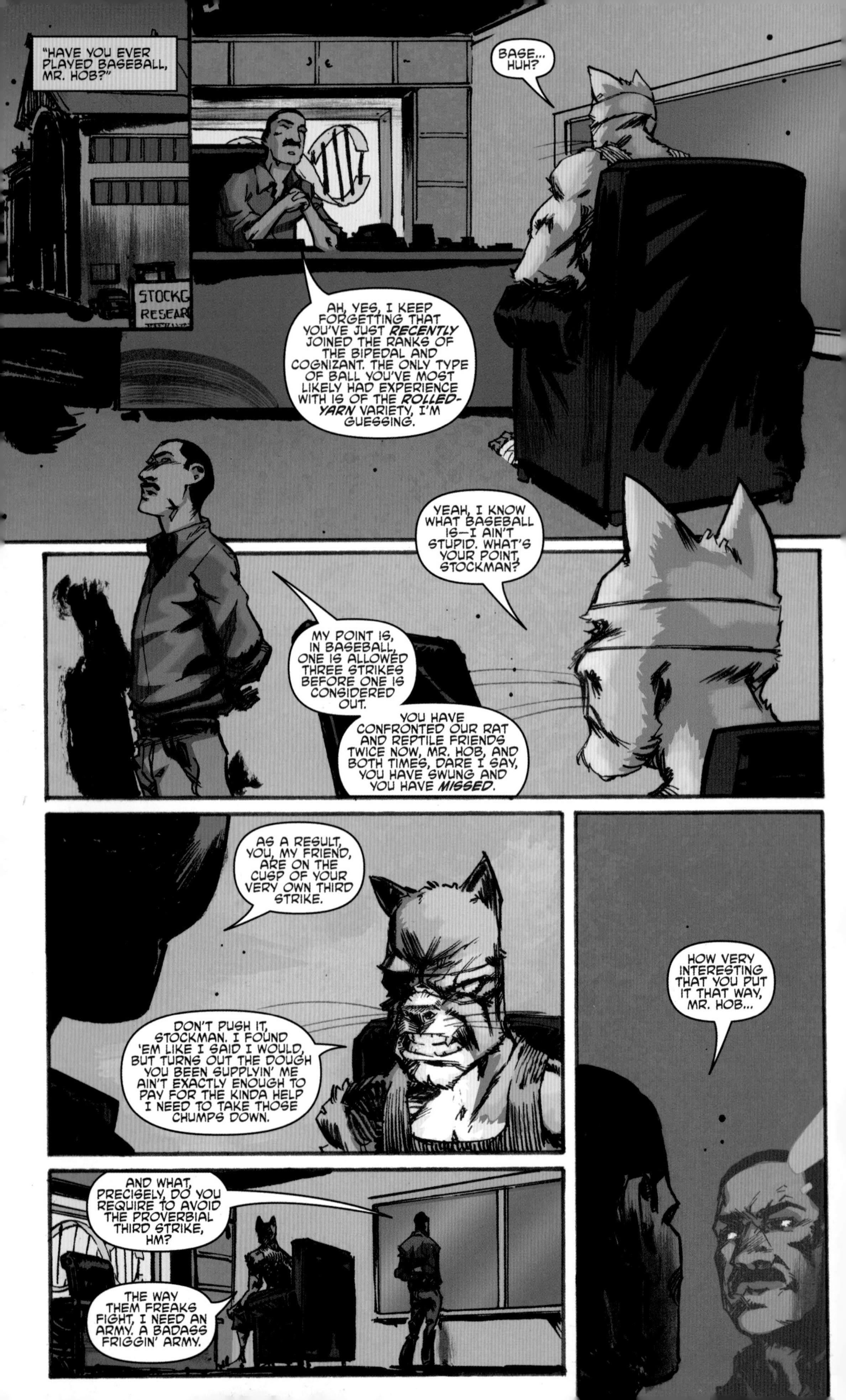
"HAVE YOU EVER PLAYED BASEBALL, MR. HOB?"
BASE... HUH?
STOCKG RESEAR
AH, YES, I KEEP FORGETTING THAT YOU'VE JUST RECENTLY JOINED THE RANKS OF THE BIPEDAL AND COGNIZANT. THE ONLY TYPE OF BALL YOU'VE MOST LIKELY HAD EXPERIENCE WITH IS OF THE ROLLED-YARN VARIETY, I'M GUESSING.
YEAH, I KNOW WHAT BASEBALL IS—I AIN'T STUPID. WHAT'S YOUR POINT, STOCKMAN?
MY POINT IS, IN BASEBALL, ONE IS ALLOWED THREE STRIKES BEFORE ONE IS CONSIDERED OUT.
YOU HAVE CONFRONTED OUR RAT AND REPTILE FRIENDS TWICE NOW, MR. HOB, AND BOTH TIMES, DARE I SAY, YOU HAVE SWUNG AND YOU HAVE MISSED.
AS A RESULT, YOU, MY FRIEND, ARE ON THE CUSP OF YOUR VERY OWN THIRD STRIKE.
DON'T PUSH IT, STOCKMAN. I FOUND 'EM LIKE I SAID I WOULD, BUT TURNS OUT THE DOUGH YOU BEEN SUPPLYIN' ME AIN'T EXACTLY ENOUGH TO PAY FOR THE KINDA HELP I NEED TO TAKE THOSE CHUMPS DOWN.
AND WHAT, PRECISELY, DO YOU REQUIRE TO AVOID THE PROVERBIAL THIRD STRIKE, HM?
THE WAY THEM FREAKS FIGHT, I NEED AN ARMY. A BADASS FRIGGIN' ARMY.
HOW VERY INTERESTING THAT YOU PUT IT THAT WAY, MR. HOB...

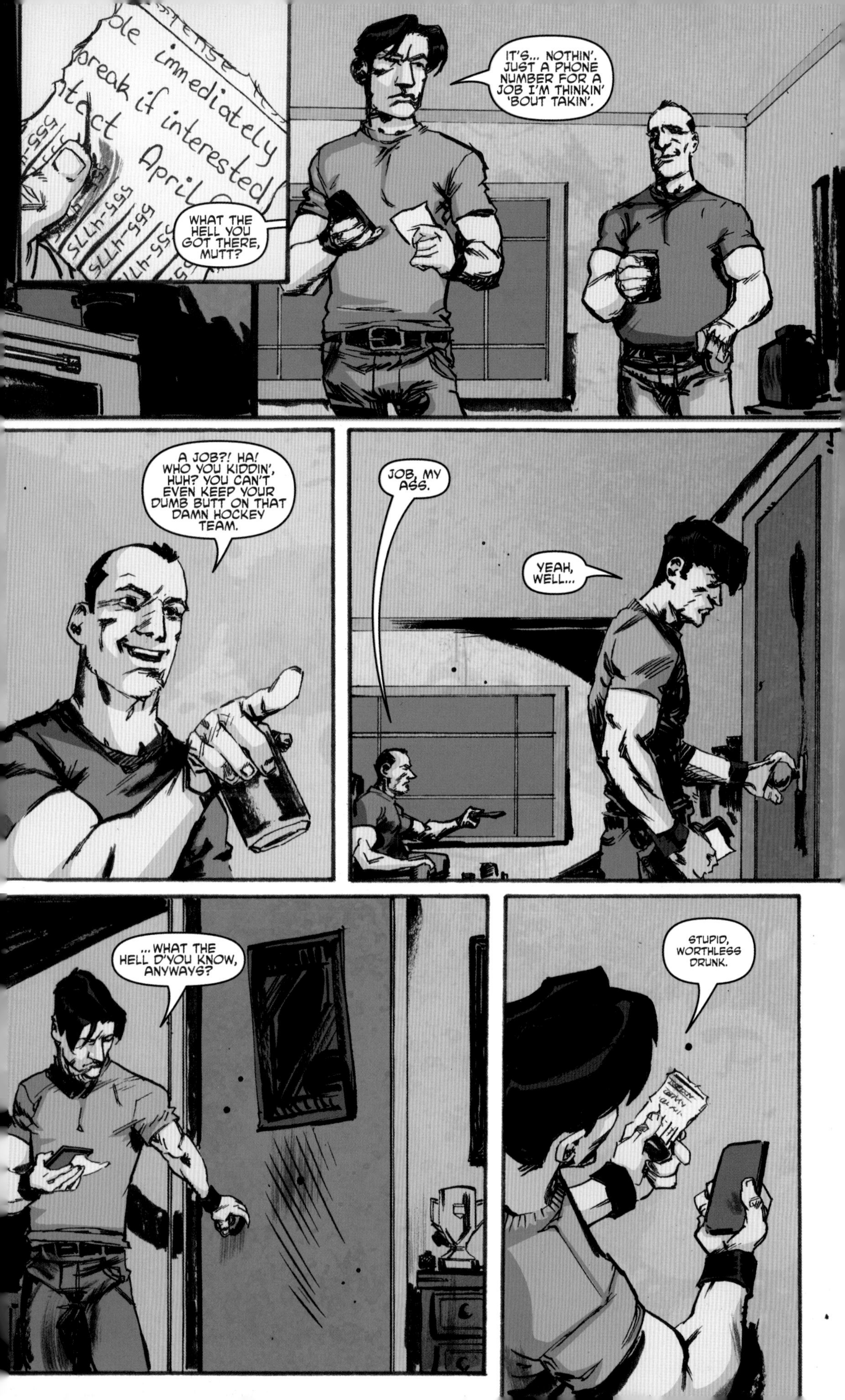
immediately
break if interested
April
555-4775
WHAT THE HELL YOU GOT THERE, MUTT?
IT'S... NOTHIN'. JUST A PHONE NUMBER FOR A JOB I'M THINKIN' 'BOUT TAKIN'.
A JOB?! HA! WHO YOU KIDDIN', HUH? YOU CAN'T EVEN KEEP YOUR DUMB BUTT ON THAT DAMN HOCKEY TEAM.
JOB, MY ASS.
YEAH, WELL...
...WHAT THE HELL D'YOU KNOW, ANYWAYS?
STUPID, WORTHLESS DRUNK.

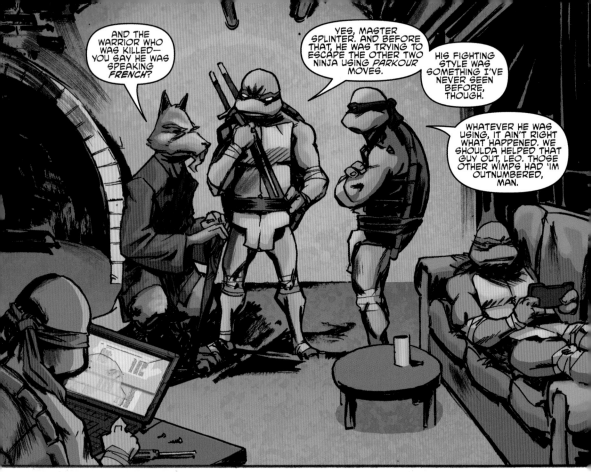

AND THE WARRIOR WHO WAS KILLED—YOU SAY HE WAS SPEAKING *FRENCH*?

YES, MASTER SPLINTER. AND BEFORE THAT, HE WAS TRYING TO ESCAPE THE OTHER TWO NINJA USING *PARKOUR* MOVES.

HIS FIGHTING STYLE WAS SOMETHING I'VE NEVER SEEN BEFORE, THOUGH.

WHATEVER HE WAS USING, IT AIN'T RIGHT WHAT HAPPENED. WE SHOULDA HELPED THAT GUY OUT, LEO. THOSE OTHER WIMPS HAD 'IM OUTNUMBERED, MAN.

BASED ON YOUR DESCRIPTIONS, THOSE TWO "WIMPS," AS YOU CALL THEM, APPEAR TO HAVE BEEN *FOOT NINJA*, JUST AS I DESCRIBED TO YOU BEFORE. IF SO, OFFERING A FAIR FIGHT IS NOT PART OF THEIR CREED, MY SON.

WHOEVER THEY WERE, THE WHOLE THING WAS MESSED UP. WE SHOULDA DONE SOMETHIN'.

AS NOBLE AS YOUR INTENTIONS WOULD HAVE BEEN, RAPHAEL, I BELIEVE IT WAS FOR THE BEST THAT THE FOUR OF YOU REMAINED NEUTRAL AS YOU DID.

WE MAY KNOW WHO SOME OF OUR ADVERSARIES ARE, BUT WE CANNOT BE CERTAIN WHO ELSE MAY BE AN ENEMY TO US—OR AN ALLY, FOR THAT MATTER.

SAVATE!

SAY WHAT?

NO, MIKEY—*SAVATE*. THE FIGHTING STYLE THE FRENCH GUY WAS USING WAS *SAVATE*. IT'S A FRENCH MARTIAL-ARTS SYSTEM THAT'S BEEN AROUND SINCE AT LEAST THE EARLY 19TH CENTURY.

FRENCH DUDE ROCKIN' FRENCH FU. MAKES SENSE.

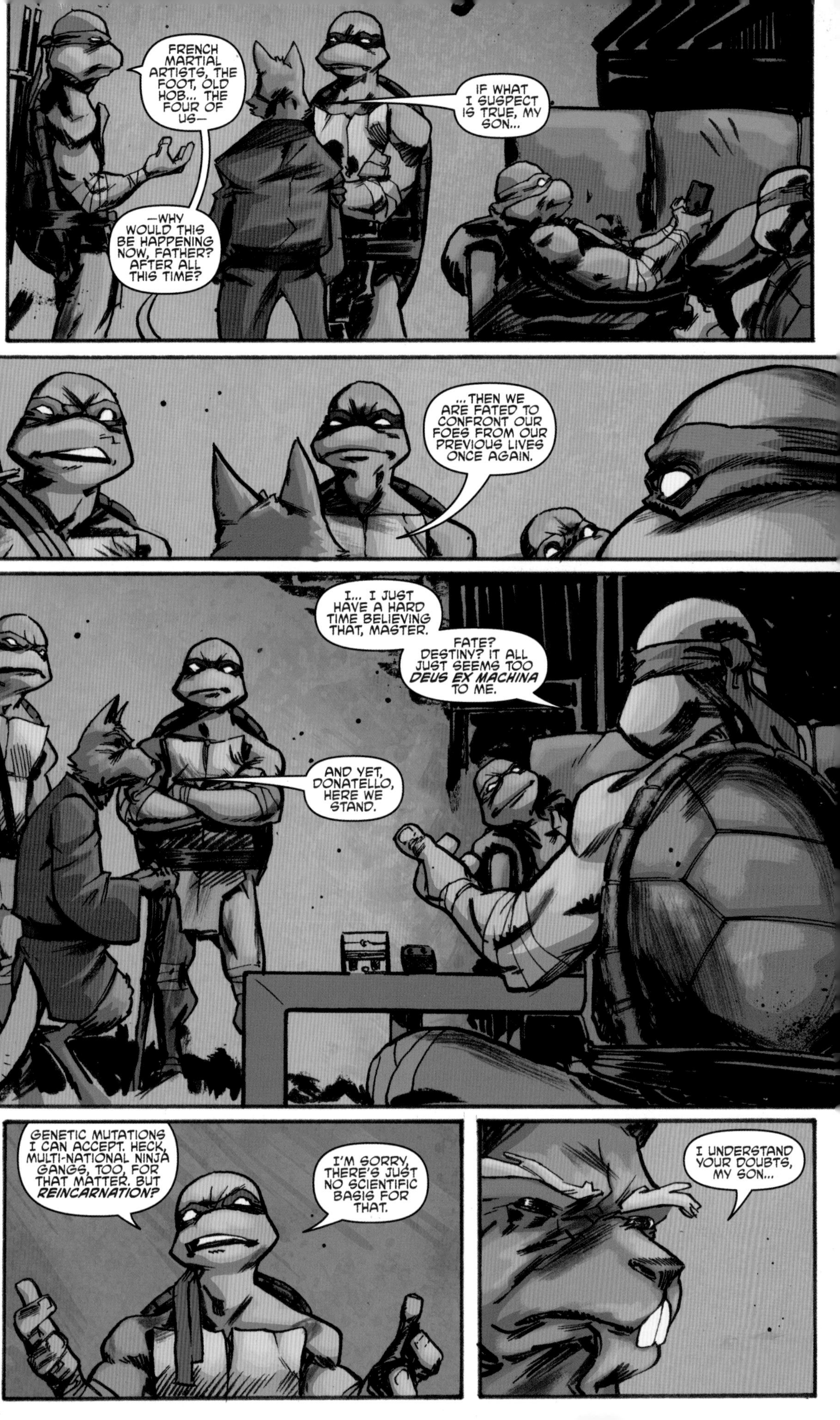
FRENCH MARTIAL ARTISTS, THE FOOT, OLD HOB... THE FOUR OF US—
—WHY WOULD THIS BE HAPPENING NOW, FATHER? AFTER ALL THIS TIME?
IF WHAT I SUSPECT IS TRUE, MY SON...
...THEN WE ARE FATED TO CONFRONT OUR FOES FROM OUR PREVIOUS LIVES ONCE AGAIN.
I... I JUST HAVE A HARD TIME BELIEVING THAT, MASTER.
FATE? DESTINY? IT ALL JUST SEEMS TOO *DEUS EX MACHINA* TO ME.
AND YET, DONATELLO, HERE WE STAND.
GENETIC MUTATIONS I CAN ACCEPT. HECK, MULTI-NATIONAL NINJA GANGS, TOO, FOR THAT MATTER. BUT *REINCARNATION?*
I'M SORRY, THERE'S JUST NO SCIENTIFIC BASIS FOR THAT.
I UNDERSTAND YOUR DOUBTS, MY SON...

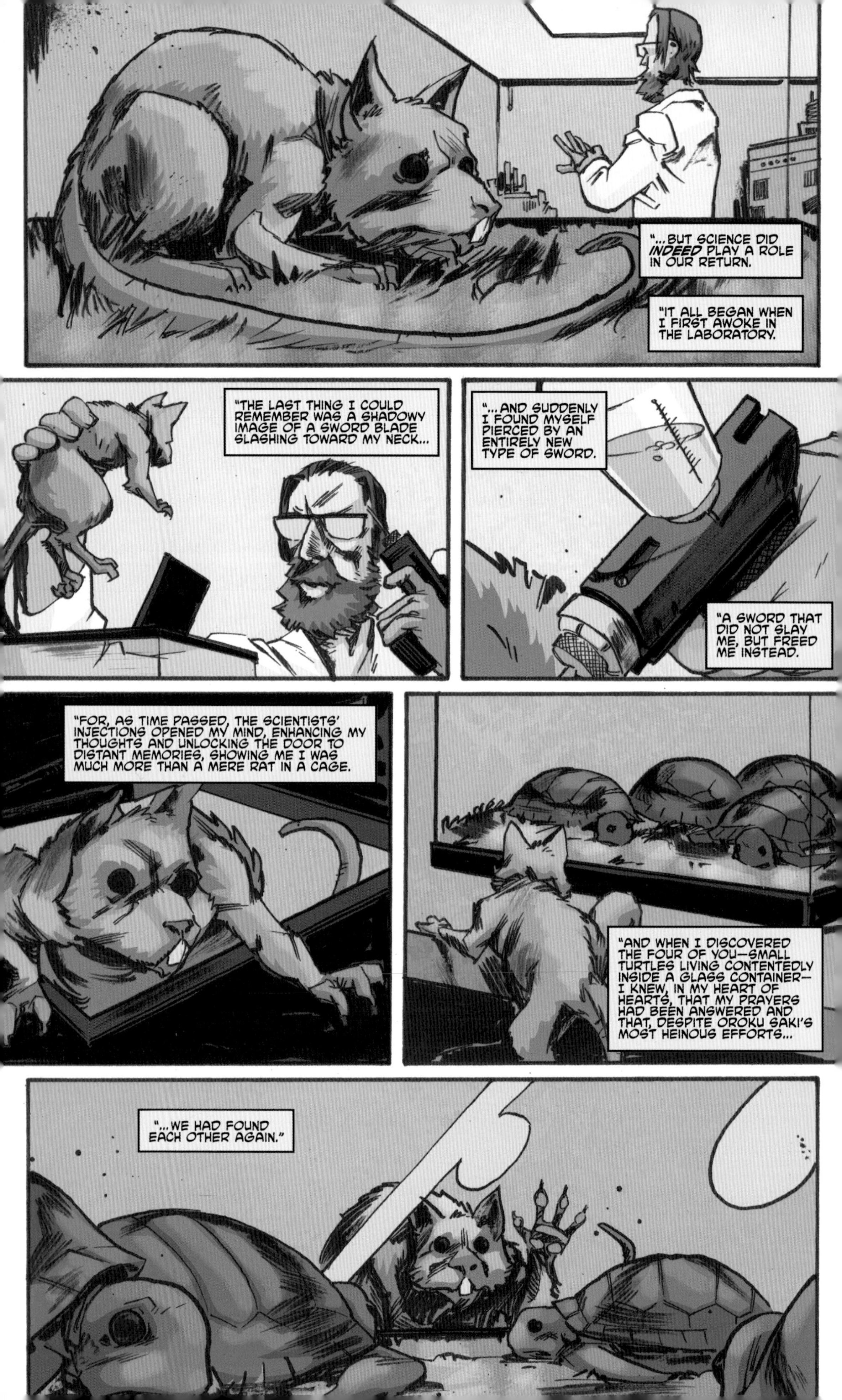
"...BUT SCIENCE DID *INDEED* PLAY A ROLE IN OUR RETURN.
"IT ALL BEGAN WHEN I FIRST AWOKE IN THE LABORATORY.
"THE LAST THING I COULD REMEMBER WAS A SHADOWY IMAGE OF A SWORD BLADE SLASHING TOWARD MY NECK...
"...AND SUDDENLY I FOUND MYSELF PIERCED BY AN ENTIRELY NEW TYPE OF SWORD.
"A SWORD THAT DID NOT SLAY ME, BUT FREED ME INSTEAD.
"FOR, AS TIME PASSED, THE SCIENTISTS' INJECTIONS OPENED MY MIND, ENHANCING MY THOUGHTS AND UNLOCKING THE DOOR TO DISTANT MEMORIES, SHOWING ME I WAS MUCH MORE THAN A MERE RAT IN A CAGE.
"AND WHEN I DISCOVERED THE FOUR OF YOU—SMALL TURTLES LIVING CONTENTEDLY INSIDE A GLASS CONTAINER—I KNEW, IN MY HEART OF HEARTS, THAT MY PRAYERS HAD BEEN ANSWERED AND THAT, DESPITE OROKU SAKI'S MOST HEINOUS EFFORTS...
"...WE HAD FOUND EACH OTHER AGAIN."

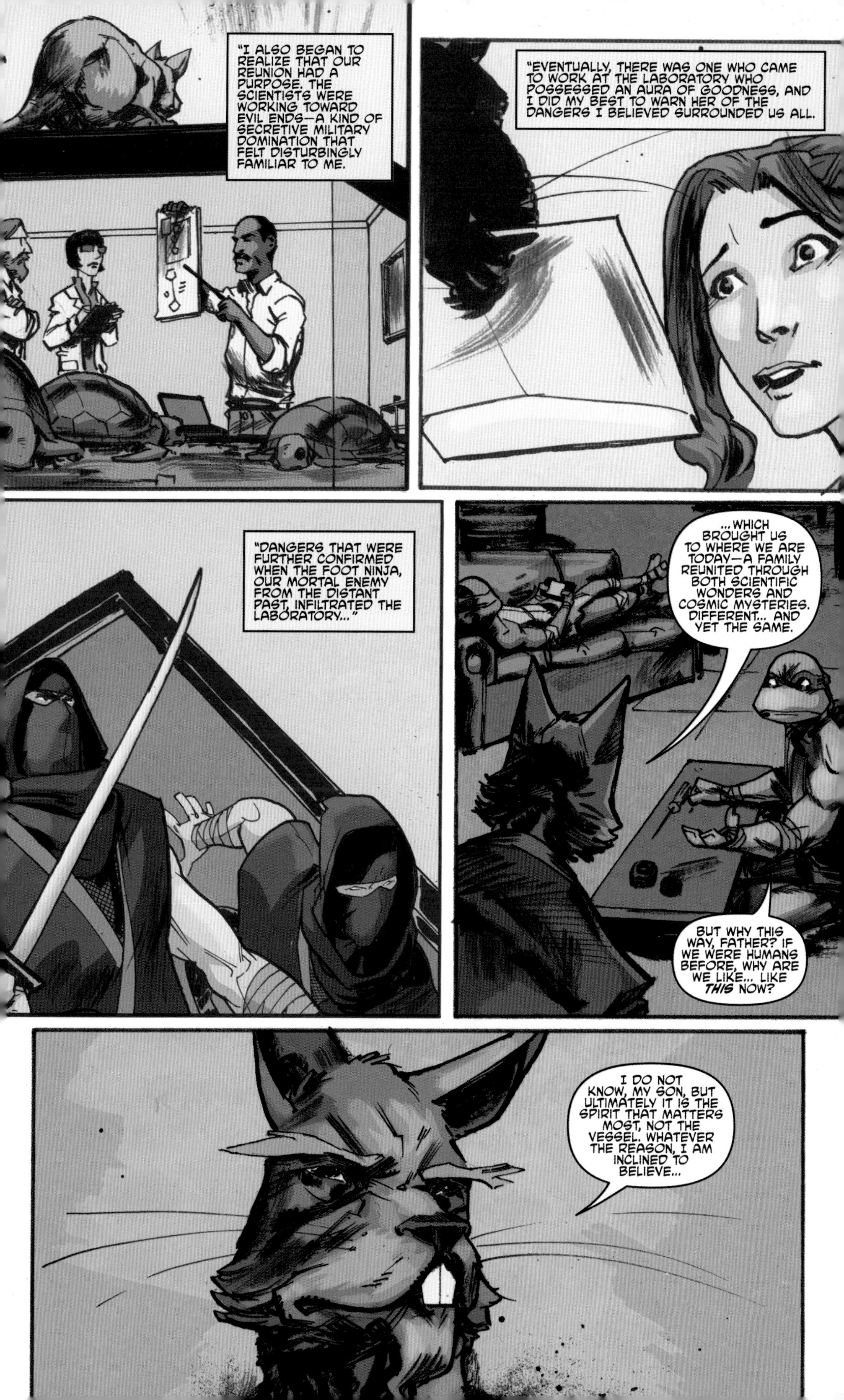
"I ALSO BEGAN TO REALIZE THAT OUR REUNION HAD A PURPOSE. THE SCIENTISTS WERE WORKING TOWARD EVIL ENDS—A KIND OF SECRETIVE MILITARY DOMINATION THAT FELT DISTURBINGLY FAMILIAR TO ME.
"EVENTUALLY, THERE WAS ONE WHO CAME TO WORK AT THE LABORATORY WHO POSSESSED AN AURA OF GOODNESS, AND I DID MY BEST TO WARN HER OF THE DANGERS I BELIEVED SURROUNDED US ALL.
"DANGERS THAT WERE FURTHER CONFIRMED WHEN THE FOOT NINJA, OUR MORTAL ENEMY FROM THE DISTANT PAST, INFILTRATED THE LABORATORY..."
...WHICH BROUGHT US TO WHERE WE ARE TODAY—A FAMILY REUNITED THROUGH BOTH SCIENTIFIC WONDERS AND COSMIC MYSTERIES. DIFFERENT... AND YET THE SAME.
BUT WHY THIS WAY, FATHER? IF WE WERE HUMANS BEFORE, WHY ARE WE LIKE... LIKE *THIS* NOW?
I DO NOT KNOW, MY SON, BUT ULTIMATELY IT IS THE SPIRIT THAT MATTERS MOST, NOT THE VESSEL. WHATEVER THE REASON, I AM INCLINED TO BELIEVE...

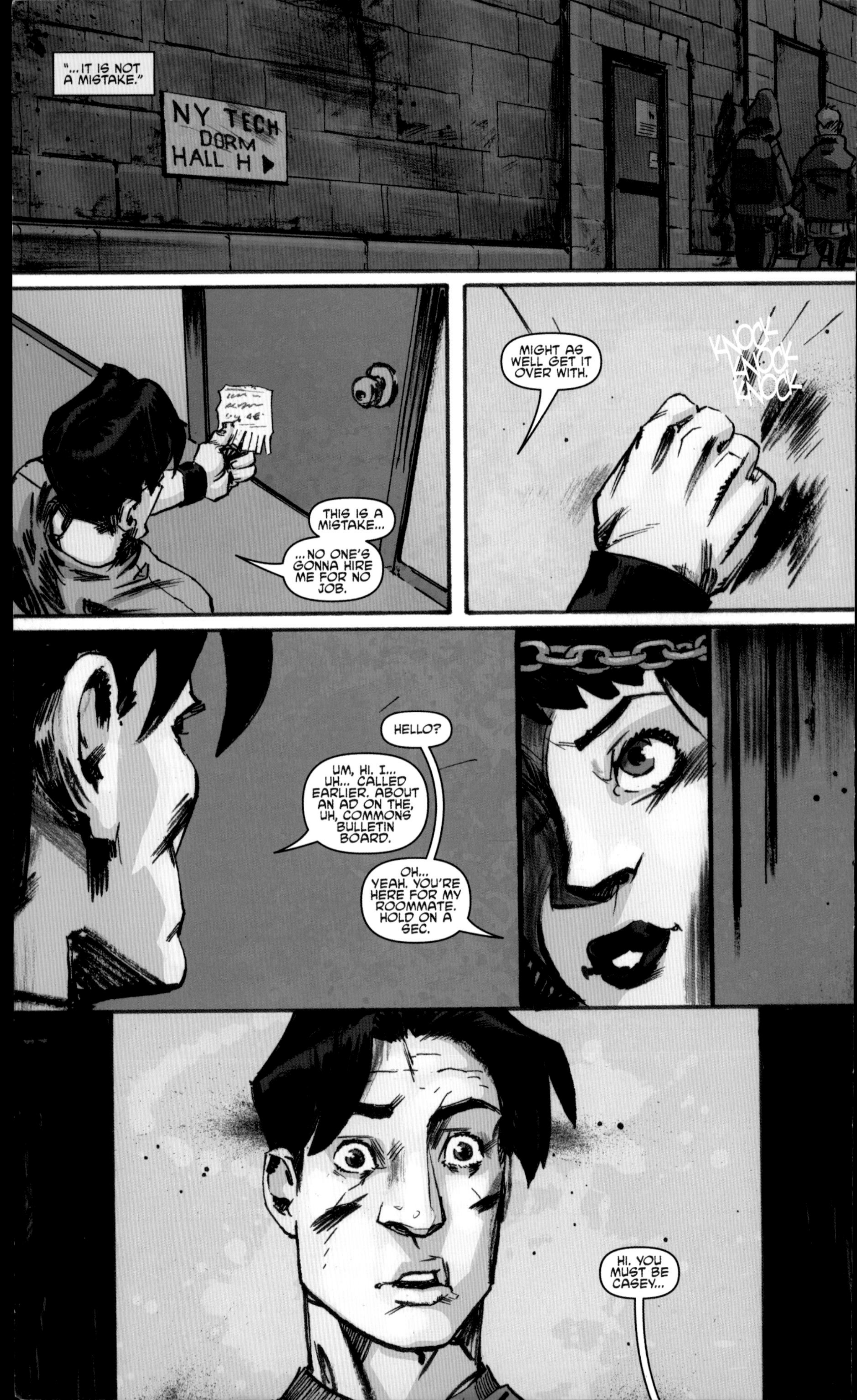
"...IT IS NOT A MISTAKE."
NY TECH DORM HALL H
THIS IS A MISTAKE...
...NO ONE'S GONNA HIRE ME FOR NO JOB.
MIGHT AS WELL GET IT OVER WITH.
KNOCK KNOCK KNOCK
HELLO?
UM, HI. I... UH... CALLED EARLIER. ABOUT AN AD ON THE, UH, COMMONS BULLETIN BOARD.
OH... YEAH. YOU'RE HERE FOR MY ROOMMATE. HOLD ON A SEC.
HI. YOU MUST BE CASEY...

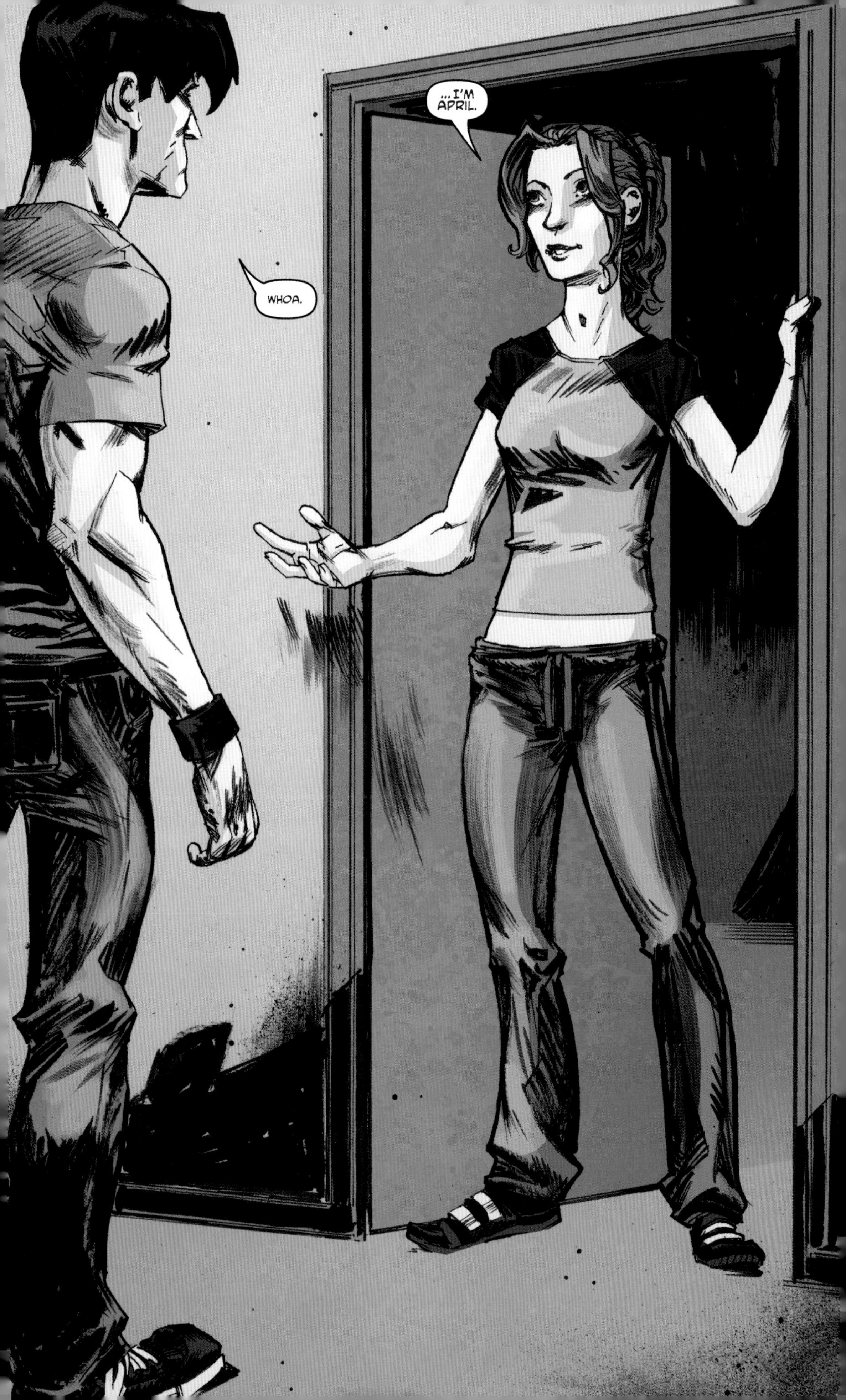
...I'M APRIL.
WHOA.

SO, MR. HOB, YOU SAY AN ARMY IS WHAT YOU REQUIRE TO FINALLY SUBDUE OUR RENEGADE RODENT AND HIS REPTILE *PROTÉGÉS,* HM?

UH, IF YOU'RE TALKIN' 'BOUT THAT SCRAWNY RAT AND THOSE SLIMY TURTLES, THEN, YEAH... AN ARMY'D BE REAL GOOD.

WELL, AS FORTUNE WOULD HAVE IT, STOCKGEN HAS BEEN DEVELOPING AN ARMY OF SORTS IN RECENT MONTHS, ONE THAT I BELIEVE CAN BE HELPFUL IN YOUR RECOVERY EFFORTS.

HOLY...

IMPRESSIVE, AREN'T THEY? WE'VE BEEN DEVELOPING THEM AS PART OF A PROGRAM TO LOCATE AND DESTROY I.E.D.S ON THE BATTLEFIELD.

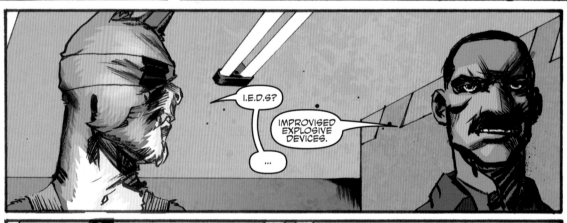

I.E.D.S?

IMPROVISED EXPLOSIVE DEVICES.

...

A BOOBY TRAP THAT GOES BOOM.

AH. GOTCHA.

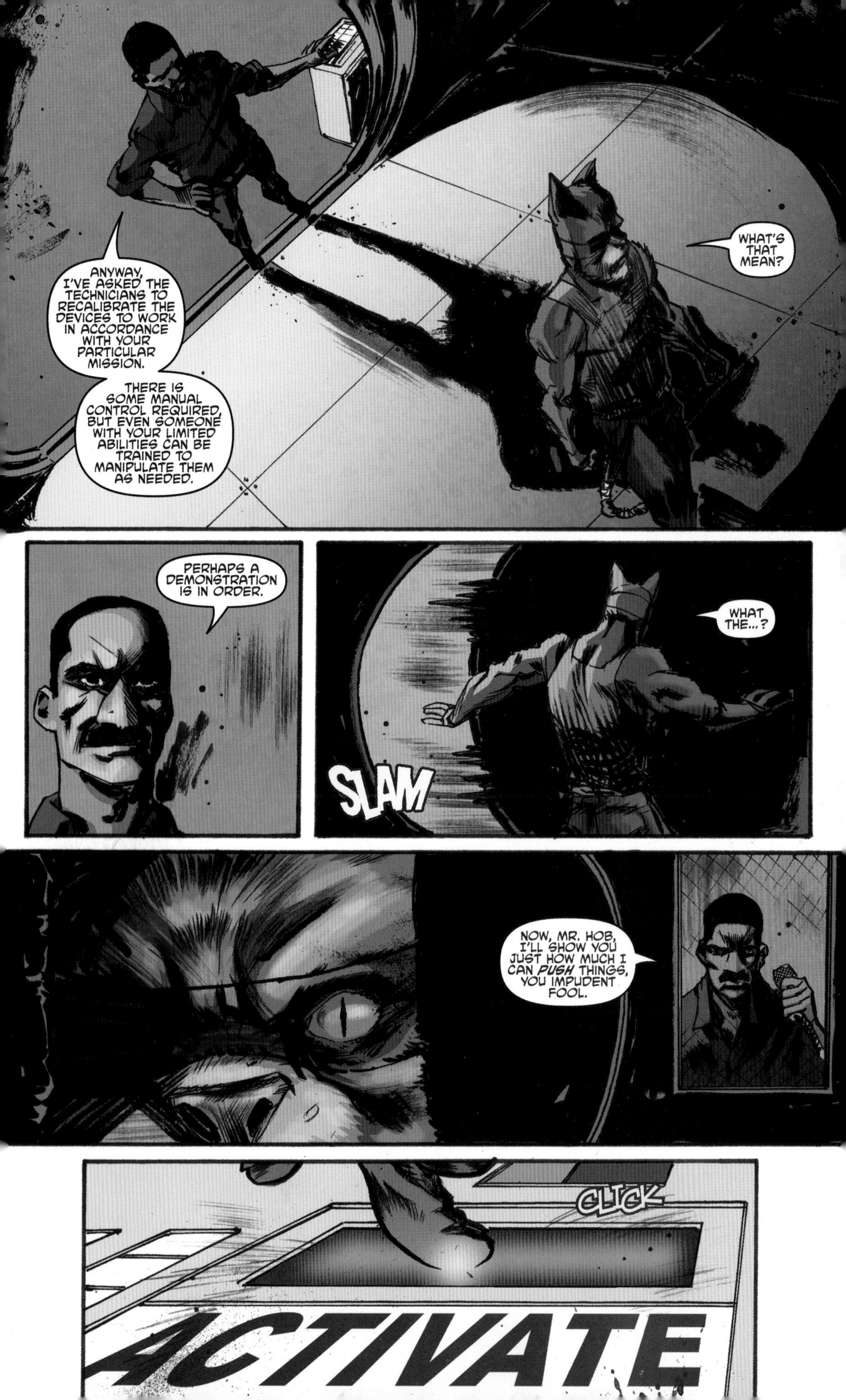
ANYWAY, I'VE ASKED THE TECHNICIANS TO RECALIBRATE THE DEVICES TO WORK IN ACCORDANCE WITH YOUR PARTICULAR MISSION.
THERE IS SOME MANUAL CONTROL REQUIRED, BUT EVEN SOMEONE WITH YOUR LIMITED ABILITIES CAN BE TRAINED TO MANIPULATE THEM AS NEEDED.
WHAT'S THAT MEAN?
PERHAPS A DEMONSTRATION IS IN ORDER.
SLAM
WHAT THE...?
NOW, MR. HOB, I'LL SHOW YOU JUST HOW MUCH I CAN *PUSH* THINGS, YOU IMPUDENT FOOL.
CLICK
ACTIVATE

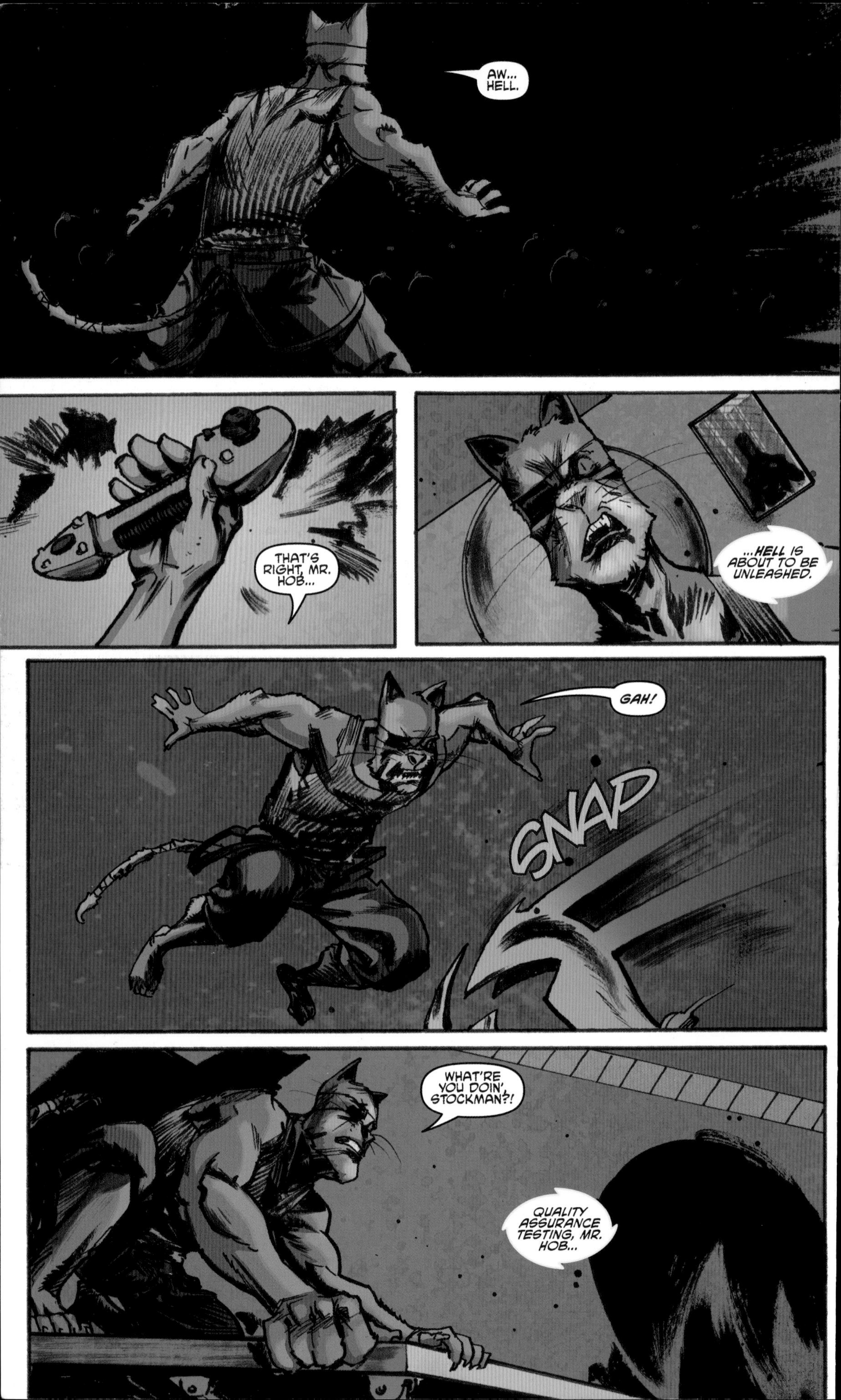
AW... HELL.
THAT'S RIGHT, MR. HOB...
...HELL IS ABOUT TO BE UNLEASHED.
GAH!
SNAP
WHAT'RE YOU DOIN', STOCKMAN?!
QUALITY ASSURANCE TESTING, MR. HOB...

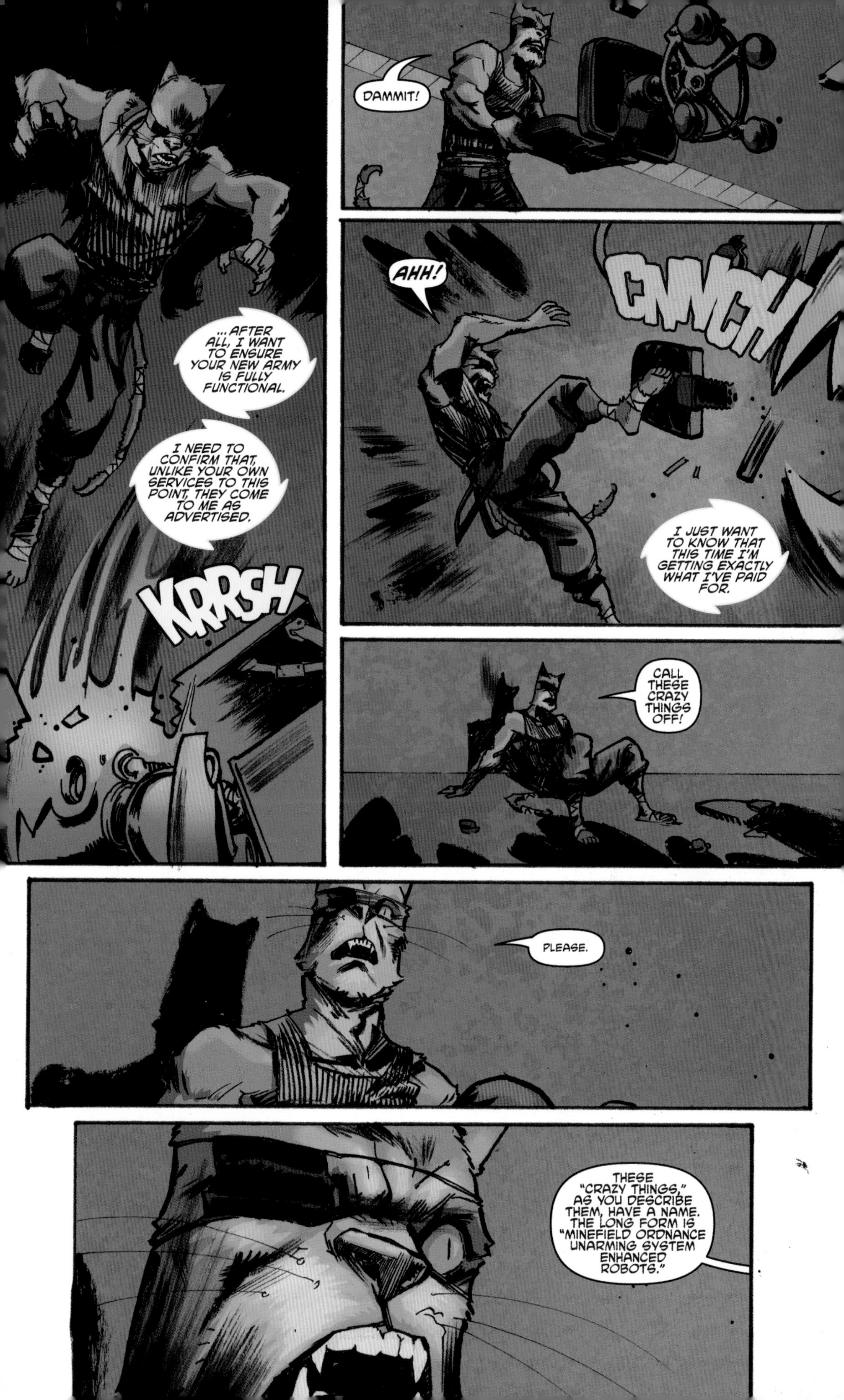
DAMMIT!
...AFTER ALL, I WANT TO ENSURE YOUR NEW ARMY IS FULLY FUNCTIONAL.
I NEED TO CONFIRM THAT, UNLIKE YOUR OWN SERVICES TO THIS POINT, THEY COME TO ME AS ADVERTISED.
KRRSH
AHH!
CHNCH
I JUST WANT TO KNOW THAT THIS TIME I'M GETTING EXACTLY WHAT I'VE PAID FOR.
CALL THESE CRAZY THINGS OFF!
PLEASE.
THESE "CRAZY THINGS," AS YOU DESCRIBE THEM, HAVE A NAME. THE LONG FORM IS "MINEFIELD ORDNANCE UNARMING SYSTEM ENHANCED ROBOTS."

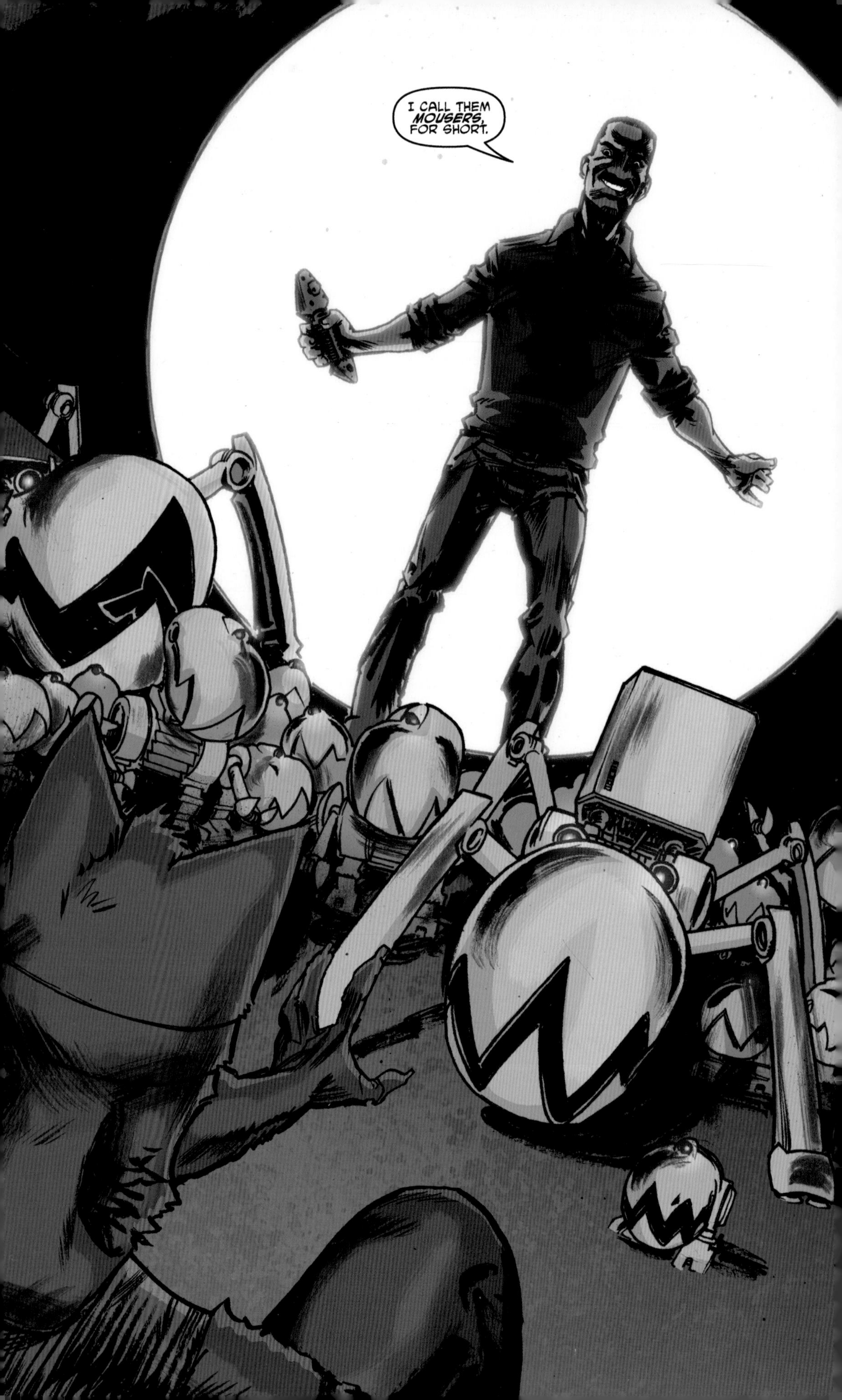
I CALL THEM *MOUSERS,* FOR SHORT.

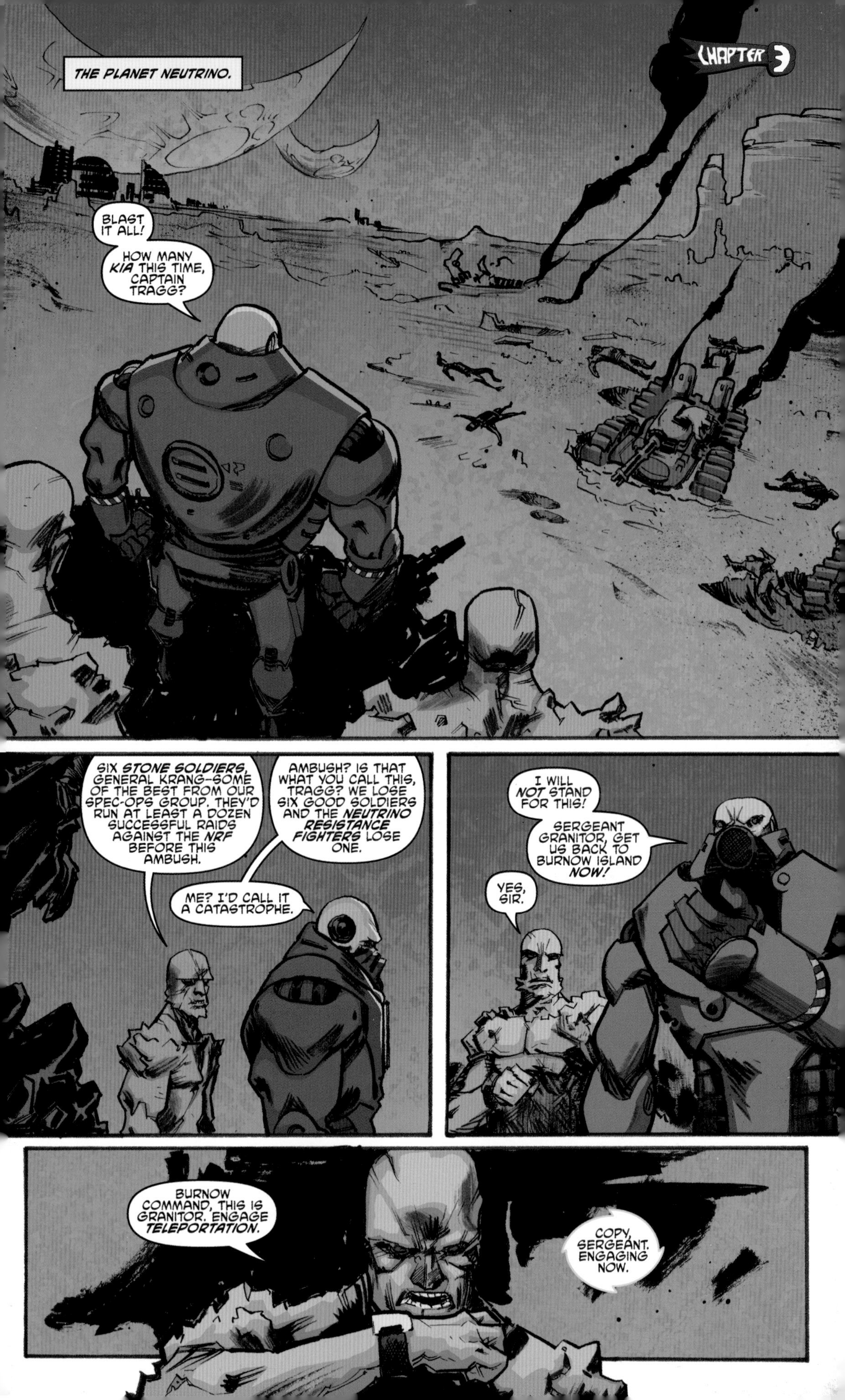
CHAPTER 3
THE PLANET NEUTRINO.
BLAST IT ALL!
HOW MANY KIA THIS TIME, CAPTAIN TRAGG?
SIX STONE SOLDIERS, GENERAL KRANG–SOME OF THE BEST FROM OUR SPEC-OPS GROUP. THEY'D RUN AT LEAST A DOZEN SUCCESSFUL RAIDS AGAINST THE NRF BEFORE THIS AMBUSH.
AMBUSH? IS THAT WHAT YOU CALL THIS, TRAGG? WE LOSE SIX GOOD SOLDIERS AND THE NEUTRINO RESISTANCE FIGHTERS LOSE ONE.
ME? I'D CALL IT A CATASTROPHE.
I WILL NOT STAND FOR THIS!
SERGEANT GRANITOR, GET US BACK TO BURNOW ISLAND NOW!
YES, SIR.
BURNOW COMMAND, THIS IS GRANITOR. ENGAGE TELEPORTATION.
COPY, SERGEANT. ENGAGING NOW.

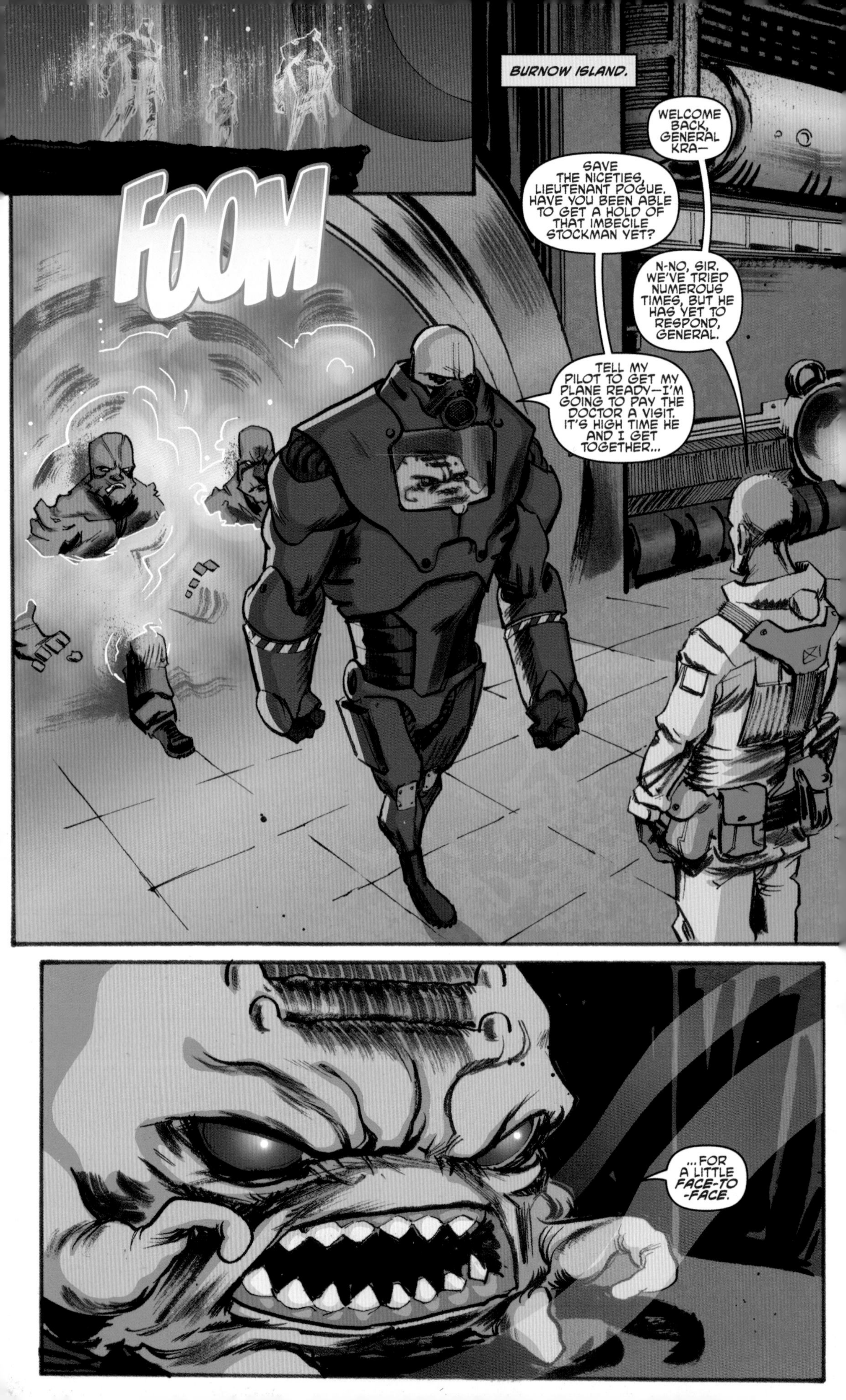
BURNOW ISLAND.
FOOM
WELCOME BACK, GENERAL KRA—
SAVE THE NICETIES, LIEUTENANT POGUE. HAVE YOU BEEN ABLE TO GET A HOLD OF THAT IMBECILE STOCKMAN YET?
N-NO, SIR. WE'VE TRIED NUMEROUS TIMES, BUT HE HAS YET TO RESPOND, GENERAL.
TELL MY PILOT TO GET MY PLANE READY—I'M GOING TO PAY THE DOCTOR A VISIT. IT'S HIGH TIME HE AND I GET TOGETHER...
...FOR A LITTLE FACE-TO-FACE.

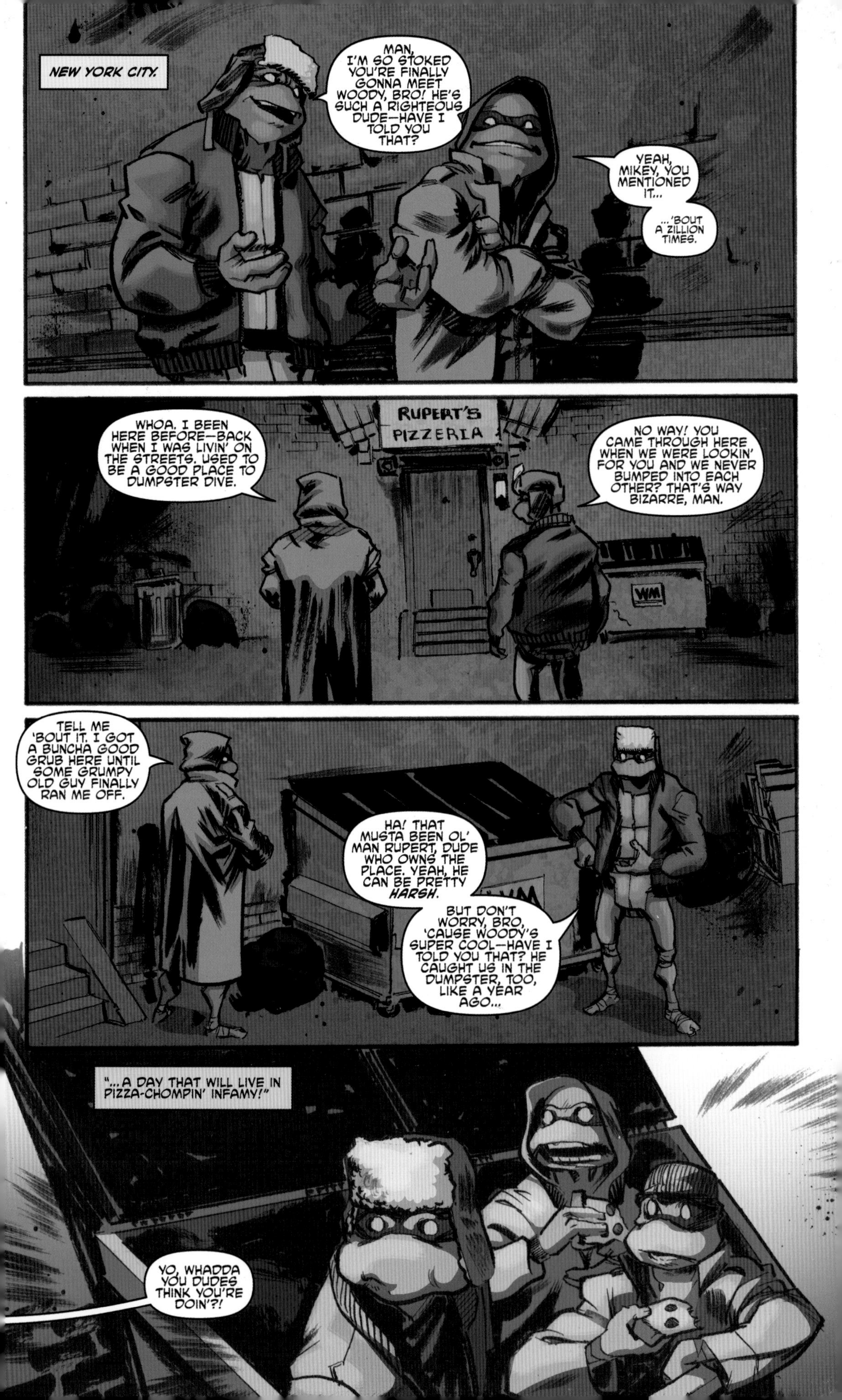
NEW YORK CITY.
MAN, I'M SO STOKED YOU'RE FINALLY GONNA MEET WOODY, BRO! HE'S SUCH A RIGHTEOUS DUDE—HAVE I TOLD YOU THAT?
YEAH, MIKEY, YOU MENTIONED IT...
...'BOUT A ZILLION TIMES.
RUPERT'S PIZZERIA
WHOA. I BEEN HERE BEFORE—BACK WHEN I WAS LIVIN' ON THE STREETS. USED TO BE A GOOD PLACE TO DUMPSTER DIVE.
NO WAY! YOU CAME THROUGH HERE WHEN WE WERE LOOKIN' FOR YOU AND WE NEVER BUMPED INTO EACH OTHER? THAT'S WAY BIZARRE, MAN.
WM
TELL ME 'BOUT IT. I GOT A BUNCHA GOOD GRUB HERE UNTIL SOME GRUMPY OLD GUY FINALLY RAN ME OFF.
HA! THAT MUSTA BEEN OL' MAN RUPERT, DUDE WHO OWNS THE PLACE. YEAH, HE CAN BE PRETTY HARSH.
BUT DON'T WORRY, BRO, 'CAUSE WOODY'S SUPER COOL—HAVE I TOLD YOU THAT? HE CAUGHT US IN THE DUMPSTER, TOO, LIKE A YEAR AGO...
"...A DAY THAT WILL LIVE IN PIZZA-CHOMPIN' INFAMY!"
YO, WHADDA YOU DUDES THINK YOU'RE DOIN'?!

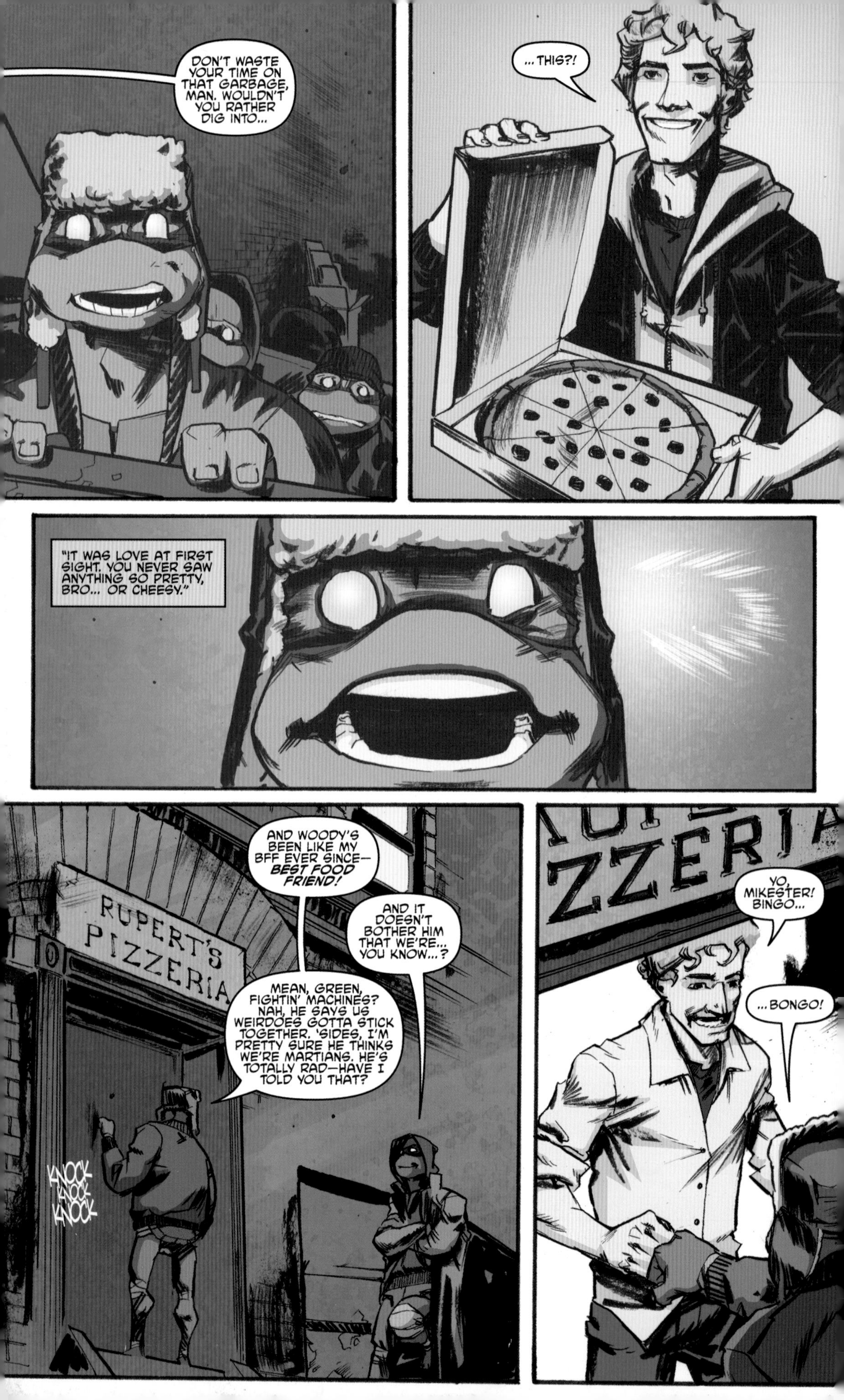
DON'T WASTE YOUR TIME ON THAT GARBAGE, MAN. WOULDN'T YOU RATHER DIG INTO...
...THIS?!
"IT WAS LOVE AT FIRST SIGHT. YOU NEVER SAW ANYTHING SO PRETTY, BRO... OR CHEESY."
AND WOODY'S BEEN LIKE MY BFF EVER SINCE— *BEST FOOD FRIEND!*
AND IT DOESN'T BOTHER HIM THAT WE'RE... YOU KNOW...?
MEAN, GREEN, FIGHTIN' MACHINES? NAH, HE SAYS US WEIRDOES GOTTA STICK TOGETHER. 'SIDES, I'M PRETTY SURE HE THINKS WE'RE MARTIANS. HE'S TOTALLY RAD—HAVE I TOLD YOU THAT?
RUPERT'S PIZZERIA
KNOCK KNOCK KNOCK
ZZERIA
YO, MIKESTER! BINGO...
...BONGO!

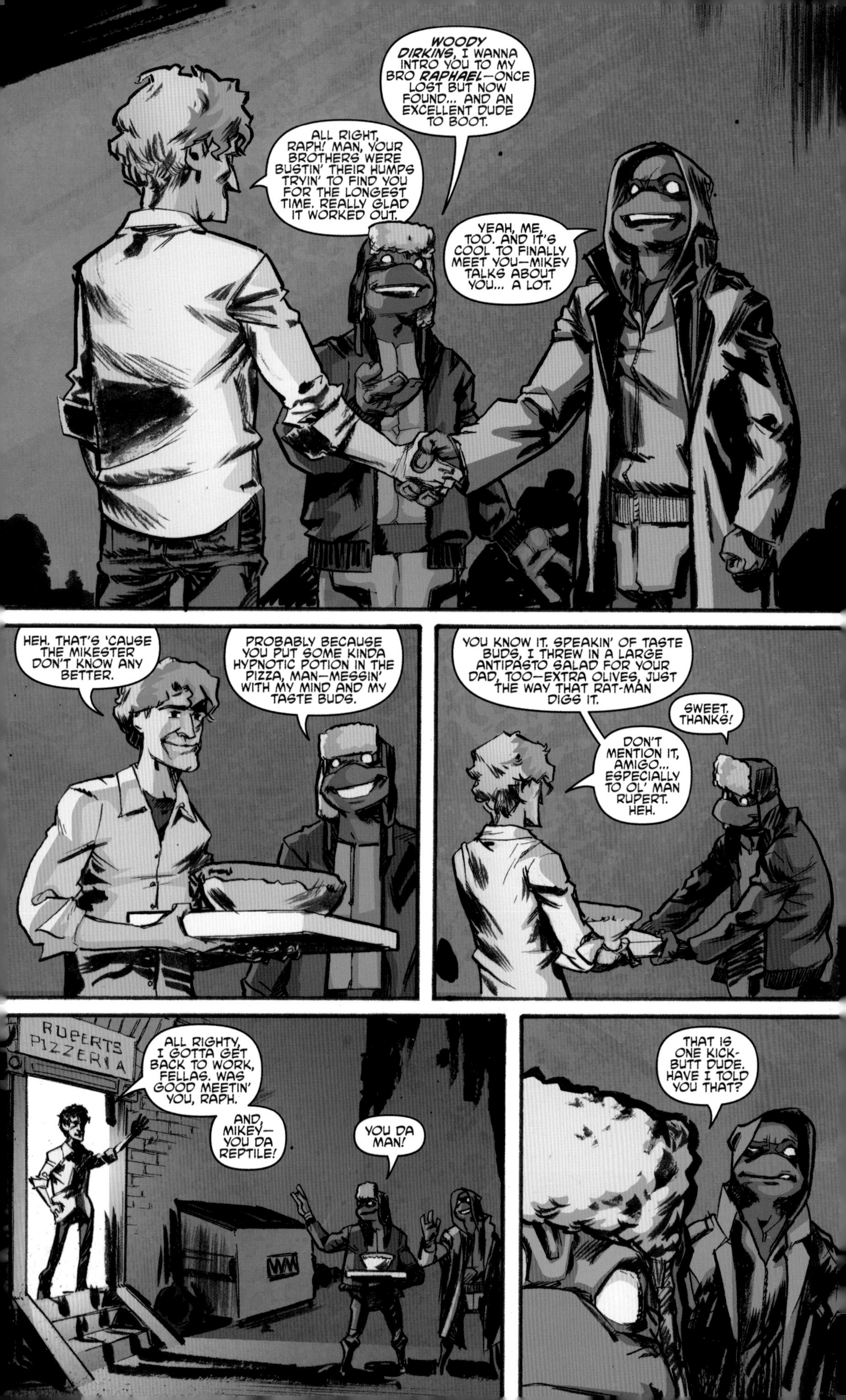
WOODY DIRKINS, I WANNA INTRO YOU TO MY BRO RAPHAEL—ONCE LOST BUT NOW FOUND... AND AN EXCELLENT DUDE TO BOOT.
ALL RIGHT, RAPH! MAN, YOUR BROTHERS WERE BUSTIN' THEIR HUMPS TRYIN' TO FIND YOU FOR THE LONGEST TIME. REALLY GLAD IT WORKED OUT.
YEAH, ME, TOO. AND IT'S COOL TO FINALLY MEET YOU—MIKEY TALKS ABOUT YOU... A LOT.
HEH. THAT'S 'CAUSE THE MIKESTER DON'T KNOW ANY BETTER.
PROBABLY BECAUSE YOU PUT SOME KINDA HYPNOTIC POTION IN THE PIZZA, MAN—MESSIN' WITH MY MIND AND MY TASTE BUDS.
YOU KNOW IT. SPEAKIN' OF TASTE BUDS, I THREW IN A LARGE ANTIPASTO SALAD FOR YOUR DAD, TOO—EXTRA OLIVES, JUST THE WAY THAT RAT-MAN DIGS IT.
SWEET. THANKS!
DON'T MENTION IT, AMIGO... ESPECIALLY TO OL' MAN RUPERT. HEH.
RUPERTS PIZZERIA
ALL RIGHTY, I GOTTA GET BACK TO WORK, FELLAS. WAS GOOD MEETIN' YOU, RAPH.
AND, MIKEY— YOU DA REPTILE!
YOU DA MAN!
THAT IS ONE KICK-BUTT DUDE. HAVE I TOLD YOU THAT?

*As seen in **TMNT** #6 – B.C.

I JUST DON'T BUY IT, LEO. I... ...I JUST CAN'T.

BUT YOU SAW IT FOR YOURSELF, DONNIE—THOSE WERE *FOOT NINJA* ON THAT ROOF FIGHTING AGAINST THAT FRENCH GUY.*

NO, I SAW NINJA FIGHTING THE *SAVATE* DUDE— IT WAS MASTER SPLINTER WHO SAID THEY WERE FOOT NINJA, AND HE WASN'T EVEN THERE.

YEAH, BUT WE DESCRIBED THEM TO HIM PRETTY ACCURATELY. IF ANYONE KNOWS WHAT A FOOT NINJA LOOKS LIKE, IT'S FATHER.

AND THERE'S *THAT*, TOO, MAN. FATHER SAYS HE KNOWS WHAT THE FOOT LOOK LIKE BECAUSE HE USED TO BE ONE IN FEUDAL JAPAN... WHICH IS CRAZY.

C'MON, LEO... *REINCARNATION?* THAT SOUNDS ABOUT AS BELIEVABLE AS ONE OF MIKEY'S GOOFY COMIC BOOK STORIES.

IF IT'S TRUE, WHY IS IT HE REMEMBERS THE PAST AND WE DON'T?

YOU KNOW, I'M NOT SO SURE ABOUT THAT.

I MEAN... SOMETIMES WHEN I'M DREAMING, I... SEE THINGS. LITTLE FLASHES THAT SEEM SO REAL, LIKE... LIKE THEY HAPPENED TO ME. SOMETIMES I EVEN SEE...

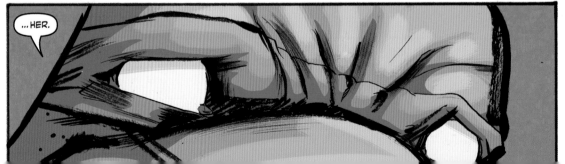

...HER.

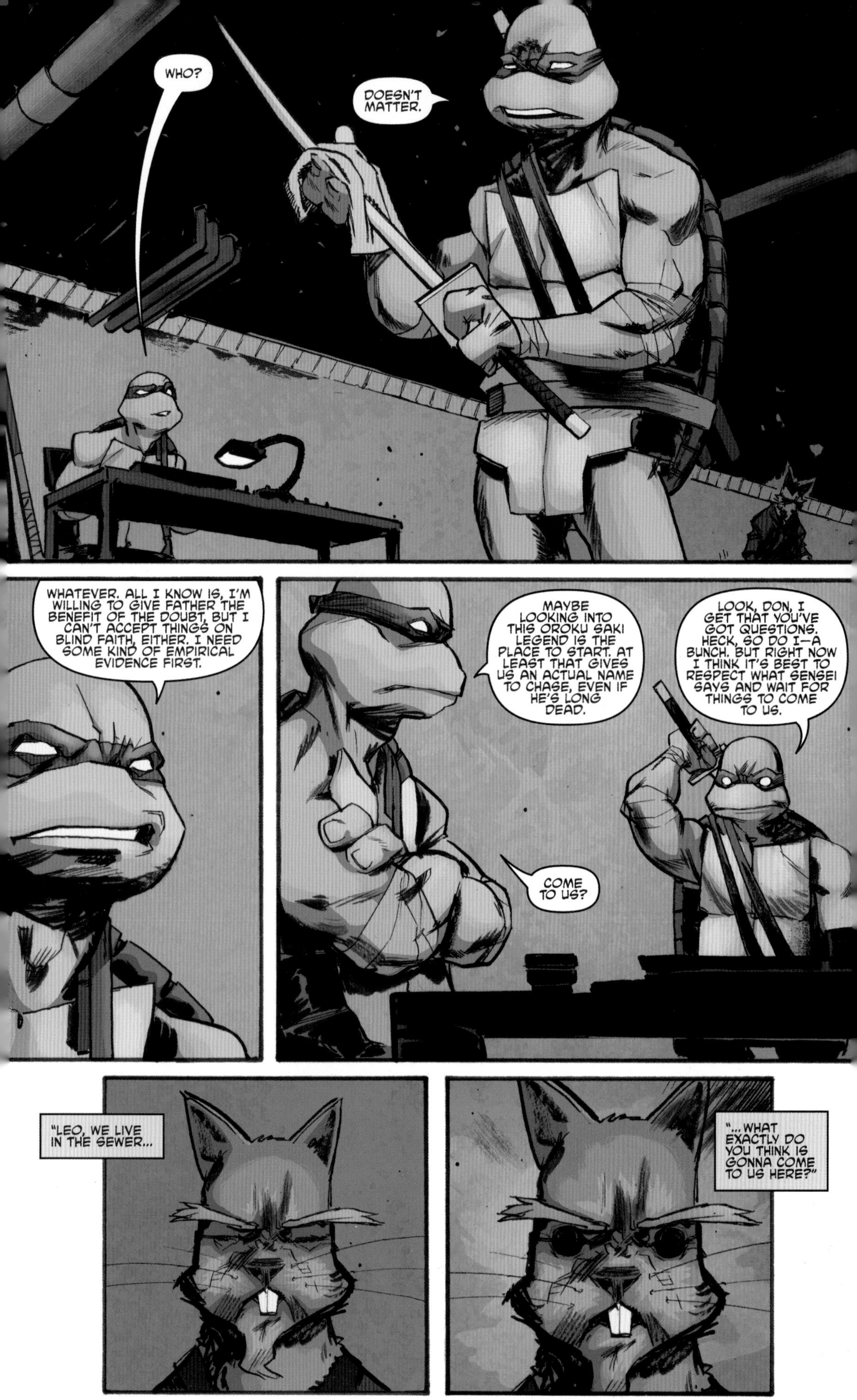
WHO?
DOESN'T MATTER.
WHATEVER. ALL I KNOW IS, I'M WILLING TO GIVE FATHER THE BENEFIT OF THE DOUBT, BUT I CAN'T ACCEPT THINGS ON BLIND FAITH, EITHER. I NEED SOME KIND OF EMPIRICAL EVIDENCE FIRST.
MAYBE LOOKING INTO THIS OROKU SAKI LEGEND IS THE PLACE TO START. AT LEAST THAT GIVES US AN ACTUAL NAME TO CHASE, EVEN IF HE'S LONG DEAD.
LOOK, DON, I GET THAT YOU'VE GOT QUESTIONS. HECK, SO DO I—A BUNCH. BUT RIGHT NOW I THINK IT'S BEST TO RESPECT WHAT SENSEI SAYS AND WAIT FOR THINGS TO COME TO US.
COME TO US?
"LEO, WE LIVE IN THE SEWER...
"...WHAT EXACTLY DO YOU THINK IS GONNA COME TO US HERE?"

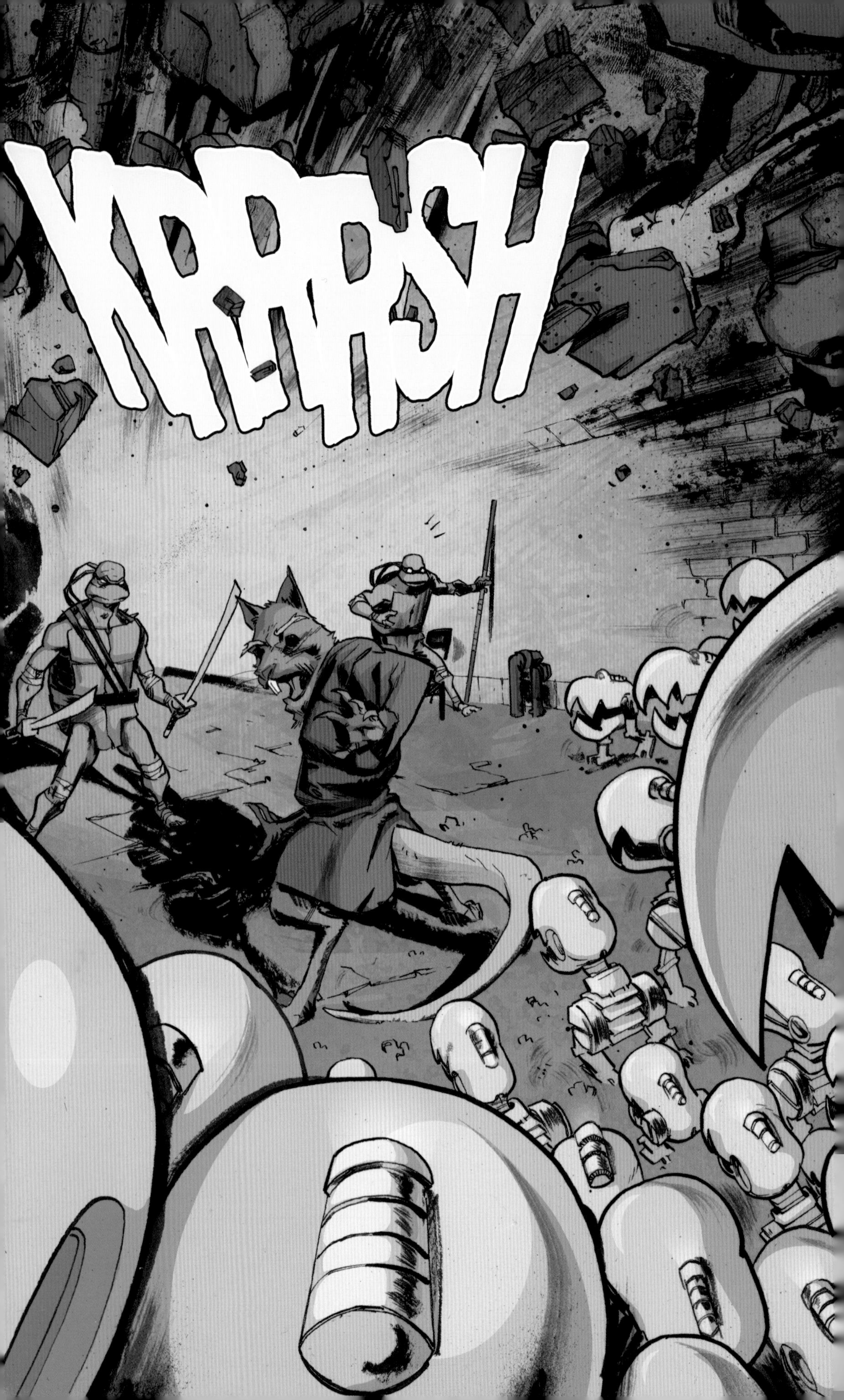
KRRRSH

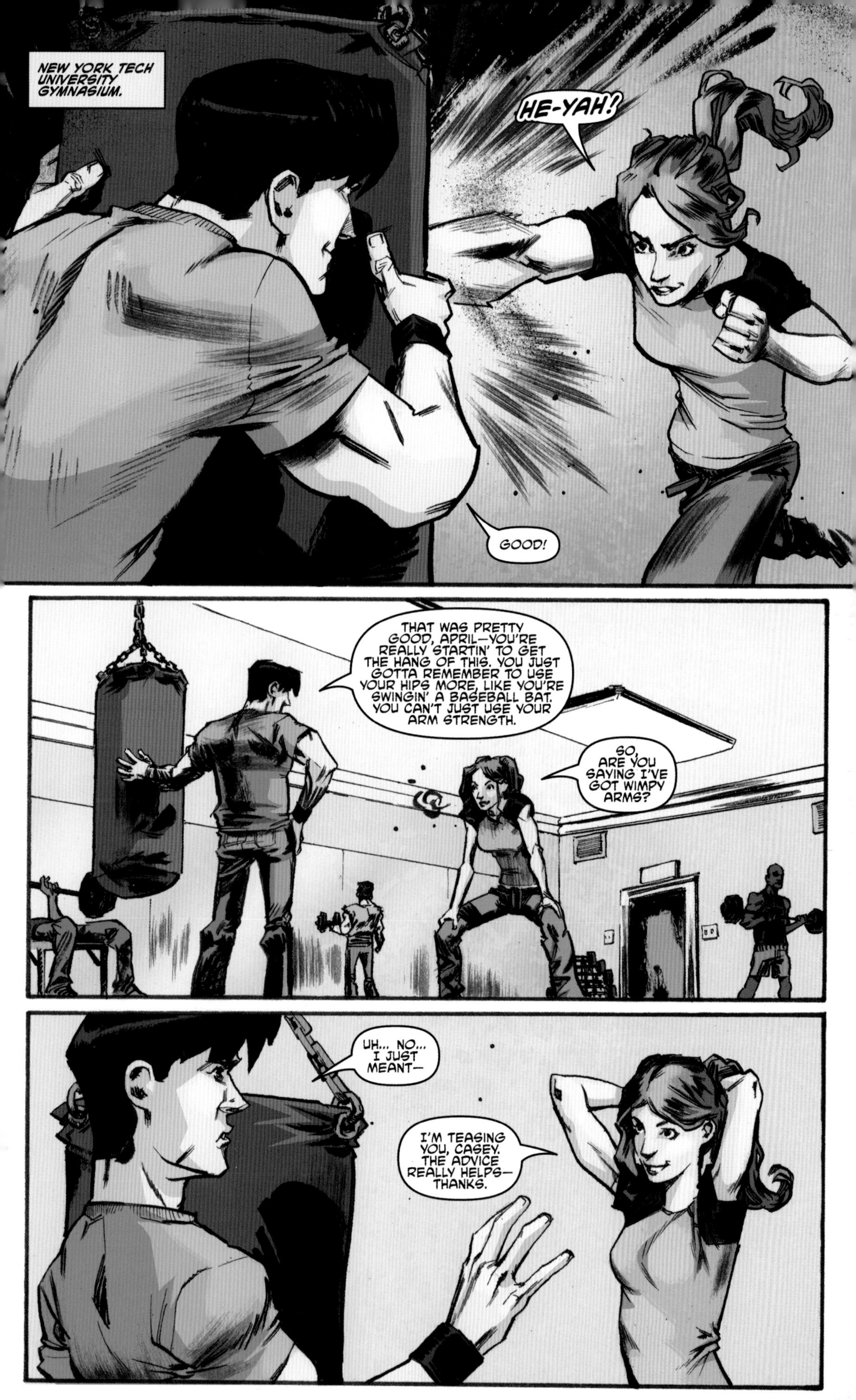
NEW YORK TECH UNIVERSITY GYMNASIUM.
HE-YAH!
GOOD!
THAT WAS PRETTY GOOD, APRIL—YOU'RE REALLY STARTIN' TO GET THE HANG OF THIS. YOU JUST GOTTA REMEMBER TO USE YOUR HIPS MORE, LIKE YOU'RE SWINGIN' A BASEBALL BAT. YOU CAN'T JUST USE YOUR ARM STRENGTH.
SO, ARE YOU SAYING I'VE GOT WIMPY ARMS?
UH... NO... I JUST MEANT—
I'M TEASING YOU, CASEY. THE ADVICE REALLY HELPS—THANKS.

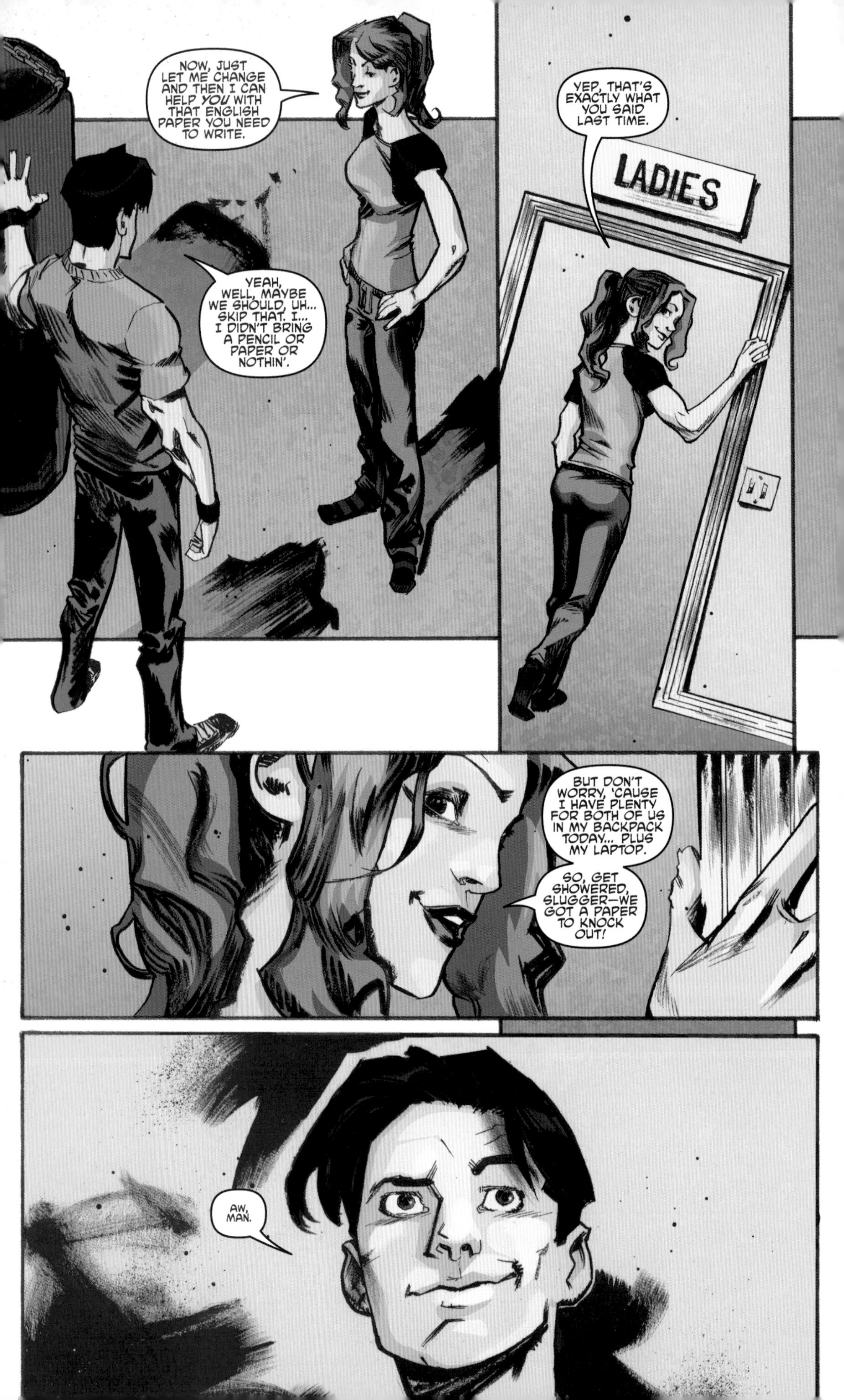
NOW, JUST LET ME CHANGE AND THEN I CAN HELP *YOU* WITH THAT ENGLISH PAPER YOU NEED TO WRITE.
YEAH, WELL, MAYBE WE SHOULD, UH... SKIP THAT. I... I DIDN'T BRING A PENCIL OR PAPER OR NOTHIN'.
YEP, THAT'S EXACTLY WHAT YOU SAID LAST TIME.
LADIES
BUT DON'T WORRY, 'CAUSE I HAVE PLENTY FOR BOTH OF US IN MY BACKPACK TODAY... PLUS MY LAPTOP.
SO, GET SHOWERED, SLUGGER—WE GOT A PAPER TO KNOCK OUT!
AW, MAN.

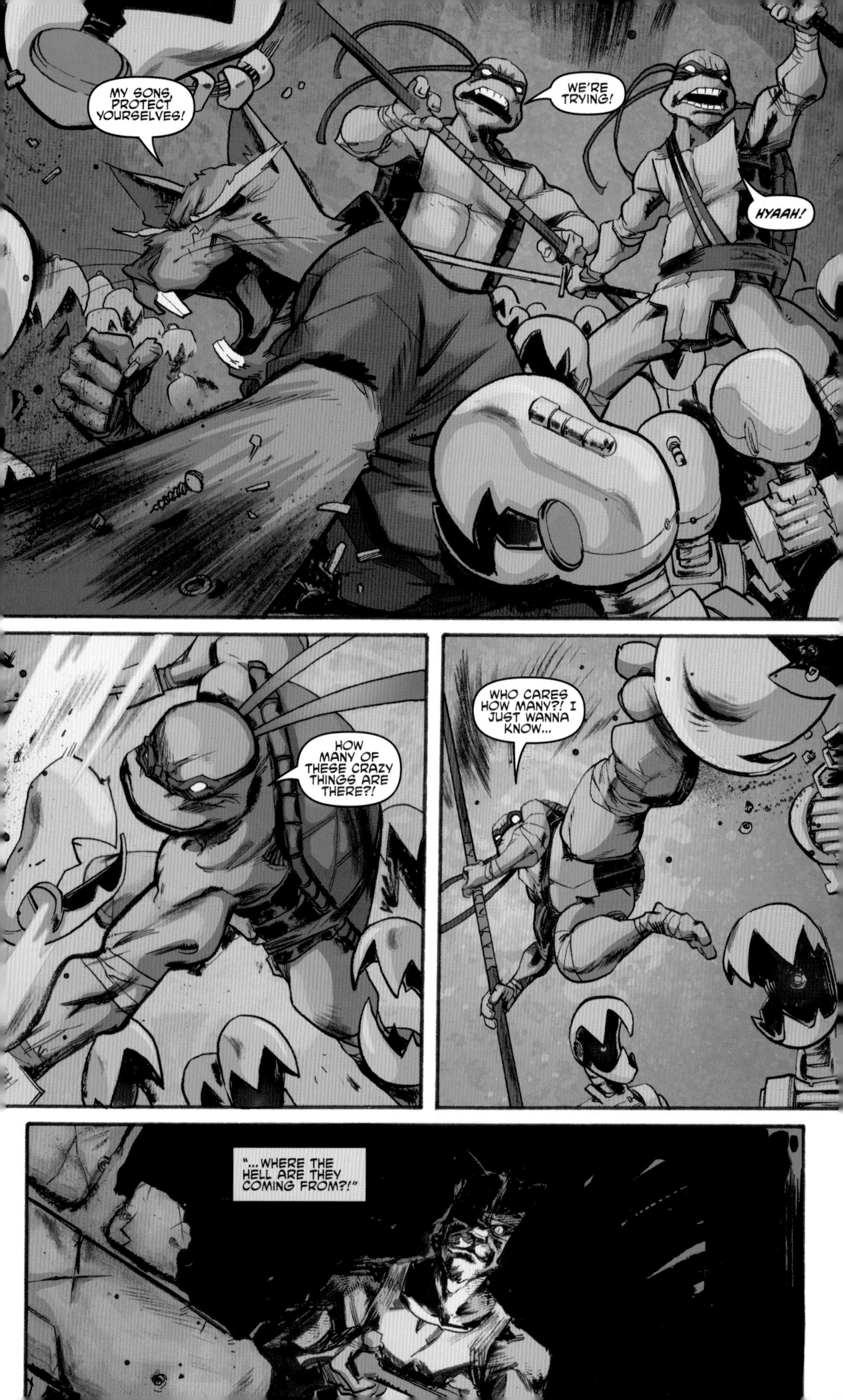
MY SONS, PROTECT YOURSELVES!
WE'RE TRYING!
HYAAH!
HOW MANY OF THESE CRAZY THINGS ARE THERE?!
WHO CARES HOW MANY?! I JUST WANNA KNOW...
"...WHERE THE HELL ARE THEY COMING FROM?!"

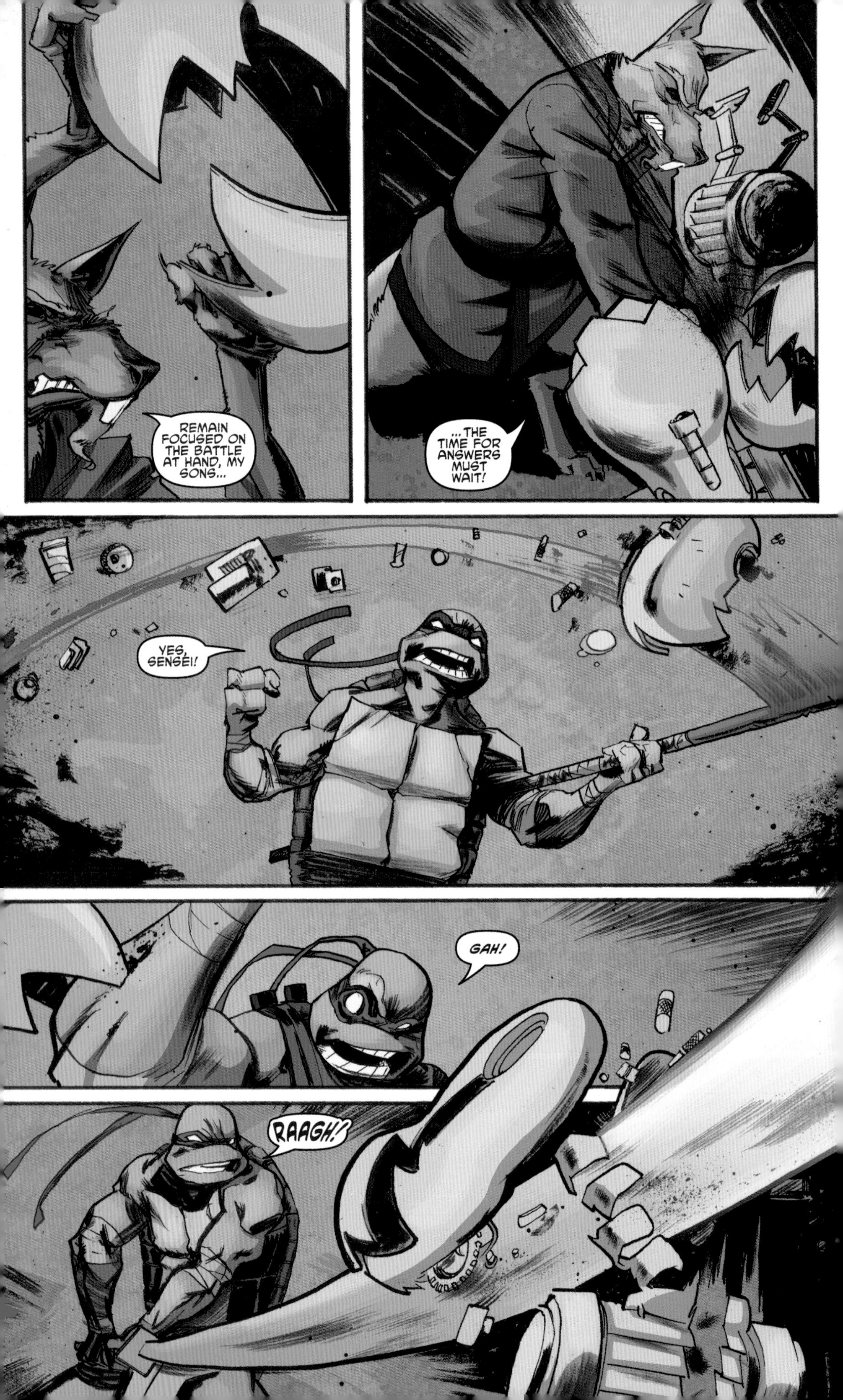
REMAIN FOCUSED ON THE BATTLE AT HAND, MY SONS...
...THE TIME FOR ANSWERS MUST WAIT!
YES, SENSEI!
GAH!
RAAGH!

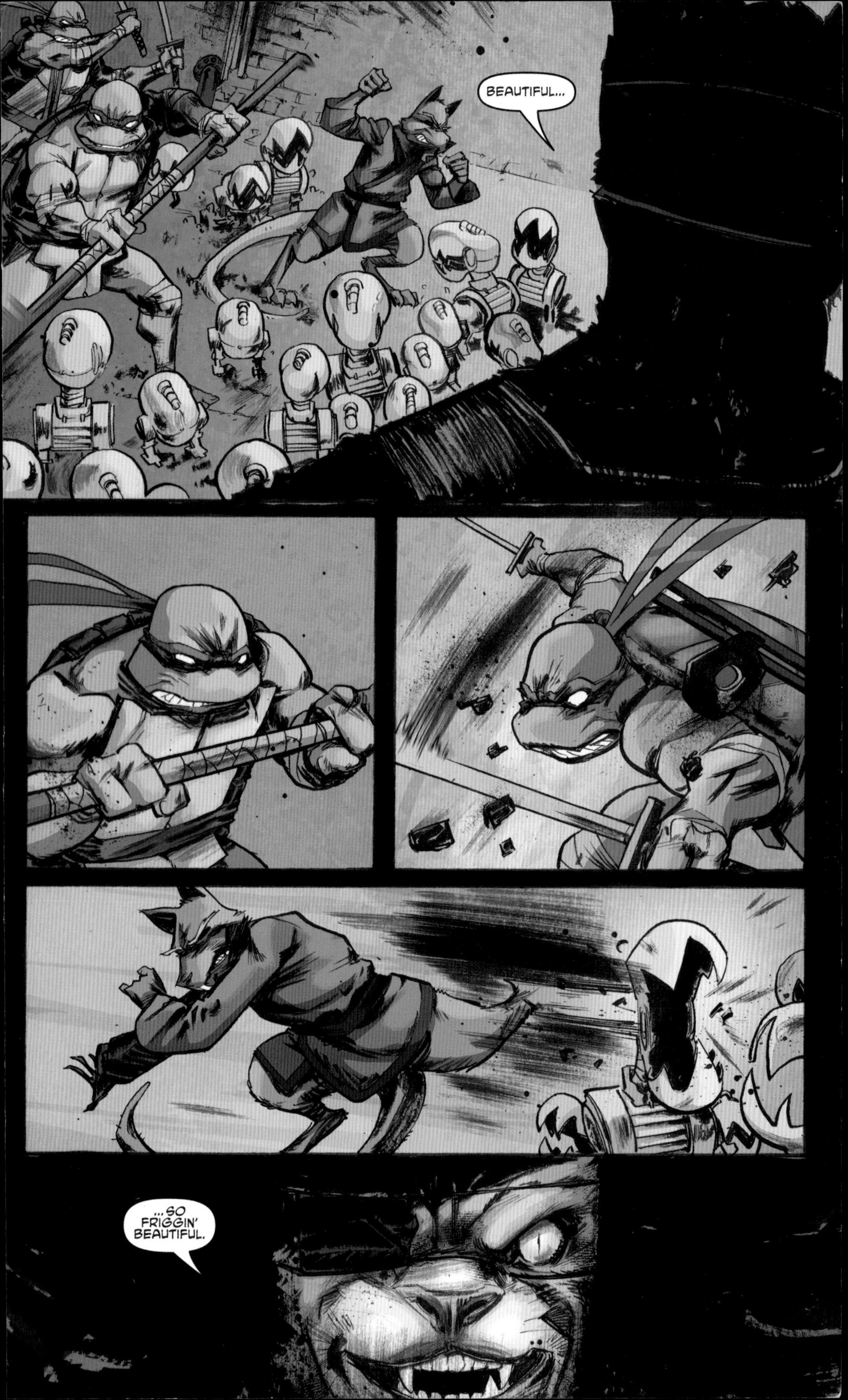
BEAUTIFUL...
...SO FRIGGIN' BEAUTIFUL.

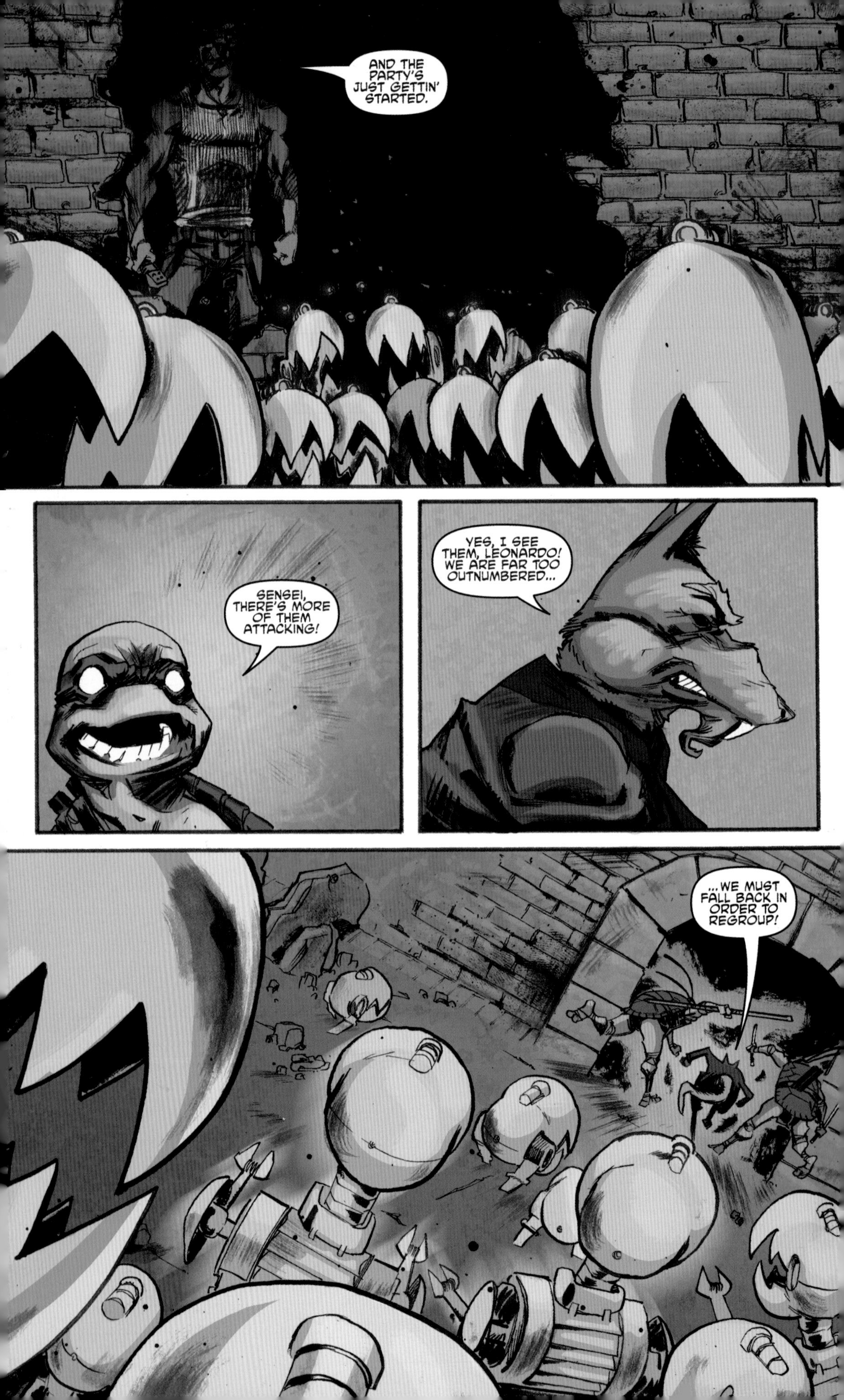
AND THE PARTY'S JUST GETTIN' STARTED.
SENSEI, THERE'S MORE OF THEM ATTACKING!
YES, I SEE THEM, LEONARDO! WE ARE FAR TOO OUTNUMBERED...
...WE MUST FALL BACK IN ORDER TO REGROUP!

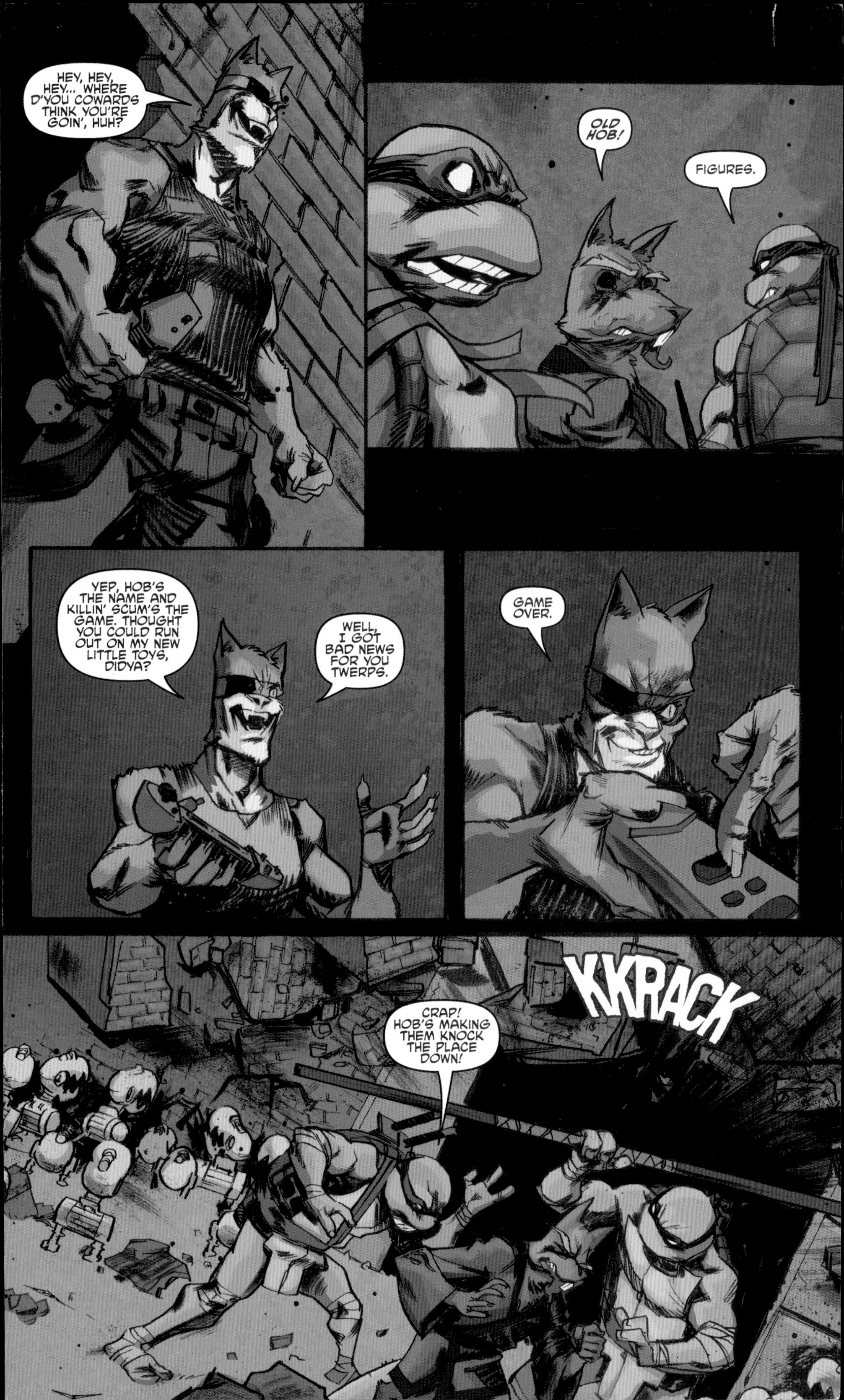
HEY, HEY, HEY... WHERE D'YOU COWARDS THINK YOU'RE GOIN', HUH?
OLD HOB!
FIGURES.
YEP, HOB'S THE NAME AND KILLIN' SCUM'S THE GAME. THOUGHT YOU COULD RUN OUT ON MY NEW LITTLE TOYS, DIDYA?
WELL, I GOT BAD NEWS FOR YOU TWERPS.
GAME OVER.
KKRACK
CRAP! HOB'S MAKING THEM KNOCK THE PLACE DOWN!

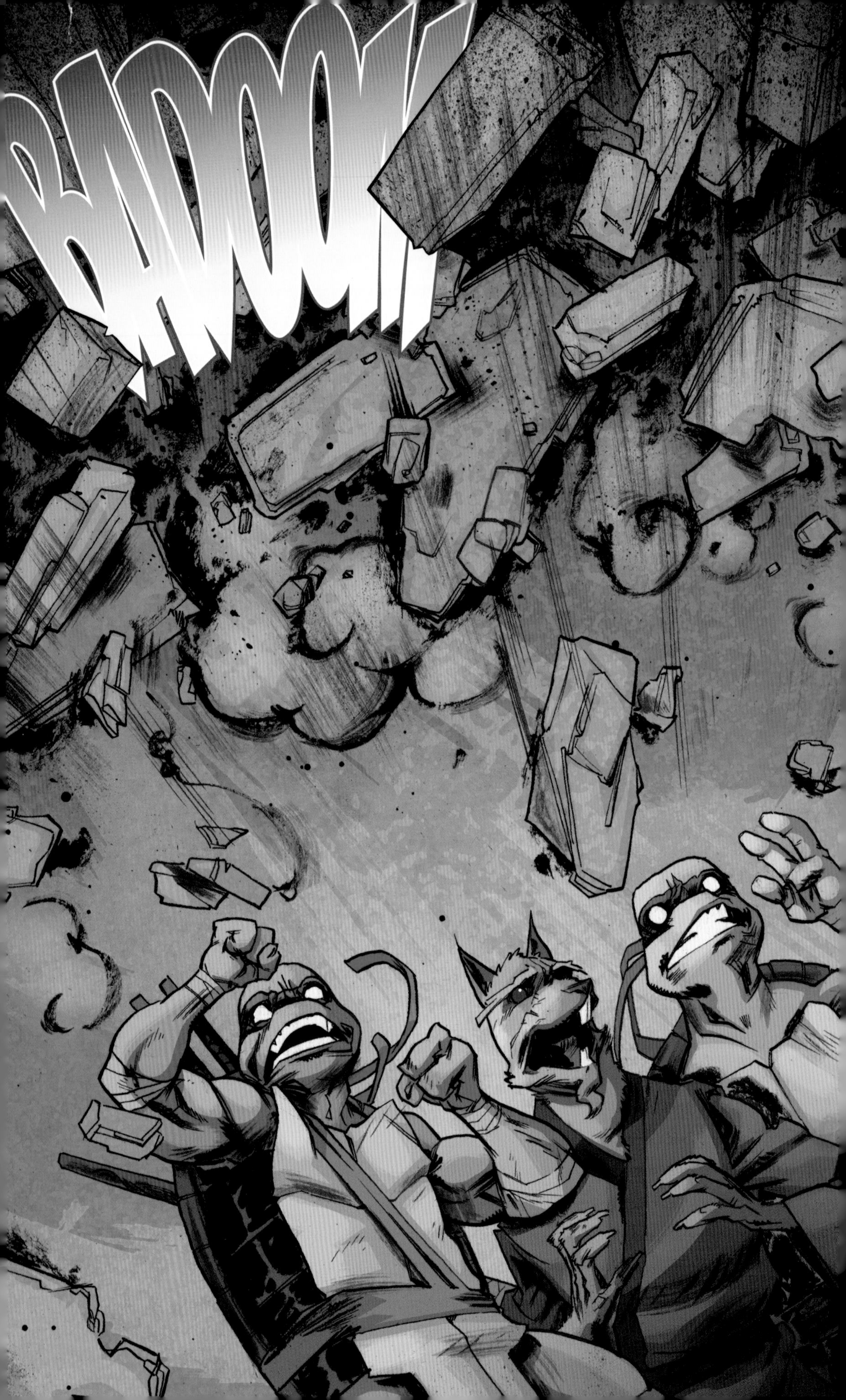
BADOOM!

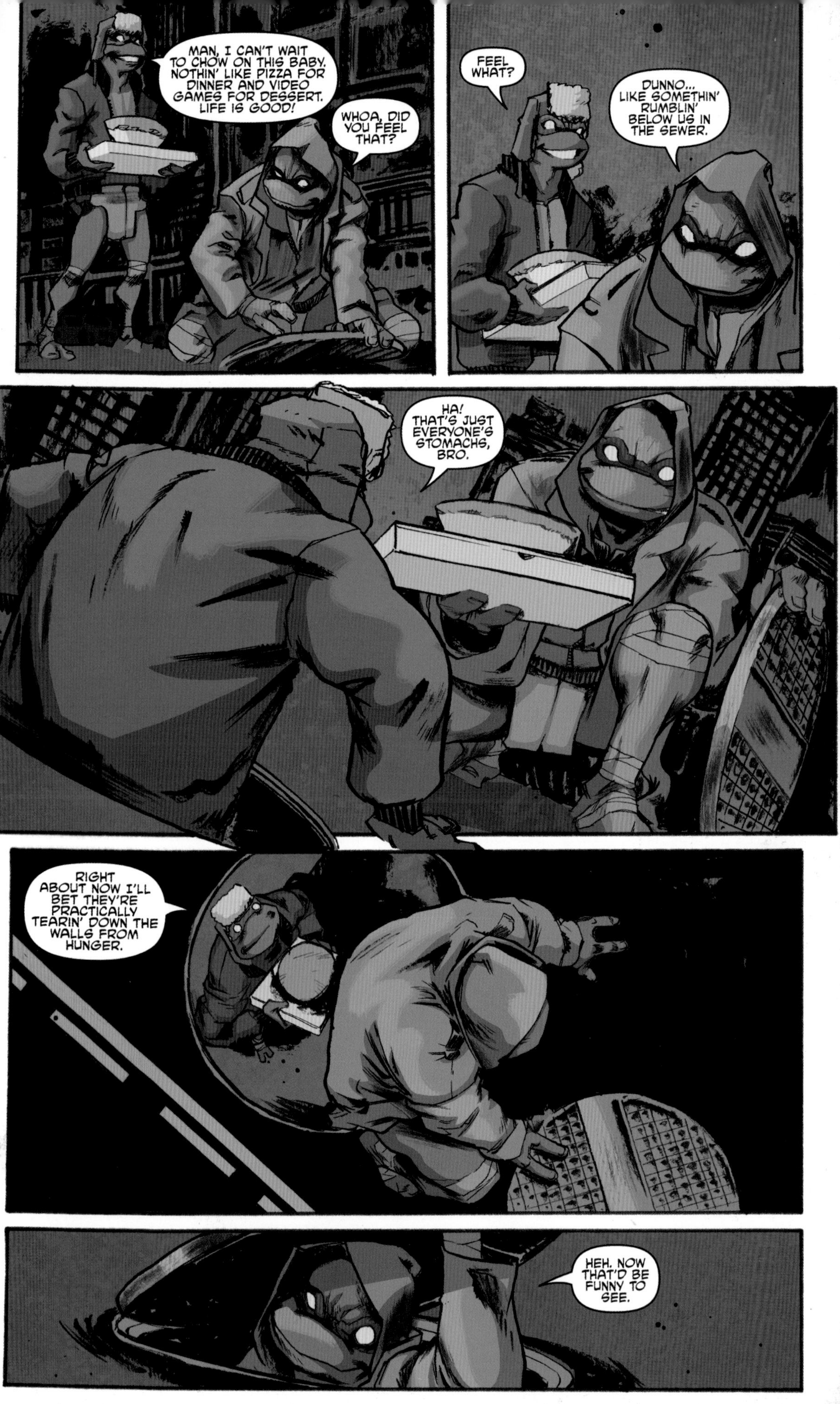
MAN, I CAN'T WAIT TO CHOW ON THIS BABY. NOTHIN' LIKE PIZZA FOR DINNER AND VIDEO GAMES FOR DESSERT. LIFE IS GOOD!
WHOA, DID YOU FEEL THAT?
FEEL WHAT?
DUNNO... LIKE SOMETHIN' RUMBLIN' BELOW US IN THE SEWER.
HA! THAT'S JUST EVERYONE'S STOMACHS, BRO.
RIGHT ABOUT NOW I'LL BET THEY'RE PRACTICALLY TEARIN' DOWN THE WALLS FROM HUNGER.
HEH. NOW THAT'D BE FUNNY TO SEE.

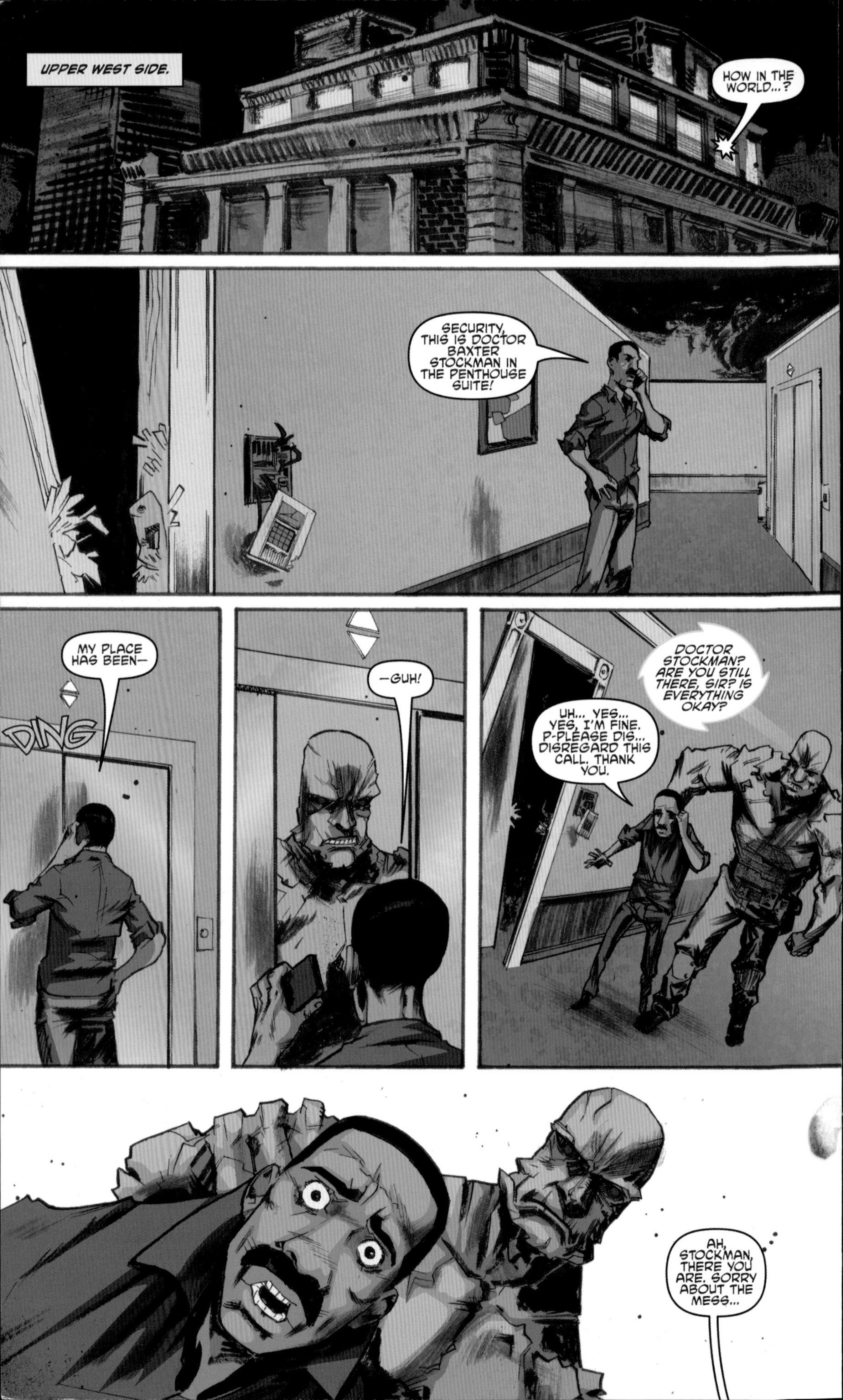
UPPER WEST SIDE.
HOW IN THE WORLD...?
SECURITY, THIS IS DOCTOR BAXTER STOCKMAN IN THE PENTHOUSE SUITE!
MY PLACE HAS BEEN—
DING
—GUH!
DOCTOR STOCKMAN? ARE YOU STILL THERE, SIR? IS EVERYTHING OKAY?
UH... YES... YES, I'M FINE. P-PLEASE DIS... DISREGARD THIS CALL. THANK YOU.
AH, STOCKMAN, THERE YOU ARE. SORRY ABOUT THE MESS...

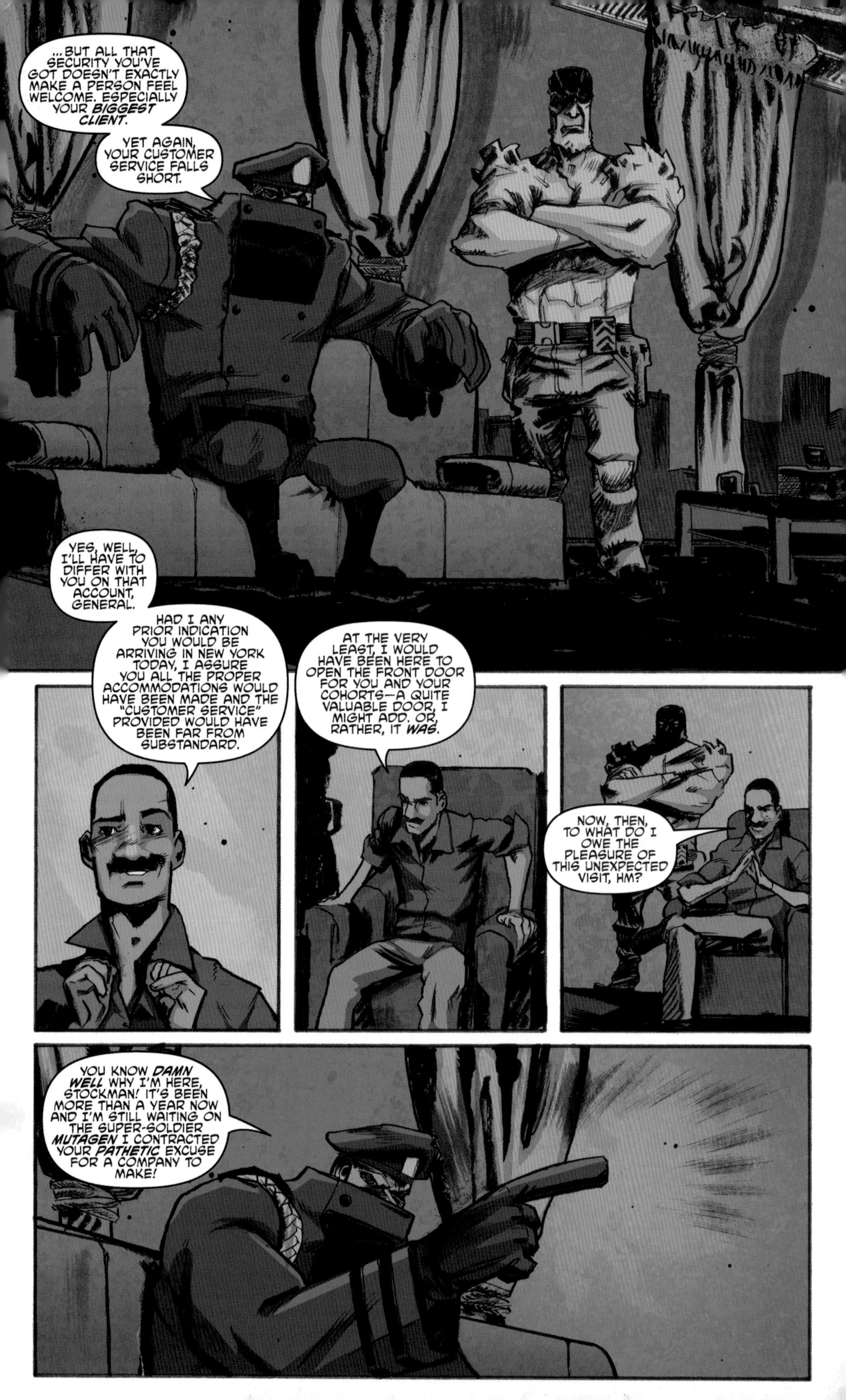
...BUT ALL THAT SECURITY YOU'VE GOT DOESN'T EXACTLY MAKE A PERSON FEEL WELCOME. ESPECIALLY YOUR *BIGGEST CLIENT*.
YET AGAIN, YOUR CUSTOMER SERVICE FALLS SHORT.
YES, WELL, I'LL HAVE TO DIFFER WITH YOU ON THAT ACCOUNT, GENERAL.
HAD I ANY PRIOR INDICATION YOU WOULD BE ARRIVING IN NEW YORK TODAY, I ASSURE YOU ALL THE PROPER ACCOMMODATIONS WOULD HAVE BEEN MADE AND THE "CUSTOMER SERVICE" PROVIDED WOULD HAVE BEEN FAR FROM SUBSTANDARD.
AT THE VERY LEAST, I WOULD HAVE BEEN HERE TO OPEN THE FRONT DOOR FOR YOU AND YOUR COHORTS—A QUITE VALUABLE DOOR, I MIGHT ADD. OR, RATHER, IT *WAS*.
NOW, THEN, TO WHAT DO I OWE THE PLEASURE OF THIS UNEXPECTED VISIT, HM?
YOU KNOW *DAMN WELL* WHY I'M HERE, STOCKMAN! IT'S BEEN MORE THAN A YEAR NOW AND I'M STILL WAITING ON THE SUPER-SOLDIER *MUTAGEN* I CONTRACTED YOUR *PATHETIC* EXCUSE FOR A COMPANY TO MAKE!

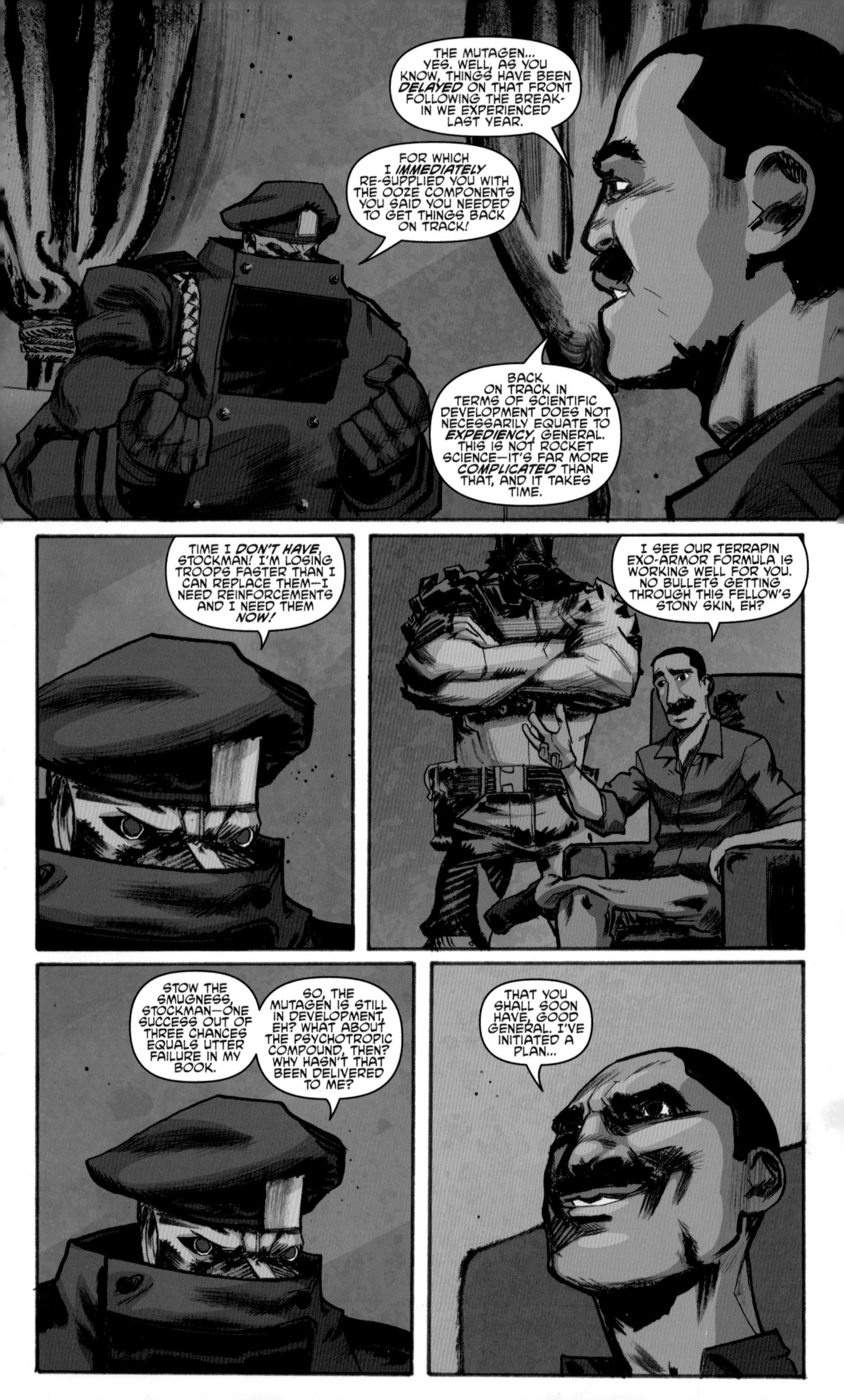
THE MUTAGEN... YES. WELL, AS YOU KNOW, THINGS HAVE BEEN DELAYED ON THAT FRONT FOLLOWING THE BREAK-IN WE EXPERIENCED LAST YEAR.
FOR WHICH I IMMEDIATELY RE-SUPPLIED YOU WITH THE OOZE COMPONENTS YOU SAID YOU NEEDED TO GET THINGS BACK ON TRACK!
BACK ON TRACK IN TERMS OF SCIENTIFIC DEVELOPMENT DOES NOT NECESSARILY EQUATE TO EXPEDIENCY, GENERAL. THIS IS NOT ROCKET SCIENCE—IT'S FAR MORE COMPLICATED THAN THAT, AND IT TAKES TIME.
TIME I DON'T HAVE, STOCKMAN! I'M LOSING TROOPS FASTER THAN I CAN REPLACE THEM—I NEED REINFORCEMENTS AND I NEED THEM NOW!
I SEE OUR TERRAPIN EXO-ARMOR FORMULA IS WORKING WELL FOR YOU. NO BULLETS GETTING THROUGH THIS FELLOW'S STONY SKIN, EH?
STOW THE SMUGNESS, STOCKMAN—ONE SUCCESS OUT OF THREE CHANCES EQUALS UTTER FAILURE IN MY BOOK.
SO, THE MUTAGEN IS STILL IN DEVELOPMENT, EH? WHAT ABOUT THE PSYCHOTROPIC COMPOUND, THEN? WHY HASN'T THAT BEEN DELIVERED TO ME?
THAT YOU SHALL SOON HAVE, GOOD GENERAL. I'VE INITIATED A PLAN...

"...ONE THAT WILL TAKE A HUGE BITE OUT OF THAT PARTICULAR SETBACK."
HOLY...
I TAKE IT BACK—AIN'T *NOTHIN'* FUNNY ABOUT THIS.
GET BACK, DAMMIT!
CRAP! THAT'S LEO! C'MON!
RAPH! MIKE! HURRY!

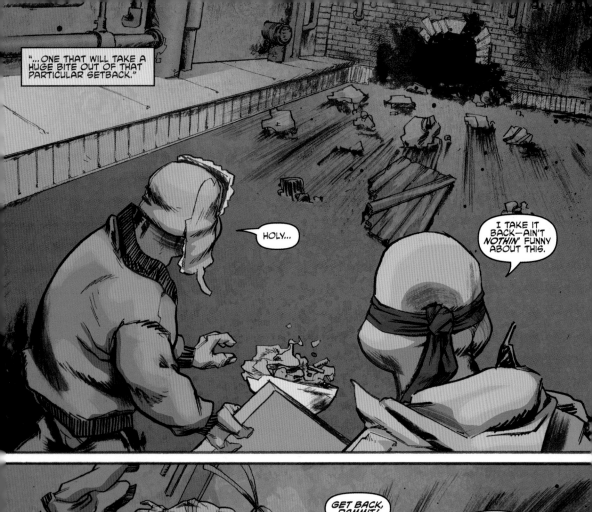

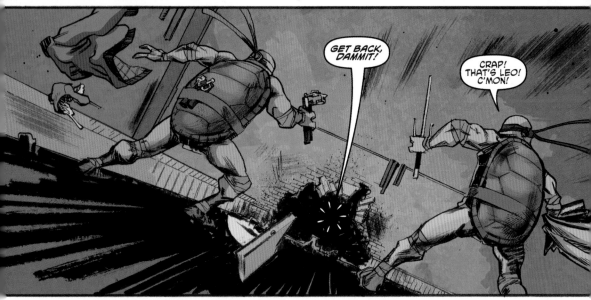

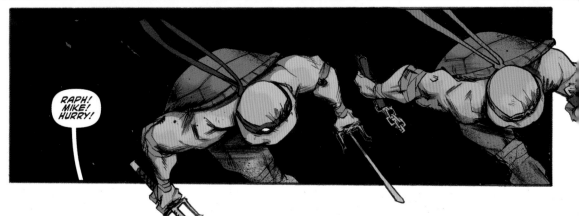

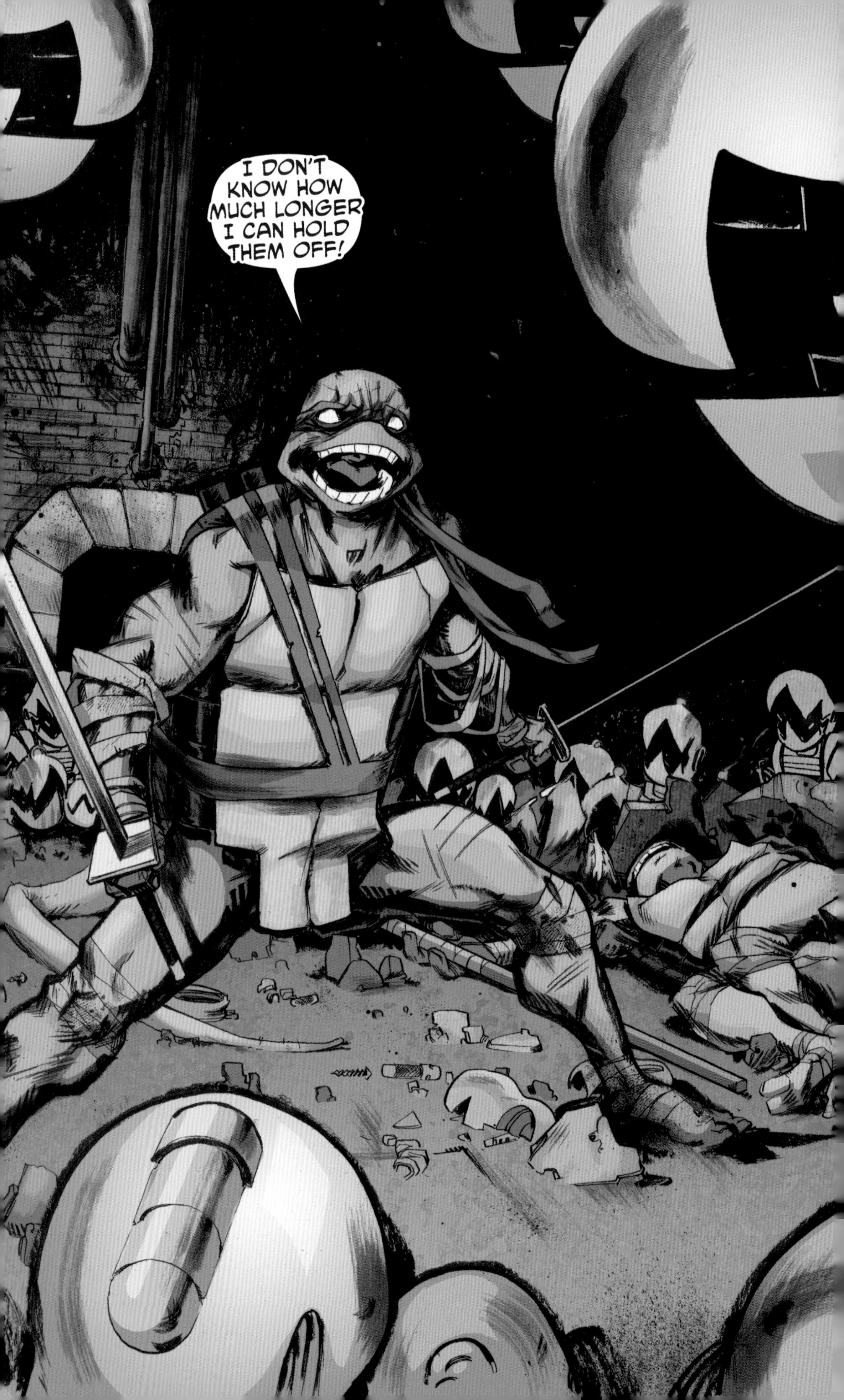
I DON'T KNOW HOW MUCH LONGER I CAN HOLD THEM OFF!

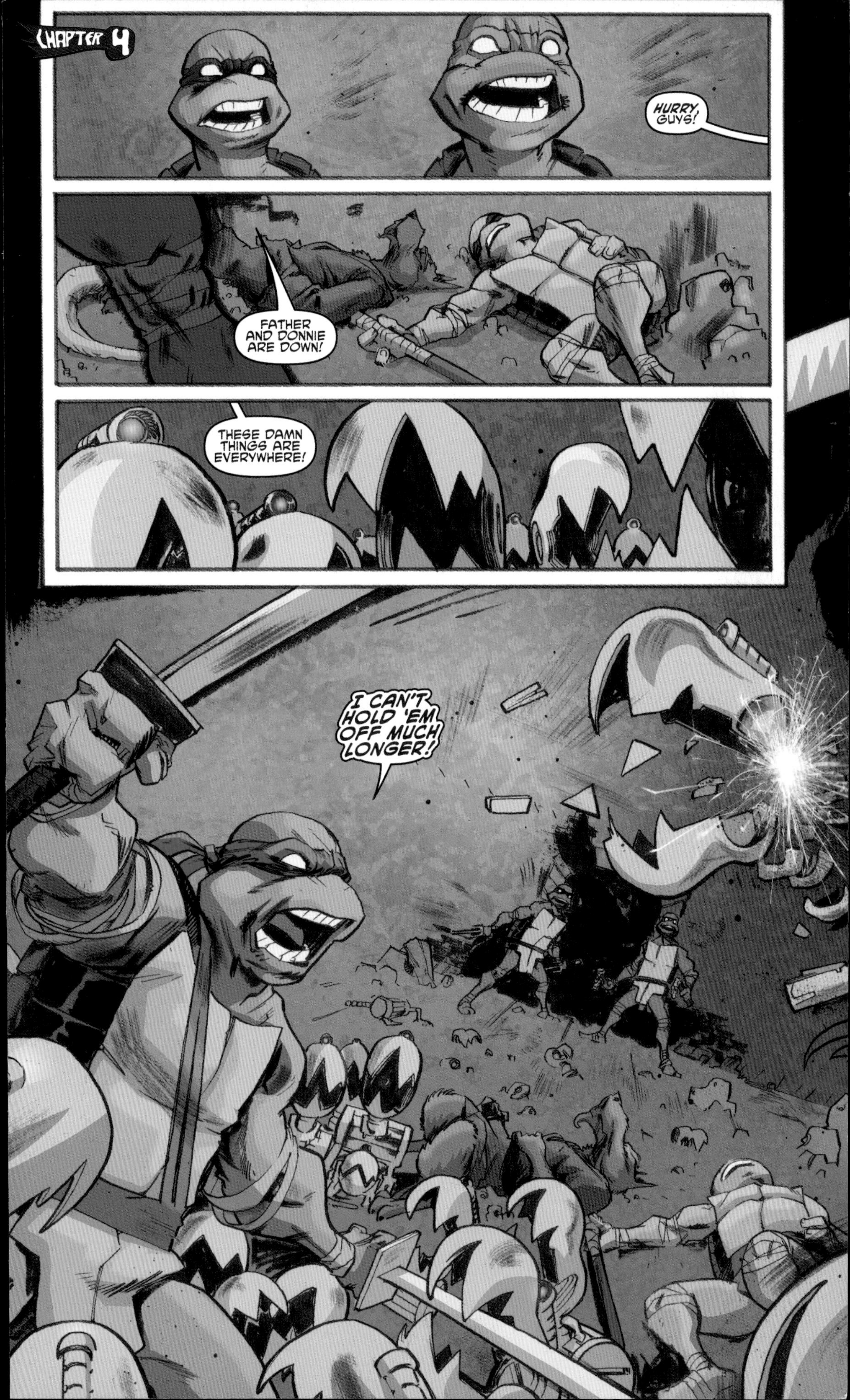
CHAPTER 4
HURRY, GUYS!
FATHER AND DONNIE ARE DOWN!
THESE DAMN THINGS ARE EVERYWHERE!
I CAN'T HOLD 'EM OFF MUCH LONGER!

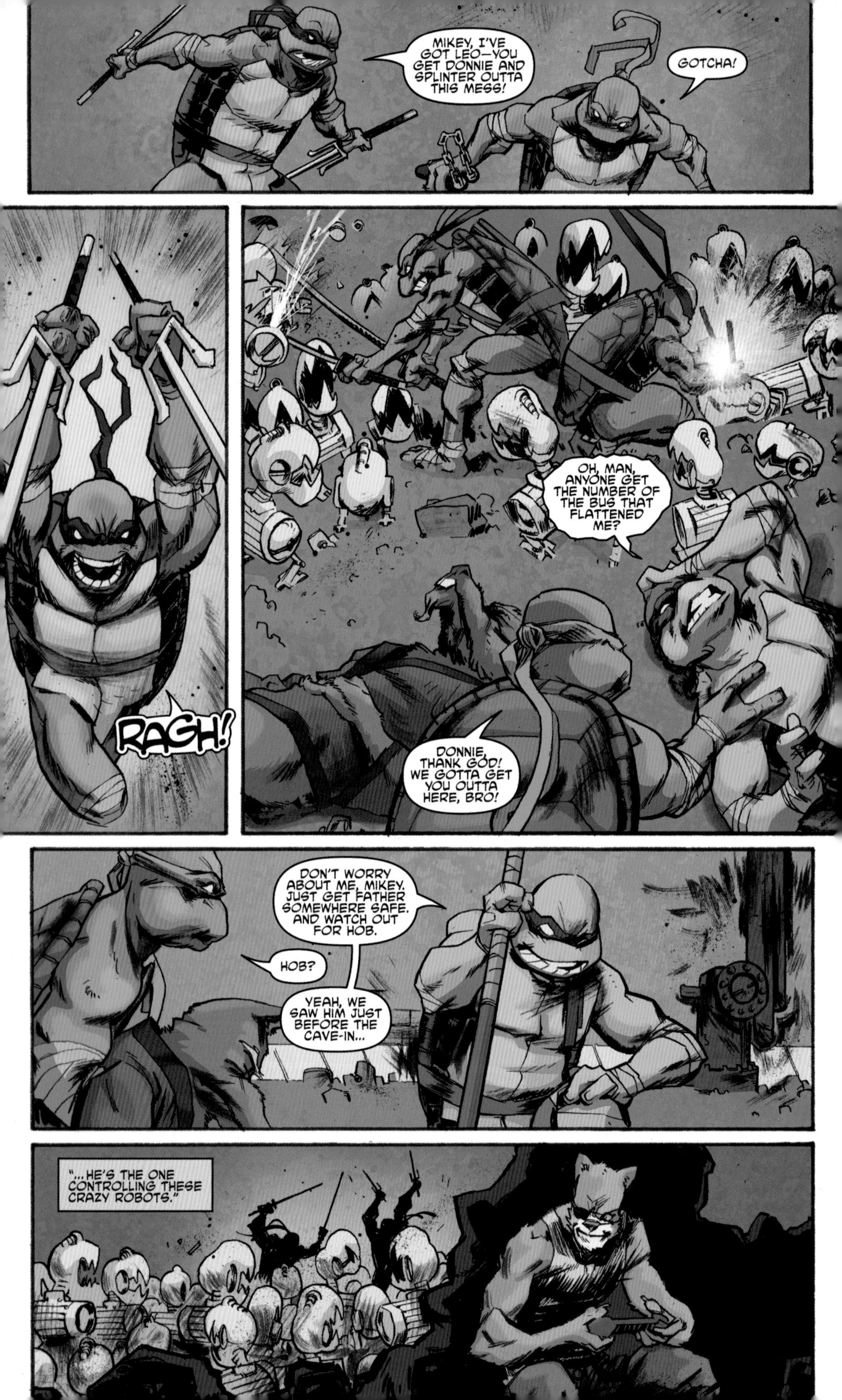
MIKEY, I'VE GOT LEO—YOU GET DONNIE AND SPLINTER OUTTA THIS MESS!
GOTCHA!
RAGH!
OH, MAN, ANYONE GET THE NUMBER OF THE BUS THAT FLATTENED ME?
DONNIE, THANK GOD! WE GOTTA GET YOU OUTTA HERE, BRO!
DON'T WORRY ABOUT ME, MIKEY. JUST GET FATHER SOMEWHERE SAFE. AND WATCH OUT FOR HOB.
HOB?
YEAH, WE SAW HIM JUST BEFORE THE CAVE-IN...
"...HE'S THE ONE CONTROLLING THESE CRAZY ROBOTS."

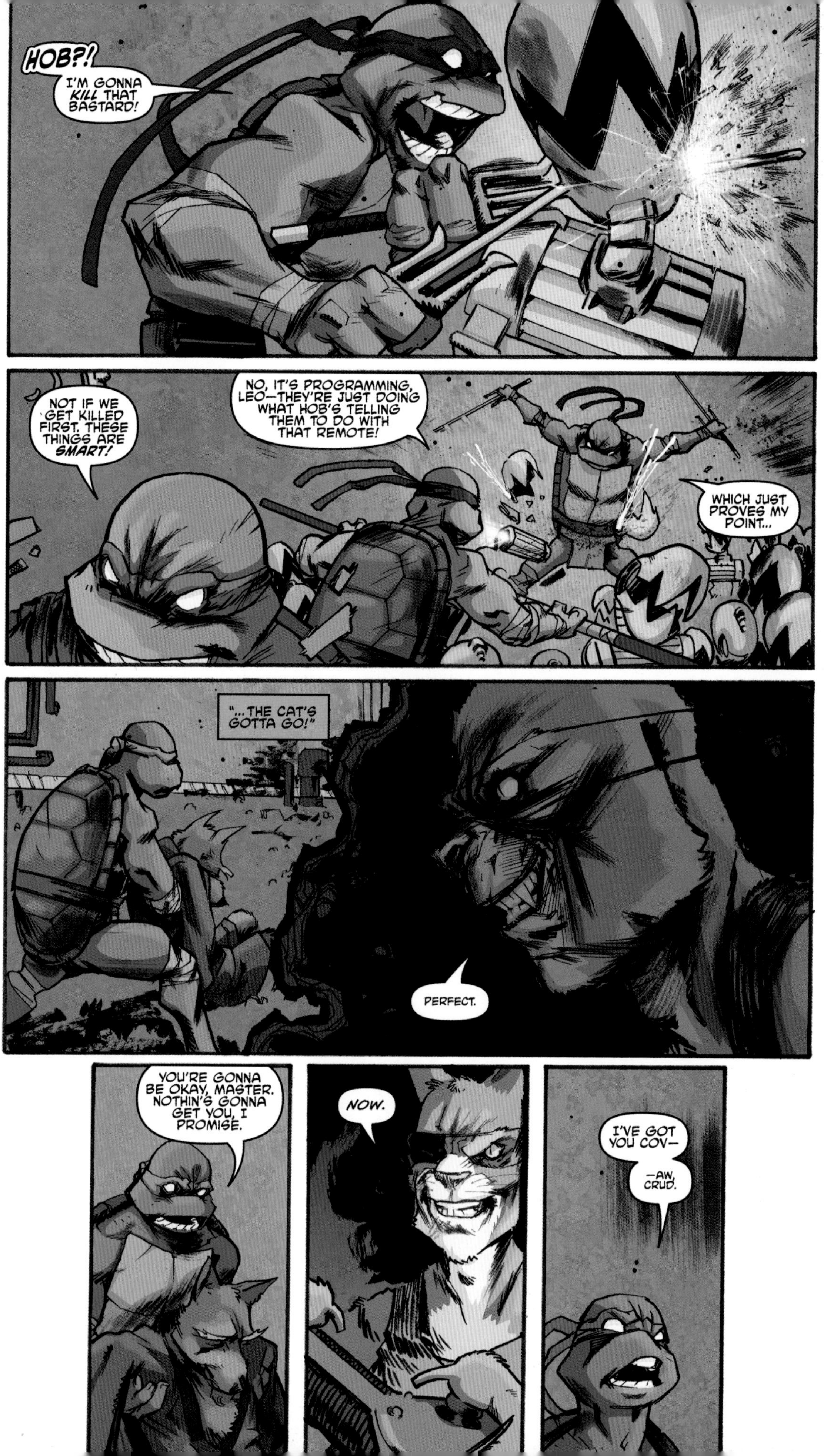
HOB?!
I'M GONNA KILL THAT BASTARD!
NOT IF WE GET KILLED FIRST. THESE THINGS ARE SMART!
NO, IT'S PROGRAMMING, LEO—THEY'RE JUST DOING WHAT HOB'S TELLING THEM TO DO WITH THAT REMOTE!
WHICH JUST PROVES MY POINT...
"...THE CAT'S GOTTA GO!"
PERFECT.
YOU'RE GONNA BE OKAY, MASTER. NOTHIN'S GONNA GET YOU, I PROMISE.
NOW.
I'VE GOT YOU COV—
—AW, CRUD.

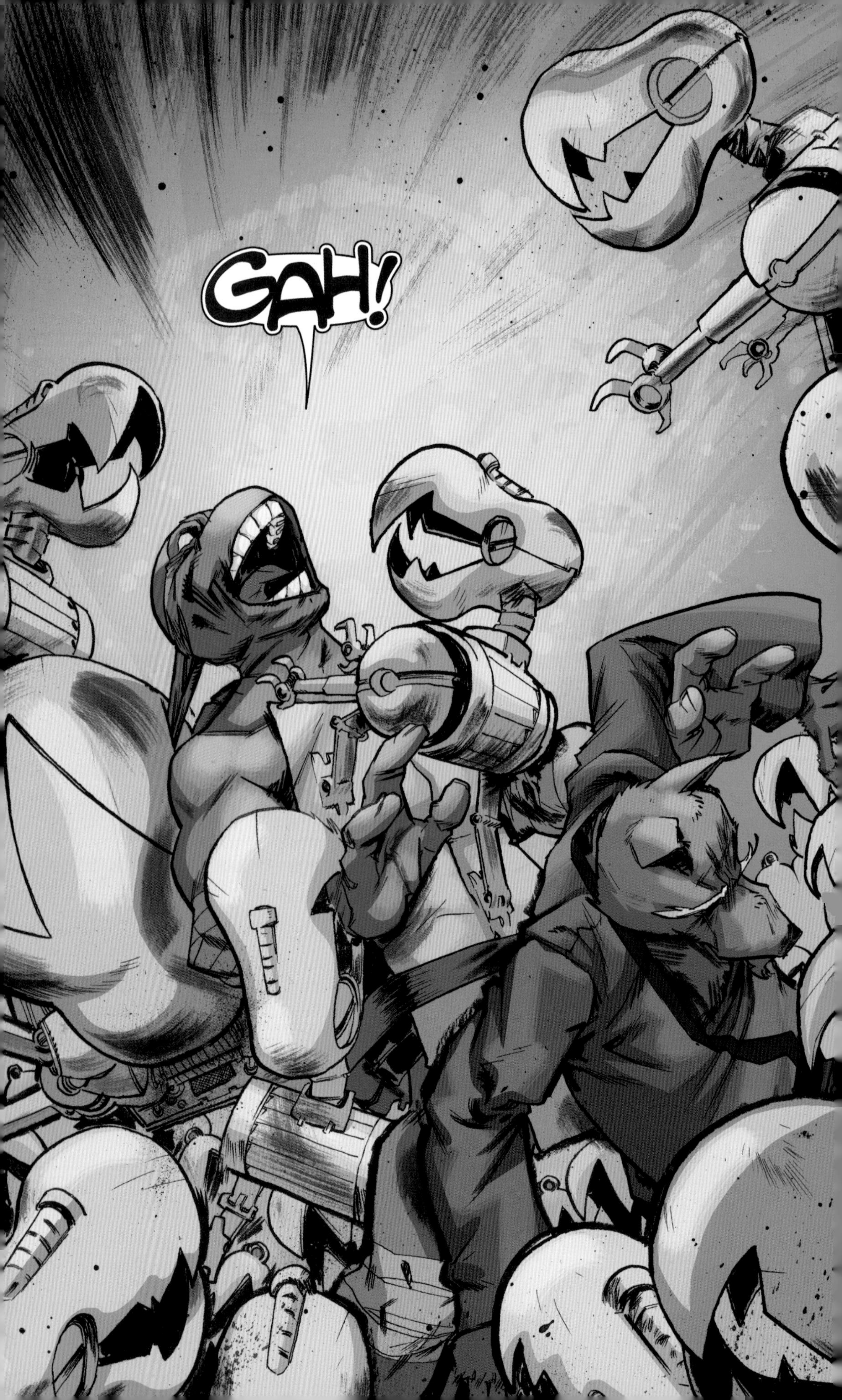
GAH!

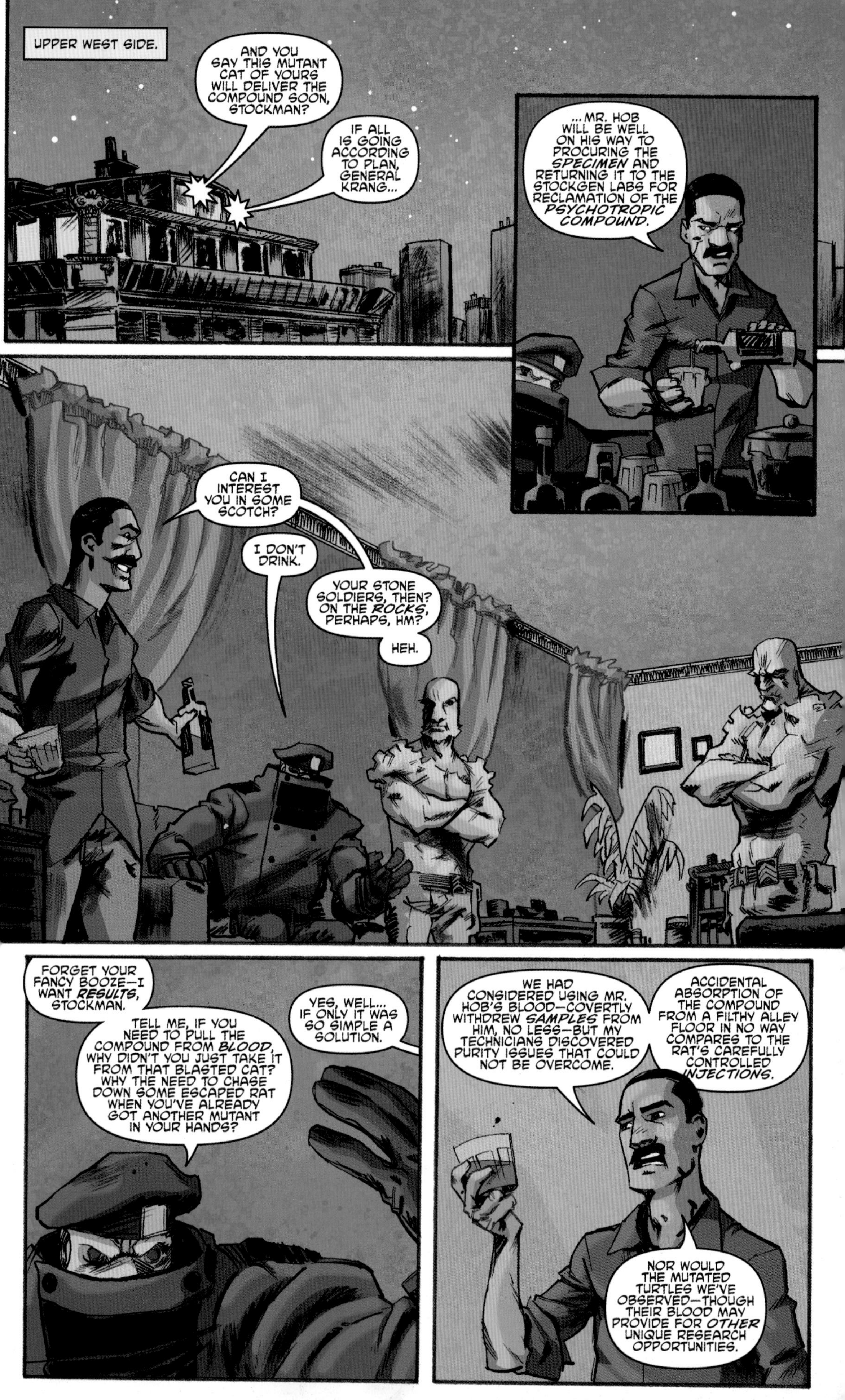
UPPER WEST SIDE.
AND YOU SAY THIS MUTANT CAT OF YOURS WILL DELIVER THE COMPOUND SOON, STOCKMAN?
IF ALL IS GOING ACCORDING TO PLAN, GENERAL KRANG...
...MR. HOB WILL BE WELL ON HIS WAY TO PROCURING THE *SPECIMEN* AND RETURNING IT TO THE STOCKGEN LABS FOR RECLAMATION OF THE *PSYCHOTROPIC COMPOUND*.
CAN I INTEREST YOU IN SOME SCOTCH?
I DON'T DRINK.
YOUR STONE SOLDIERS, THEN? ON THE *ROCKS*, PERHAPS, HM?
HEH.
FORGET YOUR FANCY BOOZE—I WANT ***RESULTS***, STOCKMAN.
TELL ME, IF YOU NEED TO PULL THE COMPOUND FROM *BLOOD*, WHY DIDN'T YOU JUST TAKE IT FROM THAT BLASTED CAT? WHY THE NEED TO CHASE DOWN SOME ESCAPED RAT WHEN YOU'VE ALREADY GOT ANOTHER MUTANT IN YOUR HANDS?
YES, WELL... IF ONLY IT WAS SO SIMPLE A SOLUTION.
WE HAD CONSIDERED USING MR. HOB'S BLOOD—COVERTLY WITHDREW *SAMPLES* FROM HIM, NO LESS—BUT MY TECHNICIANS DISCOVERED PURITY ISSUES THAT COULD NOT BE OVERCOME.
ACCIDENTAL ABSORPTION OF THE COMPOUND FROM A FILTHY ALLEY FLOOR IN NO WAY COMPARES TO THE RAT'S CAREFULLY CONTROLLED *INJECTIONS*.
NOR WOULD THE MUTATED TURTLES WE'VE OBSERVED—THOUGH THEIR BLOOD MAY PROVIDE FOR *OTHER* UNIQUE RESEARCH OPPORTUNITIES.

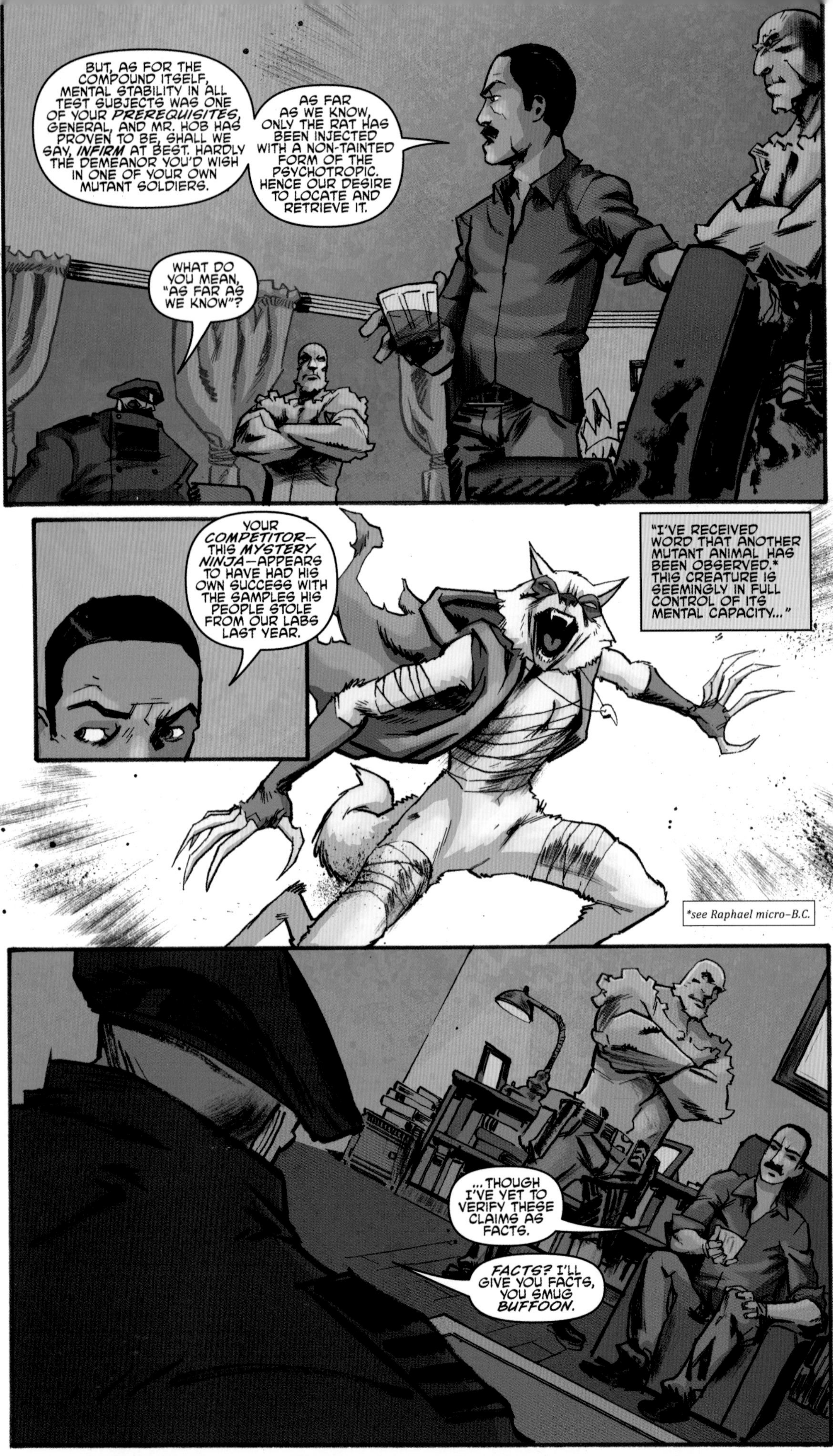
BUT, AS FOR THE COMPOUND ITSELF, MENTAL STABILITY IN ALL TEST SUBJECTS WAS ONE OF YOUR *PREREQUISITES*, GENERAL, AND MR. HOB HAS PROVEN TO BE, SHALL WE SAY, *INFIRM* AT BEST. HARDLY THE DEMEANOR YOU'D WISH IN ONE OF YOUR OWN MUTANT SOLDIERS.
AS FAR AS WE KNOW, ONLY THE RAT HAS BEEN INJECTED WITH A NON-TAINTED FORM OF THE PSYCHOTROPIC. HENCE OUR DESIRE TO LOCATE AND RETRIEVE IT.
WHAT DO YOU MEAN, "AS FAR AS WE KNOW"?
YOUR *COMPETITOR*— THIS *MYSTERY NINJA*—APPEARS TO HAVE HAD HIS OWN SUCCESS WITH THE SAMPLES HIS PEOPLE STOLE FROM OUR LABS LAST YEAR.
"I'VE RECEIVED WORD THAT ANOTHER MUTANT ANIMAL HAS BEEN OBSERVED.* THIS CREATURE IS SEEMINGLY IN FULL CONTROL OF ITS MENTAL CAPACITY..."
*see Raphael micro-B.C.
...THOUGH I'VE YET TO VERIFY THESE CLAIMS AS FACTS.
FACTS? I'LL GIVE YOU FACTS, YOU SMUG *BUFFOON*.

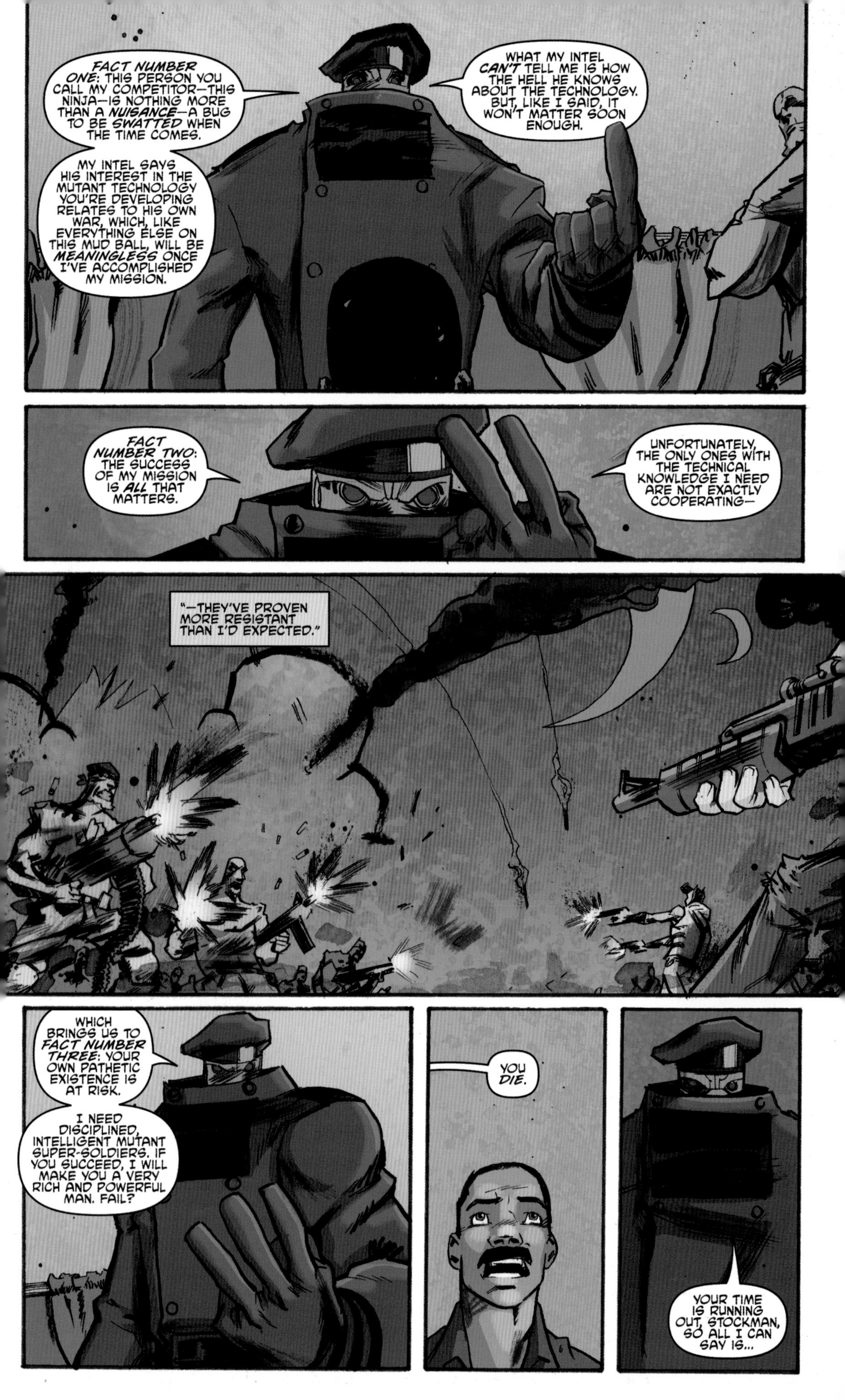
FACT NUMBER ONE: THIS PERSON YOU CALL MY COMPETITOR—THIS NINJA—IS NOTHING MORE THAN A NUISANCE—A BUG TO BE SWATTED WHEN THE TIME COMES.
MY INTEL SAYS HIS INTEREST IN THE MUTANT TECHNOLOGY YOU'RE DEVELOPING RELATES TO HIS OWN WAR, WHICH, LIKE EVERYTHING ELSE ON THIS MUD BALL, WILL BE MEANINGLESS ONCE I'VE ACCOMPLISHED MY MISSION.
WHAT MY INTEL CAN'T TELL ME IS HOW THE HELL HE KNOWS ABOUT THE TECHNOLOGY. BUT, LIKE I SAID, IT WON'T MATTER SOON ENOUGH.
FACT NUMBER TWO: THE SUCCESS OF MY MISSION IS ALL THAT MATTERS.
UNFORTUNATELY, THE ONLY ONES WITH THE TECHNICAL KNOWLEDGE I NEED ARE NOT EXACTLY COOPERATING—
"—THEY'VE PROVEN MORE RESISTANT THAN I'D EXPECTED."
WHICH BRINGS US TO FACT NUMBER THREE: YOUR OWN PATHETIC EXISTENCE IS AT RISK.
I NEED DISCIPLINED, INTELLIGENT MUTANT SUPER-SOLDIERS. IF YOU SUCCEED, I WILL MAKE YOU A VERY RICH AND POWERFUL MAN. FAIL?
YOU DIE.
YOUR TIME IS RUNNING OUT, STOCKMAN, SO ALL I CAN SAY IS...

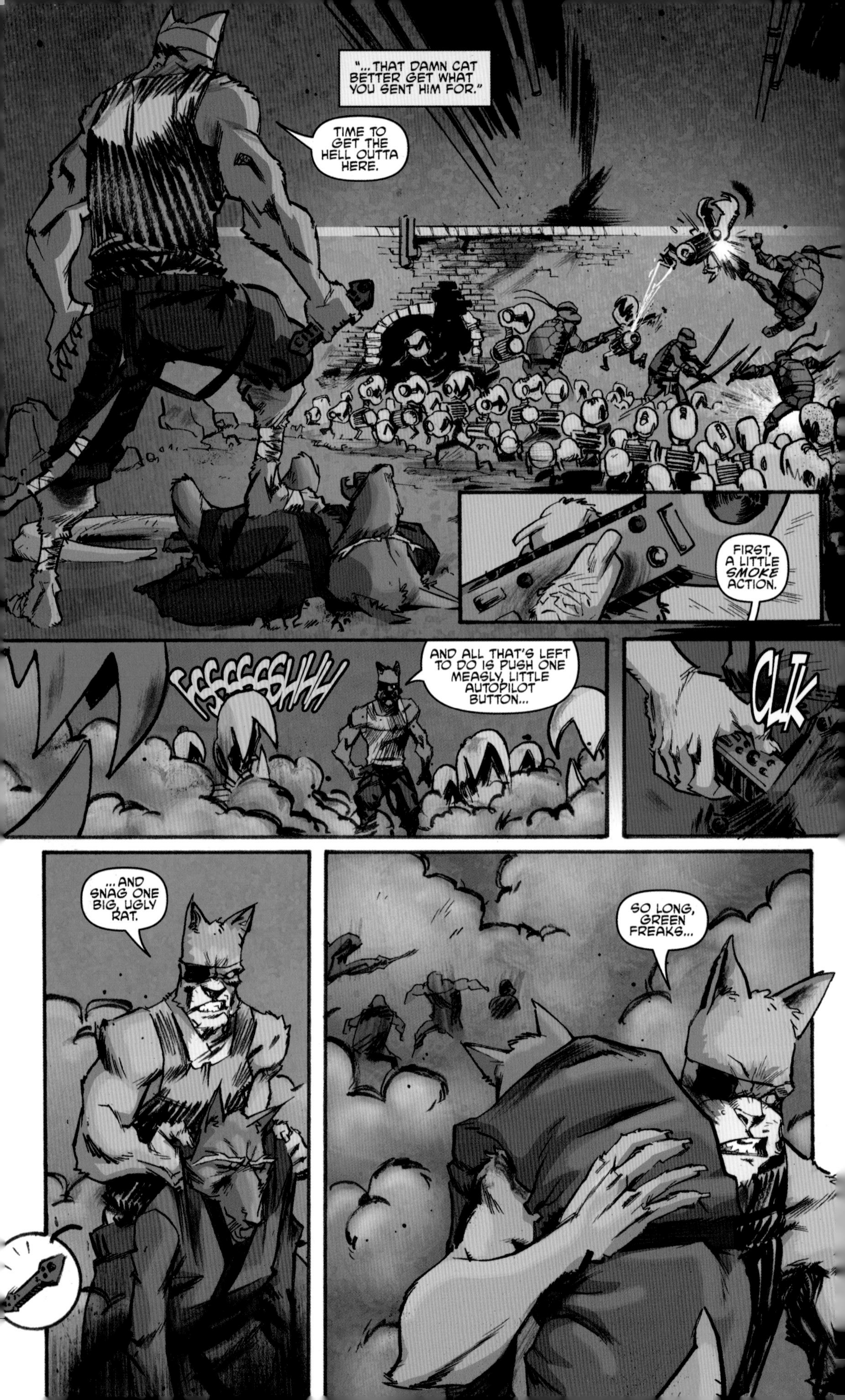
"...THAT DAMN CAT BETTER GET WHAT YOU SENT HIM FOR."
TIME TO GET THE HELL OUTTA HERE.
FIRST, A LITTLE SMOKE ACTION.
FSSSSSSHHH
AND ALL THAT'S LEFT TO DO IS PUSH ONE MEASLY, LITTLE AUTOPILOT BUTTON...
CLIK
...AND SNAG ONE BIG, UGLY RAT.
SO LONG, GREEN FREAKS...

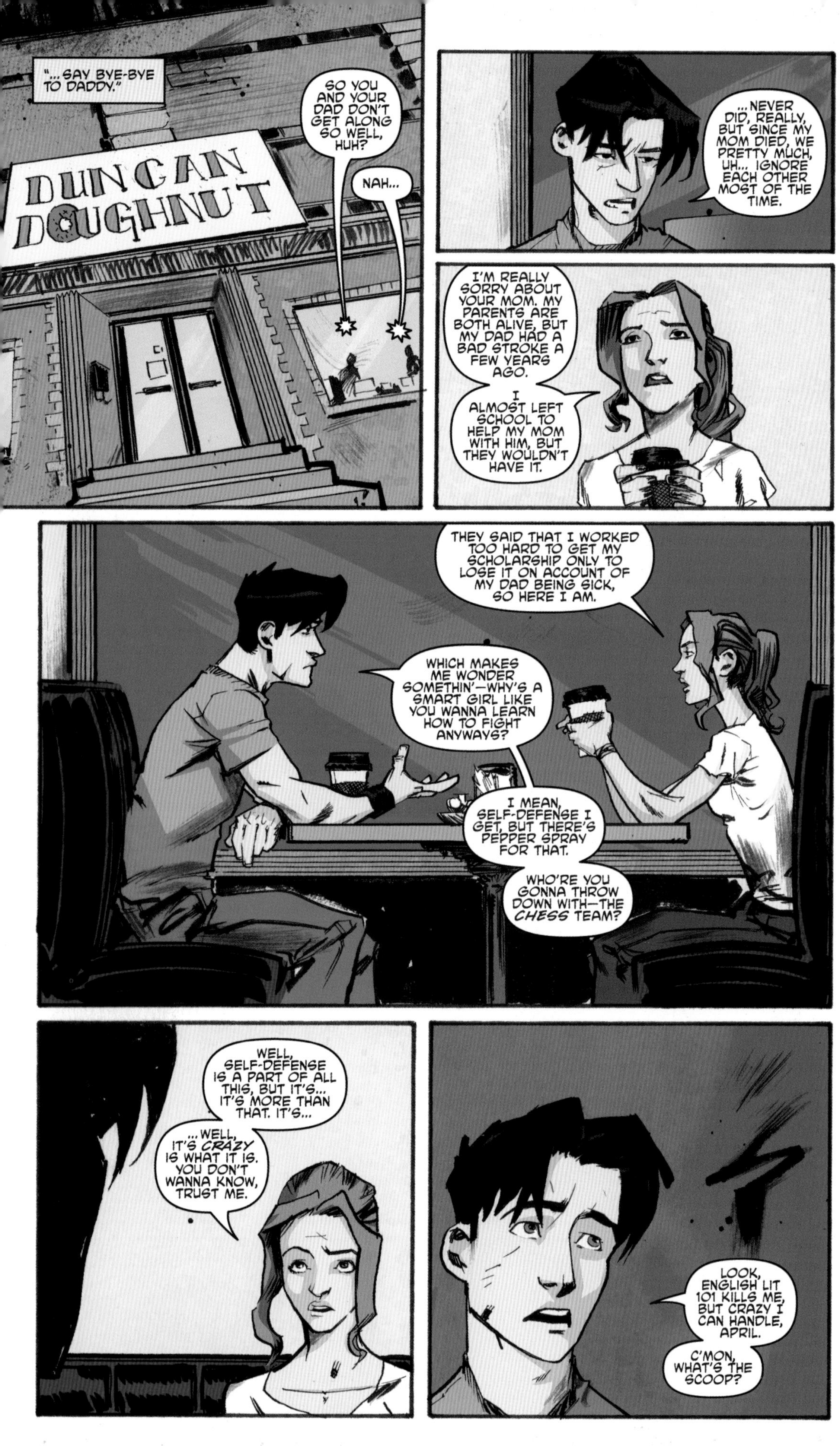
"... SAY BYE-BYE TO DADDY."
DUNCAN DOUGHNUT
SO YOU AND YOUR DAD DON'T GET ALONG SO WELL, HUH?
NAH...
... NEVER DID, REALLY, BUT SINCE MY MOM DIED, WE PRETTY MUCH, UH... IGNORE EACH OTHER MOST OF THE TIME.
I'M REALLY SORRY ABOUT YOUR MOM. MY PARENTS ARE BOTH ALIVE, BUT MY DAD HAD A BAD STROKE A FEW YEARS AGO.
I ALMOST LEFT SCHOOL TO HELP MY MOM WITH HIM, BUT THEY WOULDN'T HAVE IT.
THEY SAID THAT I WORKED TOO HARD TO GET MY SCHOLARSHIP ONLY TO LOSE IT ON ACCOUNT OF MY DAD BEING SICK, SO HERE I AM.
WHICH MAKES ME WONDER SOMETHIN'—WHY'S A SMART GIRL LIKE YOU WANNA LEARN HOW TO FIGHT ANYWAYS?
I MEAN, SELF-DEFENSE I GET, BUT THERE'S PEPPER SPRAY FOR THAT.
WHO'RE YOU GONNA THROW DOWN WITH—THE *CHESS* TEAM?
WELL, SELF-DEFENSE IS A PART OF ALL THIS, BUT IT'S... IT'S MORE THAN THAT. IT'S...
... WELL, IT'S *CRAZY* IS WHAT IT IS. YOU DON'T WANNA KNOW, TRUST ME.
LOOK, ENGLISH LIT 101 KILLS ME, BUT CRAZY I CAN HANDLE, APRIL.
C'MON, WHAT'S THE SCOOP?

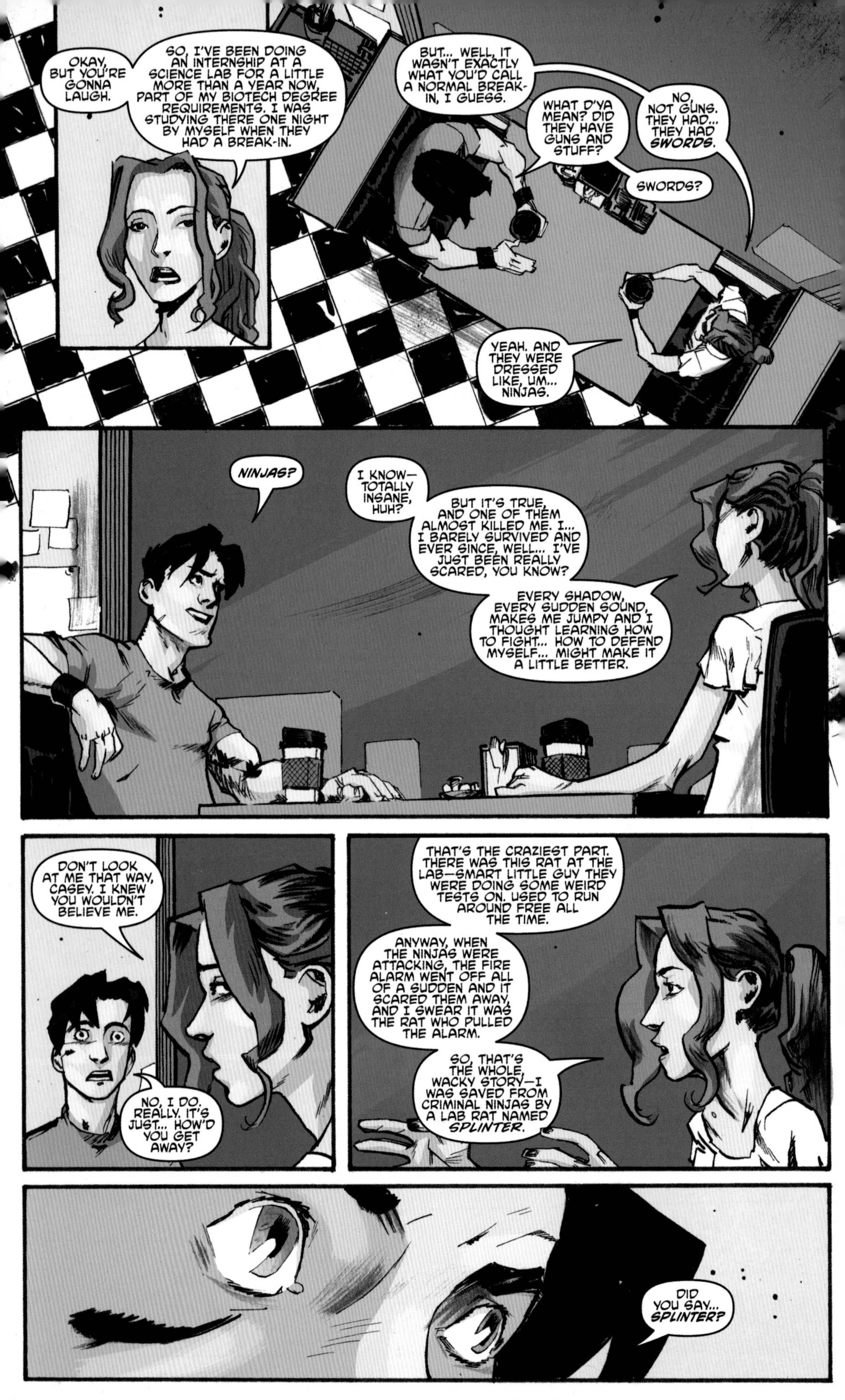
OKAY, BUT YOU'RE GONNA LAUGH.
SO, I'VE BEEN DOING AN INTERNSHIP AT A SCIENCE LAB FOR A LITTLE MORE THAN A YEAR NOW, PART OF MY BIOTECH DEGREE REQUIREMENTS. I WAS STUDYING THERE ONE NIGHT BY MYSELF WHEN THEY HAD A BREAK-IN.
BUT... WELL, IT WASN'T EXACTLY WHAT YOU'D CALL A NORMAL BREAK-IN, I GUESS.
WHAT D'YA MEAN? DID THEY HAVE GUNS AND STUFF?
NO, NOT GUNS. THEY HAD... THEY HAD SWORDS.
SWORDS?
YEAH. AND THEY WERE DRESSED LIKE, UM... NINJAS.
NINJAS?
I KNOW—TOTALLY INSANE, HUH?
BUT IT'S TRUE, AND ONE OF THEM ALMOST KILLED ME. I... I BARELY SURVIVED AND EVER SINCE, WELL... I'VE JUST BEEN REALLY SCARED, YOU KNOW?
EVERY SHADOW, EVERY SUDDEN SOUND, MAKES ME JUMPY AND I THOUGHT LEARNING HOW TO FIGHT... HOW TO DEFEND MYSELF... MIGHT MAKE IT A LITTLE BETTER.
DON'T LOOK AT ME THAT WAY, CASEY. I KNEW YOU WOULDN'T BELIEVE ME.
NO, I DO. REALLY. IT'S JUST... HOW'D YOU GET AWAY?
THAT'S THE CRAZIEST PART. THERE WAS THIS RAT AT THE LAB—SMART LITTLE GUY THEY WERE DOING SOME WEIRD TESTS ON. USED TO RUN AROUND FREE ALL THE TIME.
ANYWAY, WHEN THE NINJAS WERE ATTACKING, THE FIRE ALARM WENT OFF ALL OF A SUDDEN AND IT SCARED THEM AWAY, AND I SWEAR IT WAS THE RAT WHO PULLED THE ALARM.
SO, THAT'S THE WHOLE, WACKY STORY—I WAS SAVED FROM CRIMINAL NINJAS BY A LAB RAT NAMED SPLINTER.
DID YOU SAY... SPLINTER?

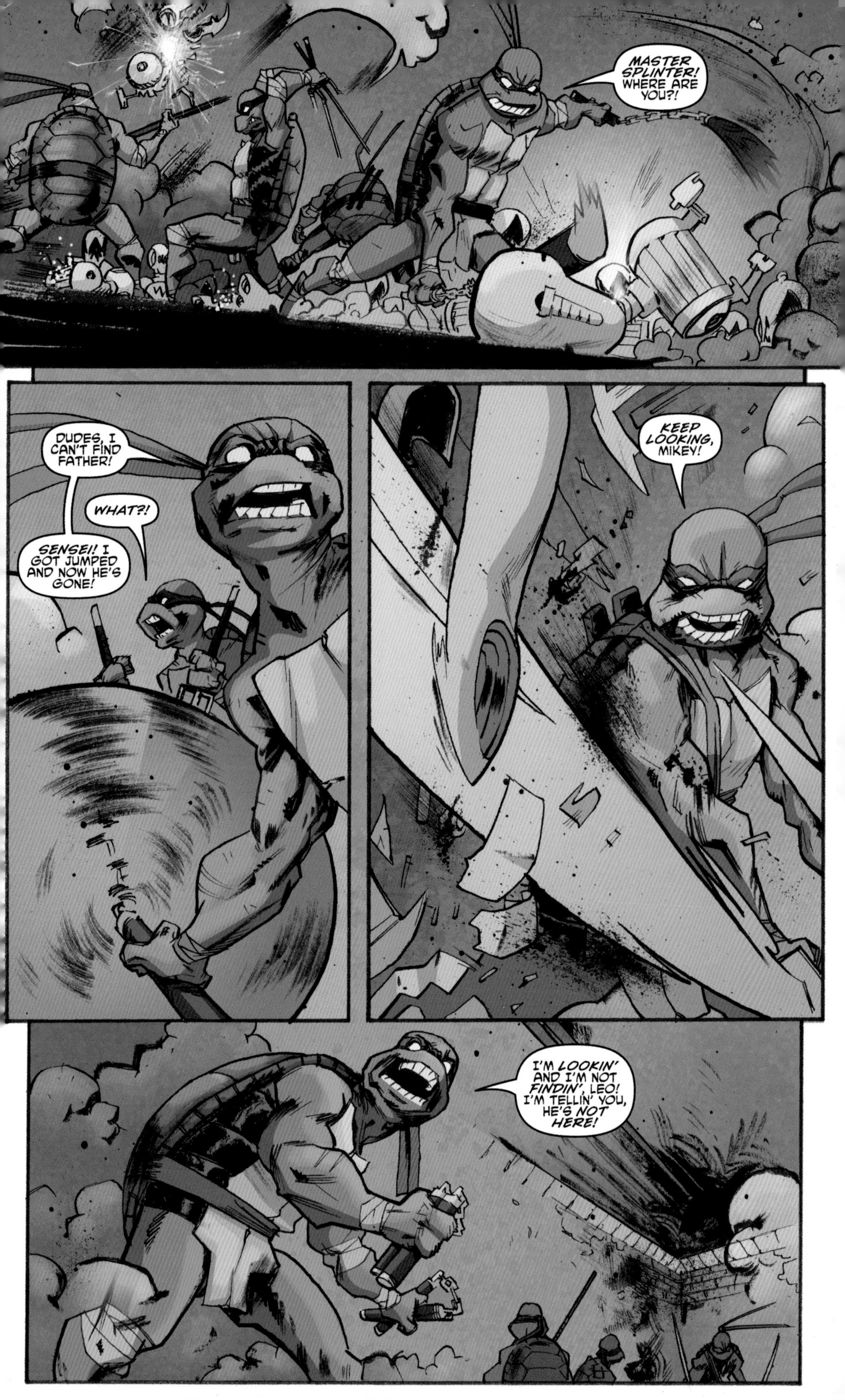
MASTER SPLINTER! WHERE ARE YOU?!
DUDES, I CAN'T FIND FATHER!
WHAT?!
SENSEI! I GOT JUMPED AND NOW HE'S GONE!
KEEP LOOKING, MIKEY!
I'M LOOKIN' AND I'M NOT FINDIN', LEO! I'M TELLIN' YOU, HE'S NOT HERE!

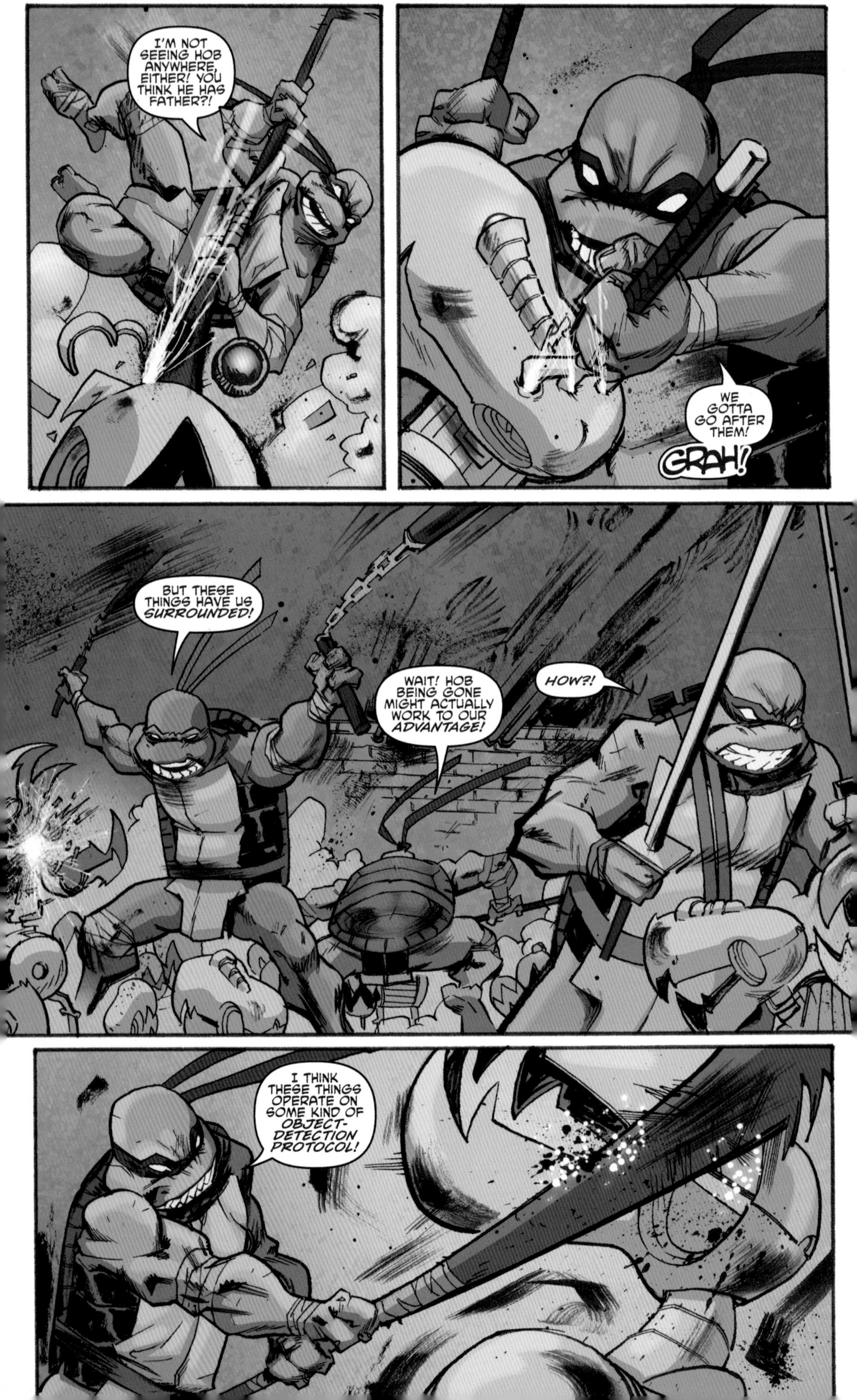
I'M NOT SEEING HOB ANYWHERE, EITHER! YOU THINK HE HAS FATHER?!
WE GOTTA GO AFTER THEM!
GRAH!
BUT THESE THINGS HAVE US SURROUNDED!
WAIT! HOB BEING GONE MIGHT ACTUALLY WORK TO OUR ADVANTAGE!
HOW?!
I THINK THESE THINGS OPERATE ON SOME KIND OF OBJECT-DETECTION PROTOCOL!

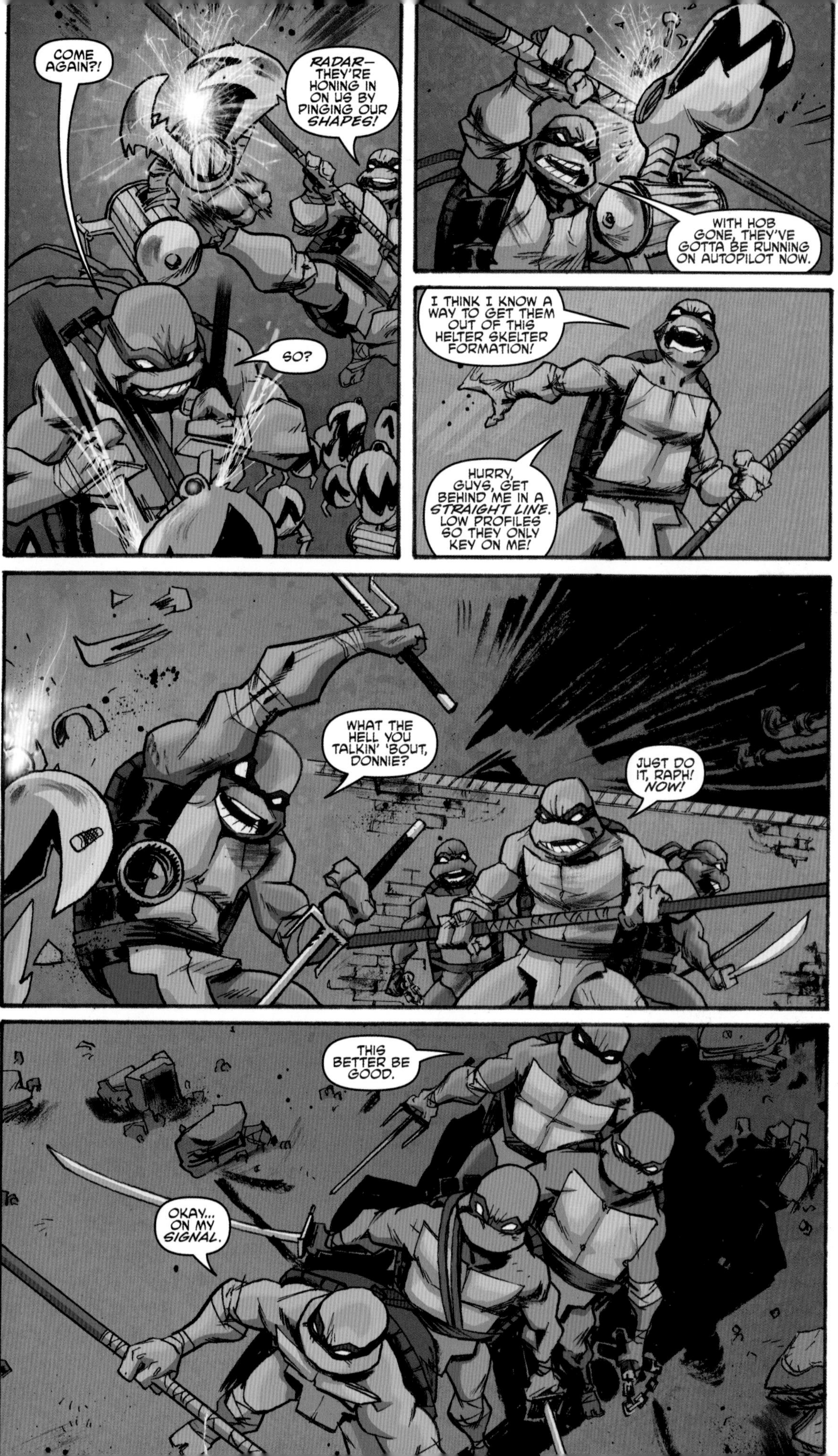
COME AGAIN?!
RADAR— THEY'RE HONING IN ON US BY PINGING OUR SHAPES!
SO?
WITH HOB GONE, THEY'VE GOTTA BE RUNNING ON AUTOPILOT NOW.
I THINK I KNOW A WAY TO GET THEM OUT OF THIS HELTER SKELTER FORMATION!
HURRY, GUYS, GET BEHIND ME IN A STRAIGHT LINE. LOW PROFILES SO THEY ONLY KEY ON ME!
WHAT THE HELL YOU TALKIN' 'BOUT, DONNIE?
JUST DO IT, RAPH! NOW!
THIS BETTER BE GOOD.
OKAY... ON MY SIGNAL.

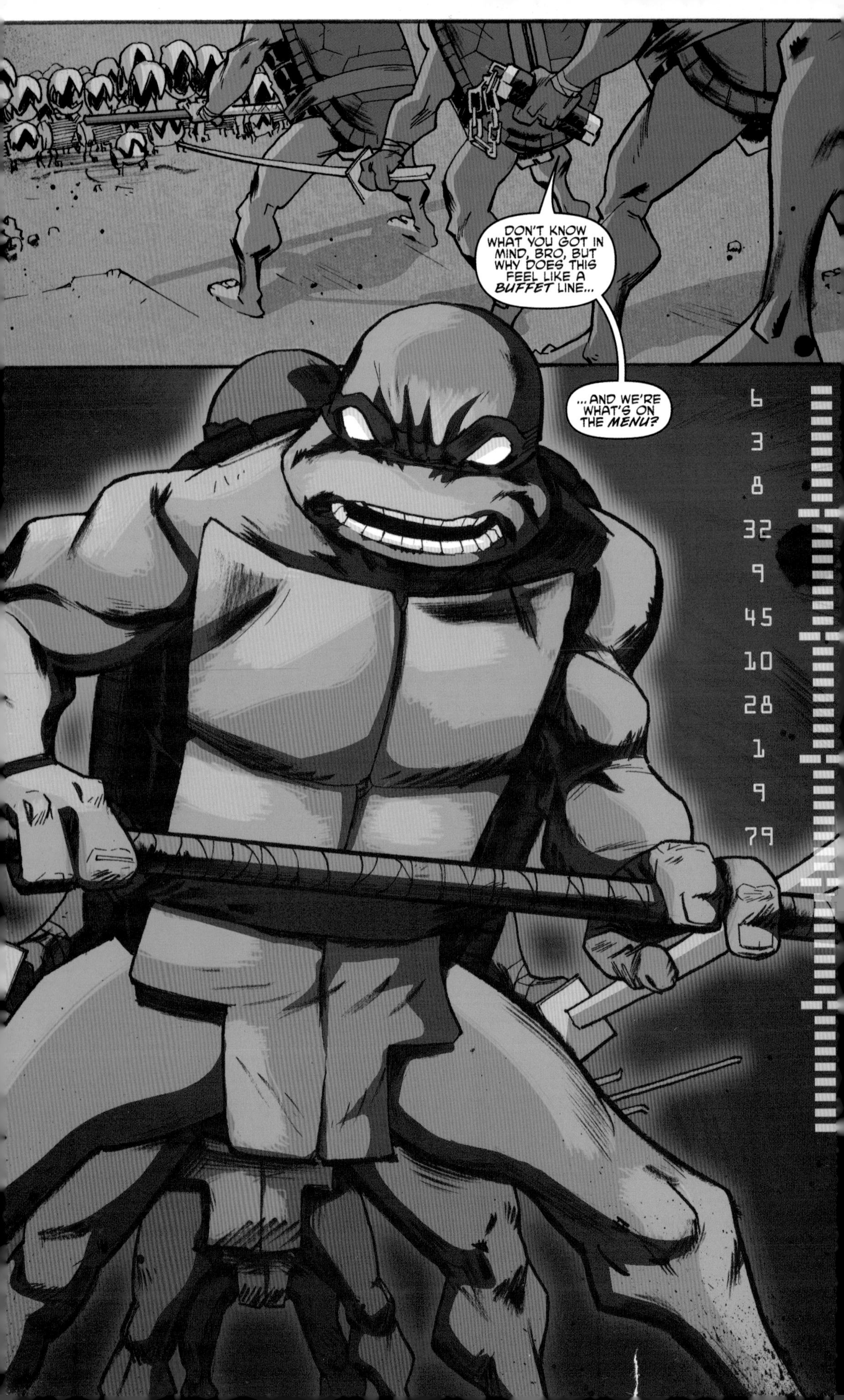
DON'T KNOW WHAT YOU GOT IN MIND, BRO, BUT WHY DOES THIS FEEL LIKE A *BUFFET* LINE...
...AND WE'RE WHAT'S ON THE *MENU*?
6
3
8
32
9
45
10
28
1
9
79

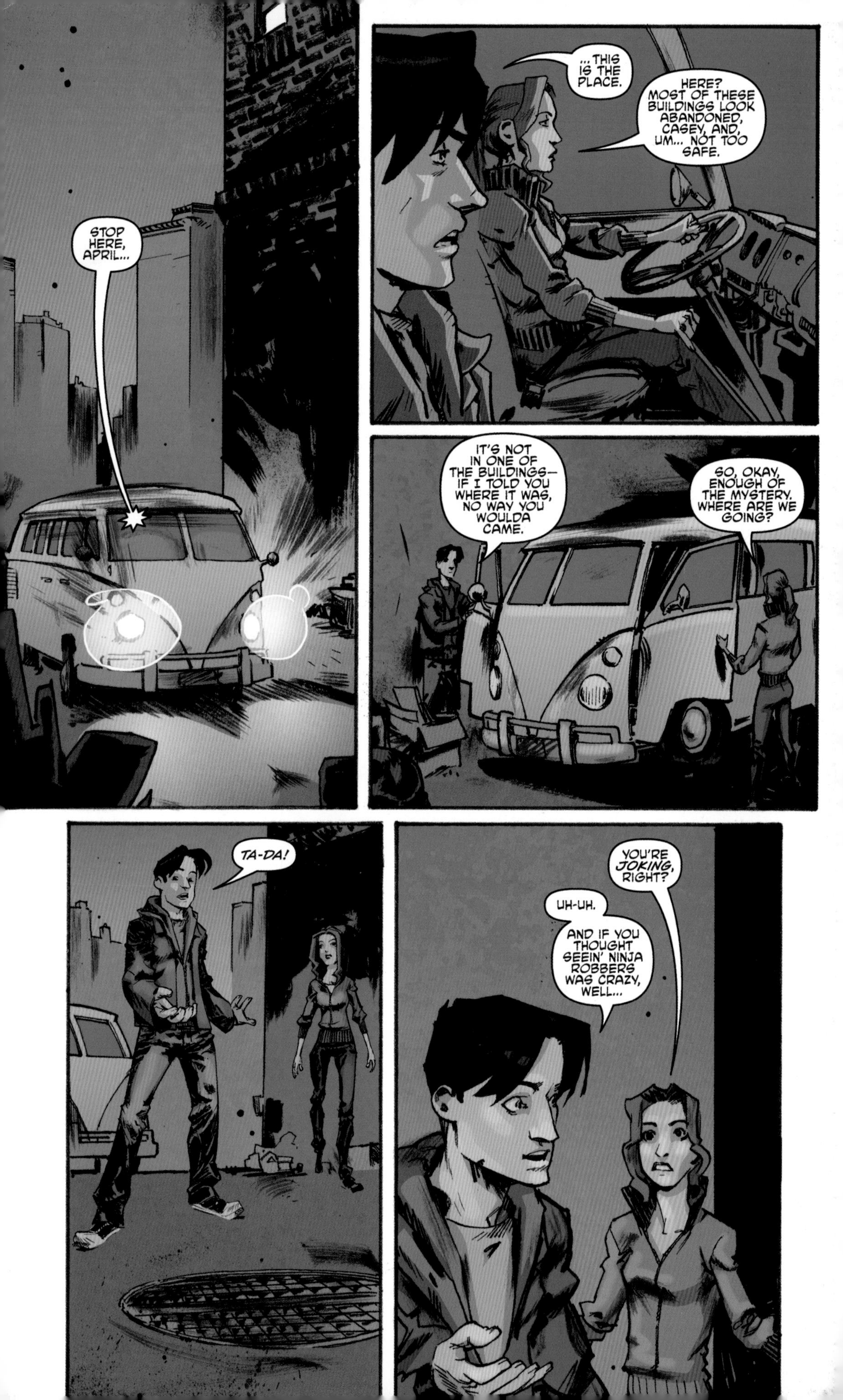
STOP HERE, APRIL...
...THIS IS THE PLACE.
HERE? MOST OF THESE BUILDINGS LOOK ABANDONED, CASEY, AND, UM... NOT TOO SAFE.
SO, OKAY, ENOUGH OF THE MYSTERY. WHERE ARE WE GOING?
IT'S NOT IN ONE OF THE BUILDINGS—IF I TOLD YOU WHERE IT WAS, NO WAY YOU WOULDA CAME.
TA-DA!
YOU'RE JOKING, RIGHT?
UH-UH.
AND IF YOU THOUGHT SEEIN' NINJA ROBBERS WAS CRAZY, WELL...

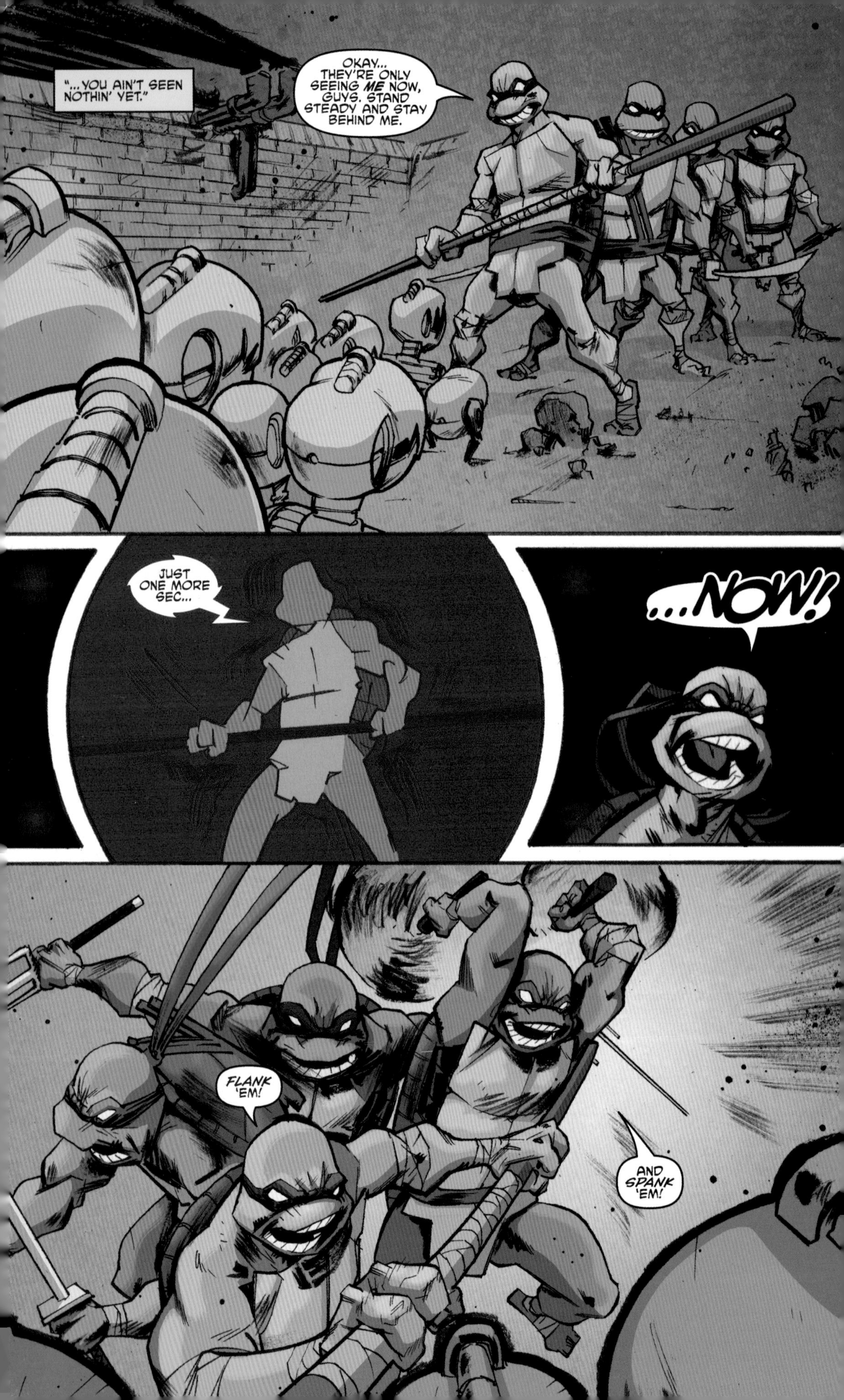
"...YOU AIN'T SEEN NOTHIN' YET."
OKAY... THEY'RE ONLY SEEING ME NOW, GUYS. STAND STEADY AND STAY BEHIND ME.
JUST ONE MORE SEC...
...NOW!
FLANK 'EM!
AND SPANK 'EM!

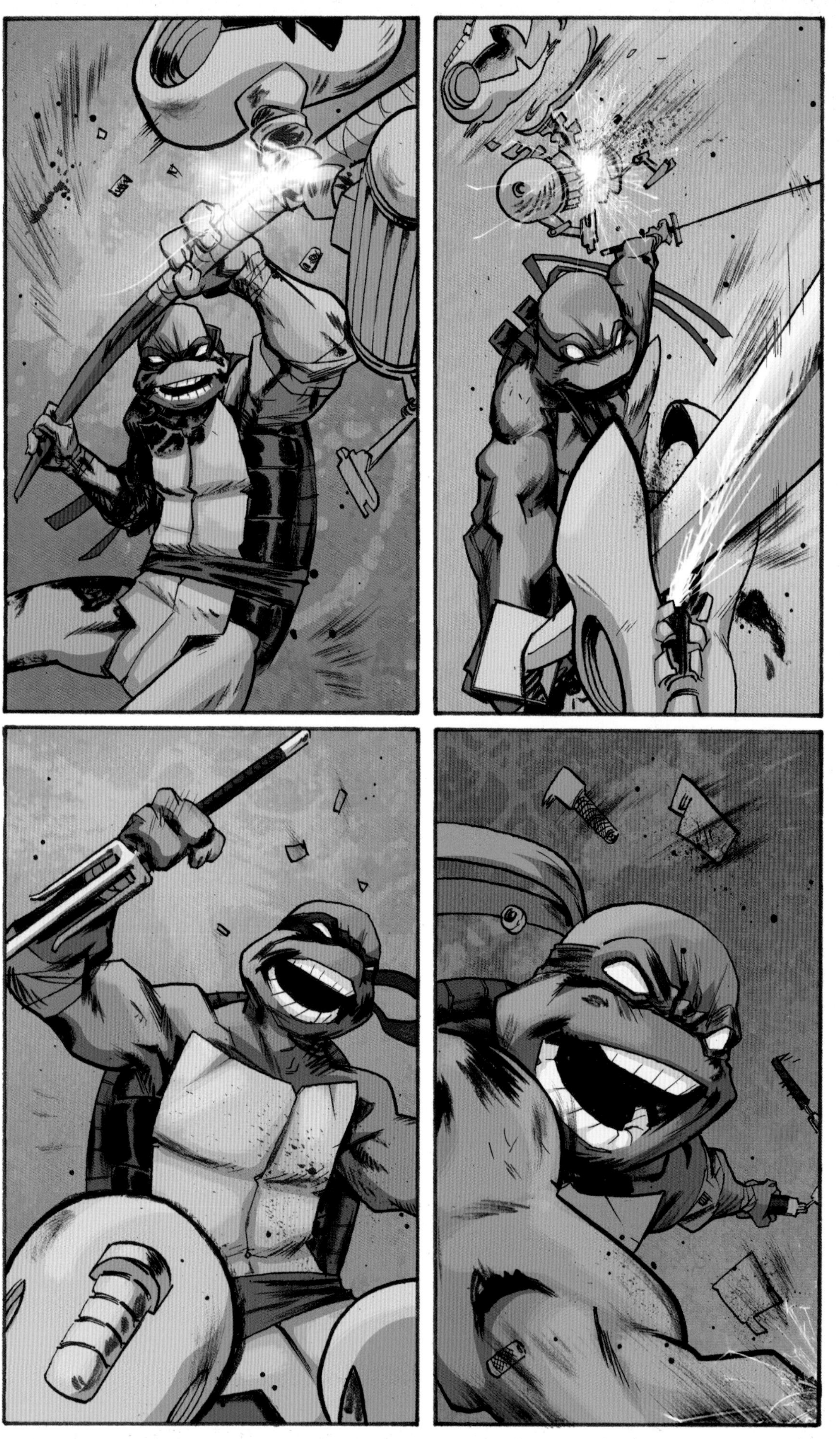

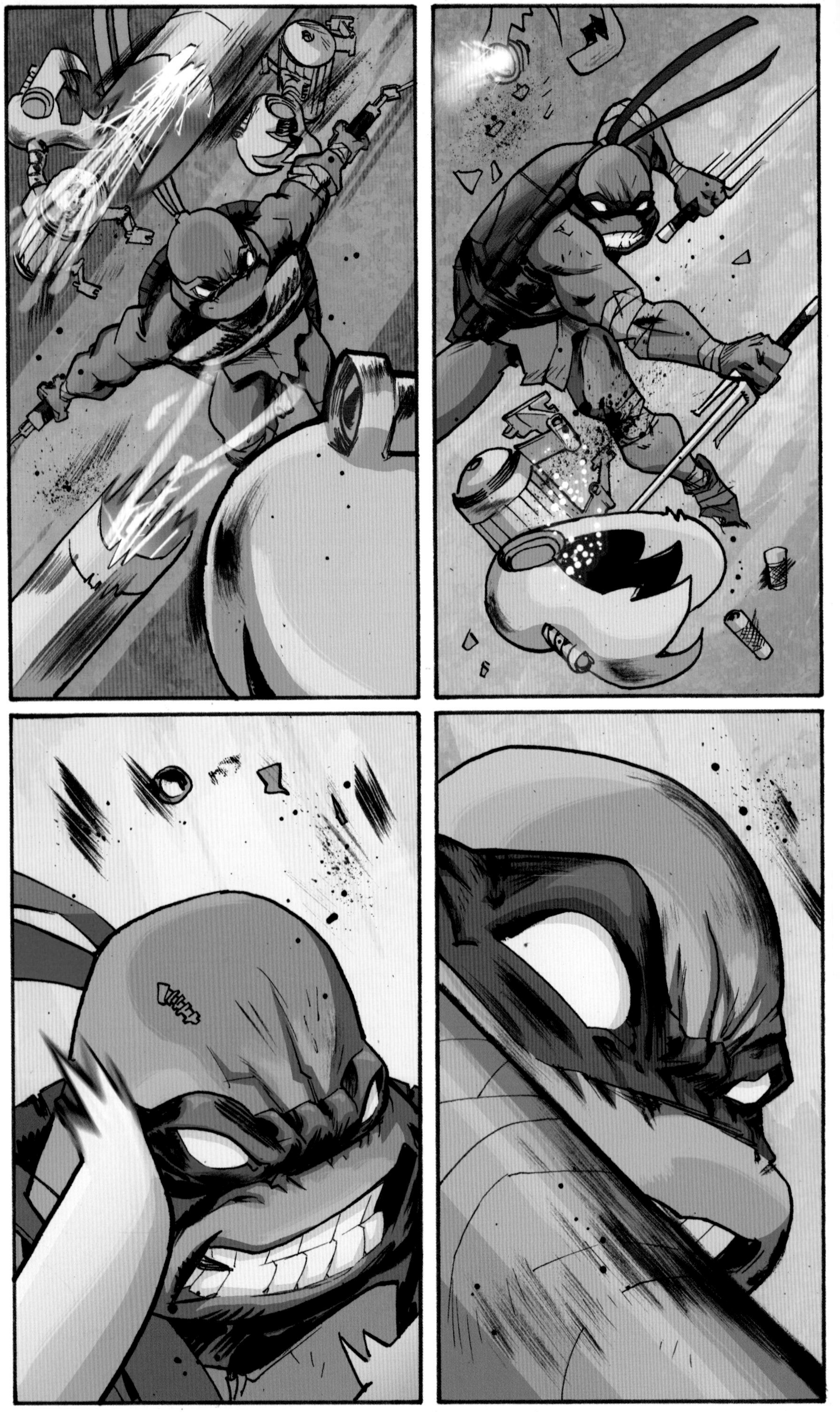

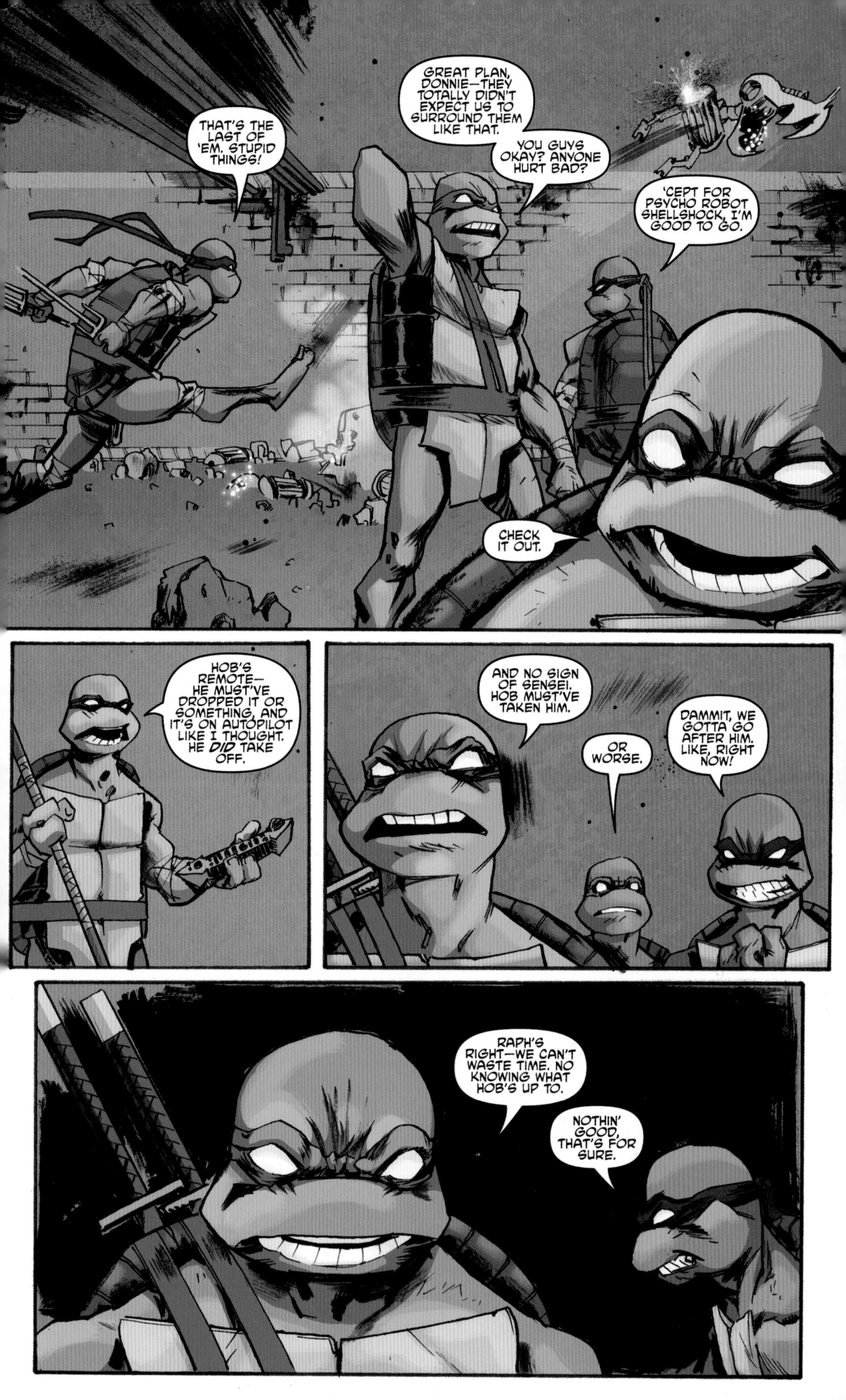
THAT'S THE LAST OF 'EM. STUPID THINGS!
GREAT PLAN, DONNIE—THEY TOTALLY DIDN'T EXPECT US TO SURROUND THEM LIKE THAT.
YOU GUYS OKAY? ANYONE HURT BAD?
'CEPT FOR PSYCHO ROBOT SHELLSHOCK, I'M GOOD TO GO.
CHECK IT OUT.
HOB'S REMOTE—HE MUST'VE DROPPED IT OR SOMETHING, AND IT'S ON AUTOPILOT LIKE I THOUGHT. HE *DID* TAKE OFF.
AND NO SIGN OF SENSEI. HOB MUST'VE TAKEN HIM.
OR WORSE.
DAMMIT, WE GOTTA GO AFTER HIM. LIKE, RIGHT NOW!
RAPH'S RIGHT—WE CAN'T WASTE TIME. NO KNOWING WHAT HOB'S UP TO.
NOTHIN' GOOD, THAT'S FOR SURE.

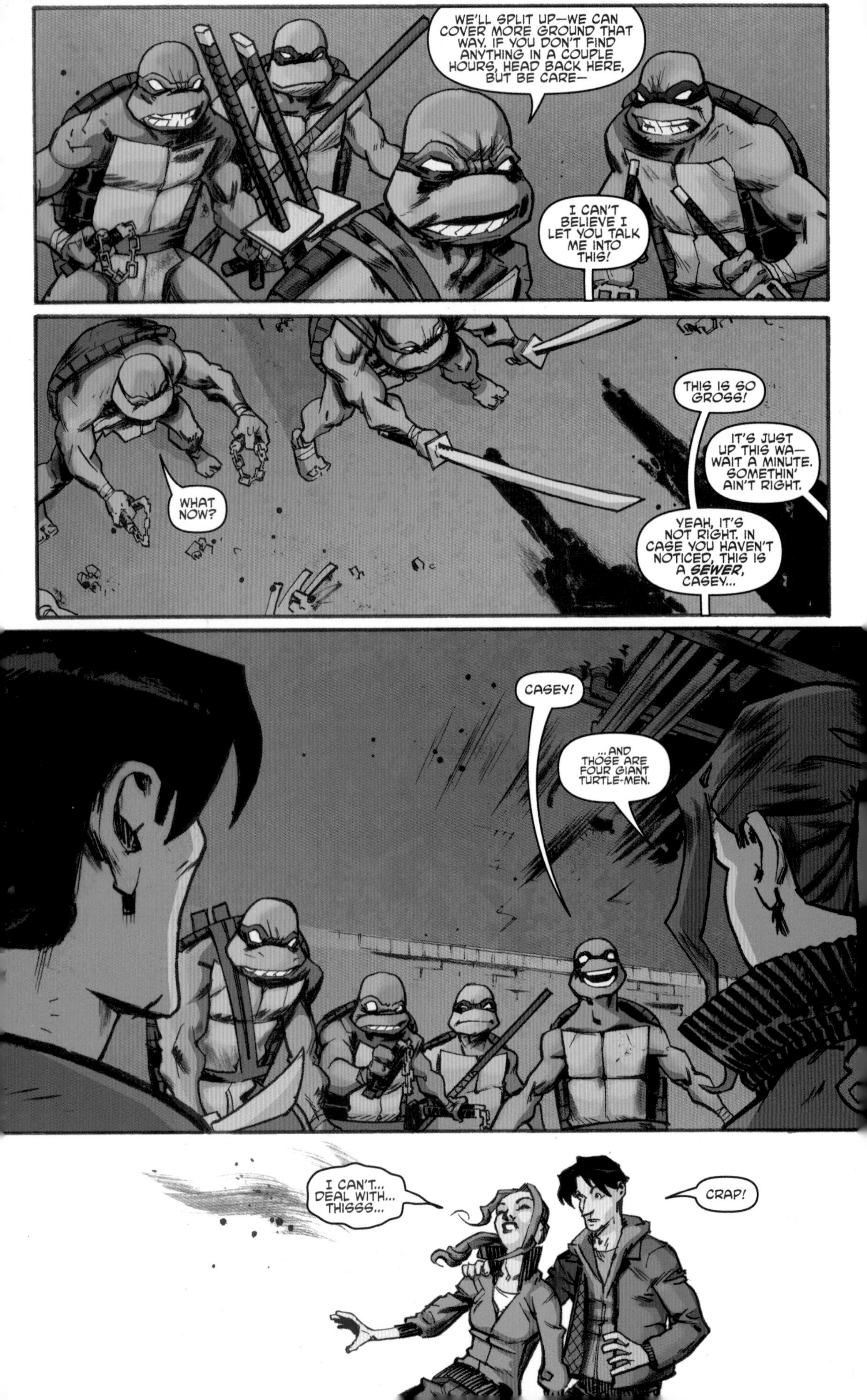
WE'LL SPLIT UP—WE CAN COVER MORE GROUND THAT WAY. IF YOU DON'T FIND ANYTHING IN A COUPLE HOURS, HEAD BACK HERE, BUT BE CARE—
I CAN'T BELIEVE I LET YOU TALK ME INTO THIS!
THIS IS SO GROSS!
WHAT NOW?
IT'S JUST UP THIS WA— WAIT A MINUTE. SOMETHIN' AIN'T RIGHT.
YEAH, IT'S NOT RIGHT. IN CASE YOU HAVEN'T NOTICED, THIS IS A SEWER, CASEY...
CASEY!
...AND THOSE ARE FOUR GIANT TURTLE-MEN.
I CAN'T... DEAL WITH... THISSS...
CRAP!

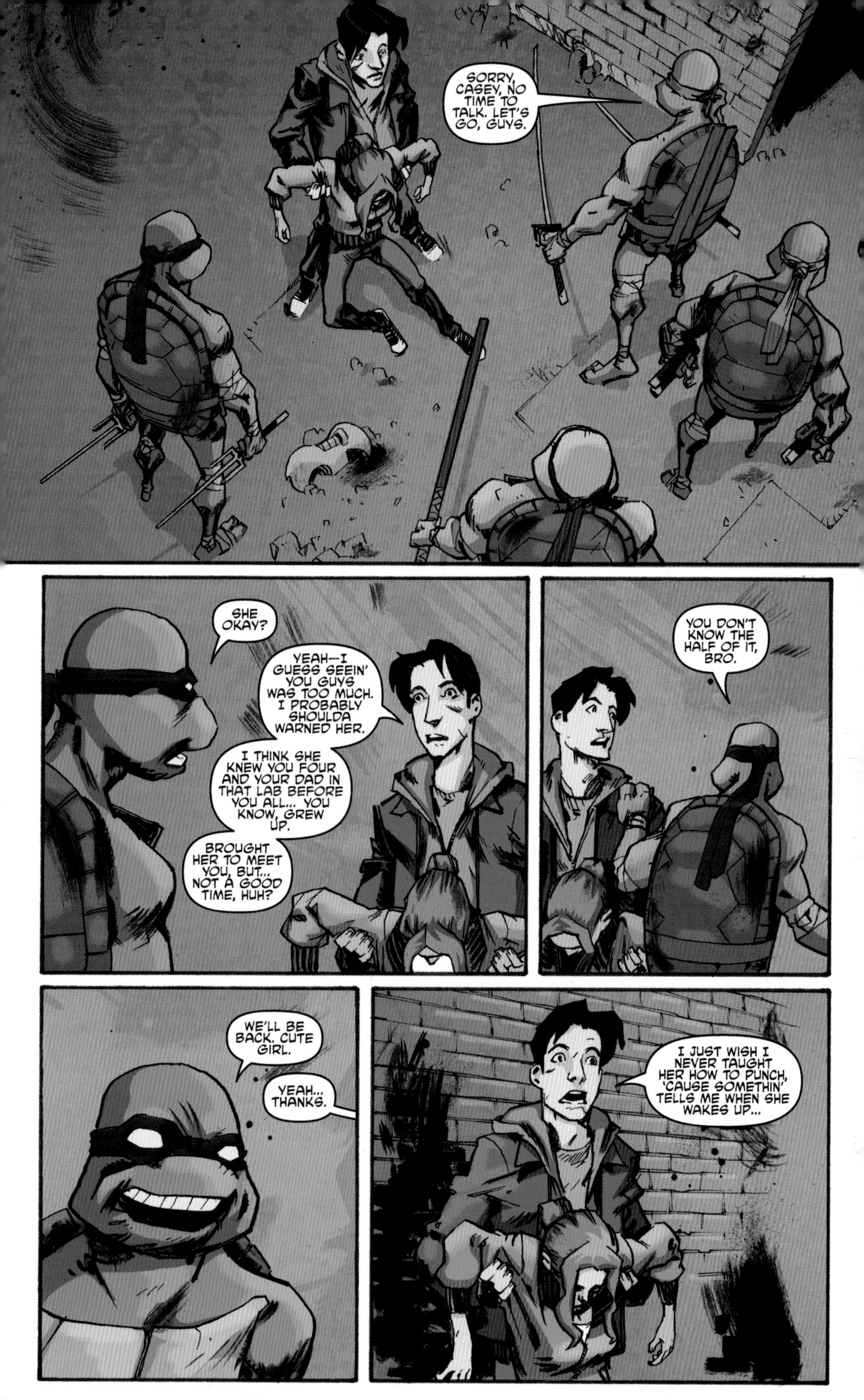
SORRY, CASEY, NO TIME TO TALK. LET'S GO, GUYS.
SHE OKAY?
YEAH—I GUESS SEEIN' YOU GUYS WAS TOO MUCH. I PROBABLY SHOULDA WARNED HER.
I THINK SHE KNEW YOU FOUR AND YOUR DAD IN THAT LAB BEFORE YOU ALL... YOU KNOW, GREW UP.
BROUGHT HER TO MEET YOU, BUT... NOT A GOOD TIME, HUH?
YOU DON'T KNOW THE HALF OF IT, BRO.
WE'LL BE BACK, CUTE GIRL.
YEAH... THANKS.
I JUST WISH I NEVER TAUGHT HER HOW TO PUNCH, 'CAUSE SOMETHIN' TELLS ME WHEN SHE WAKES UP...

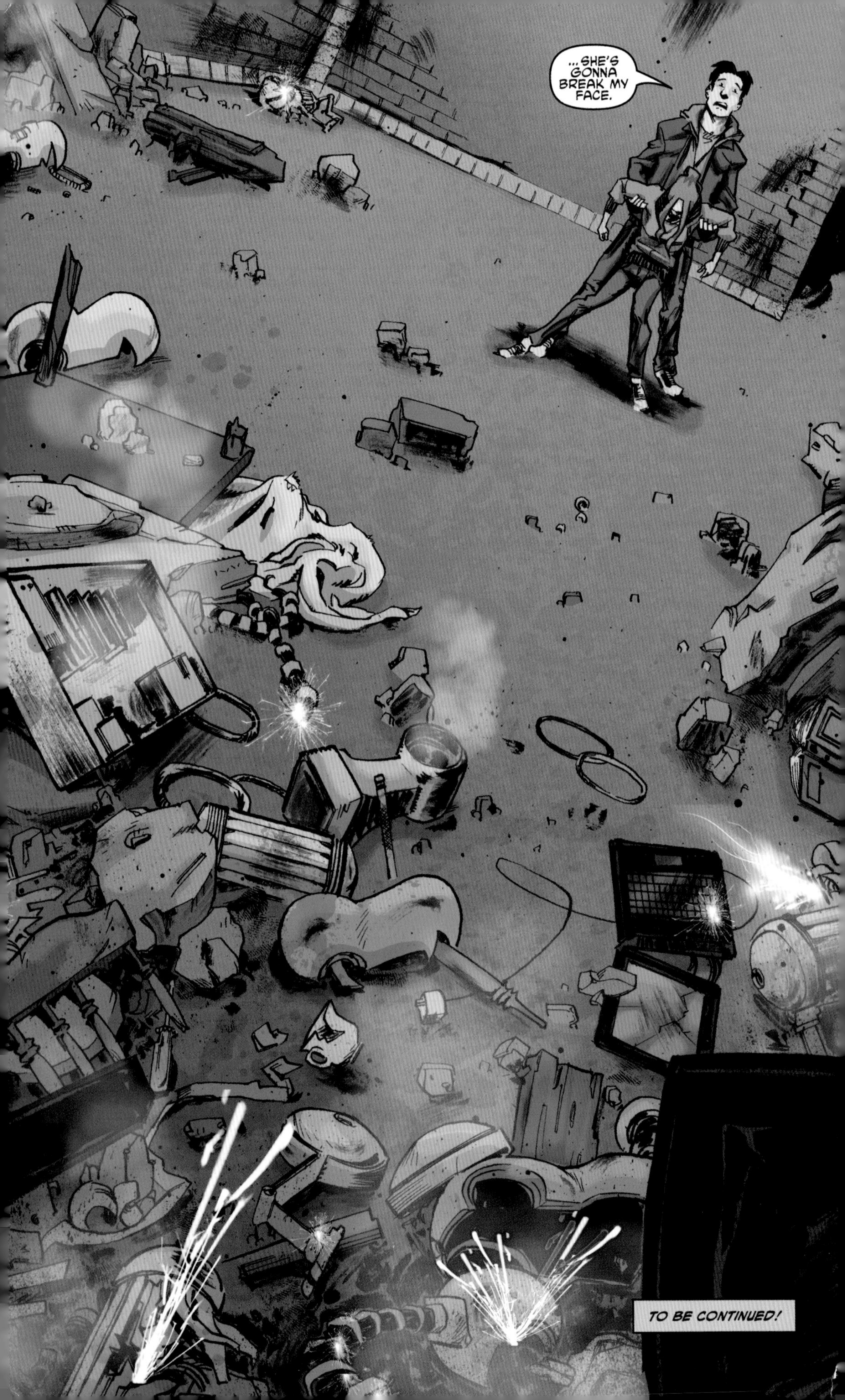
...SHE'S GONNA BREAK MY FACE.
TO BE CONTINUED!

ART GALLERY

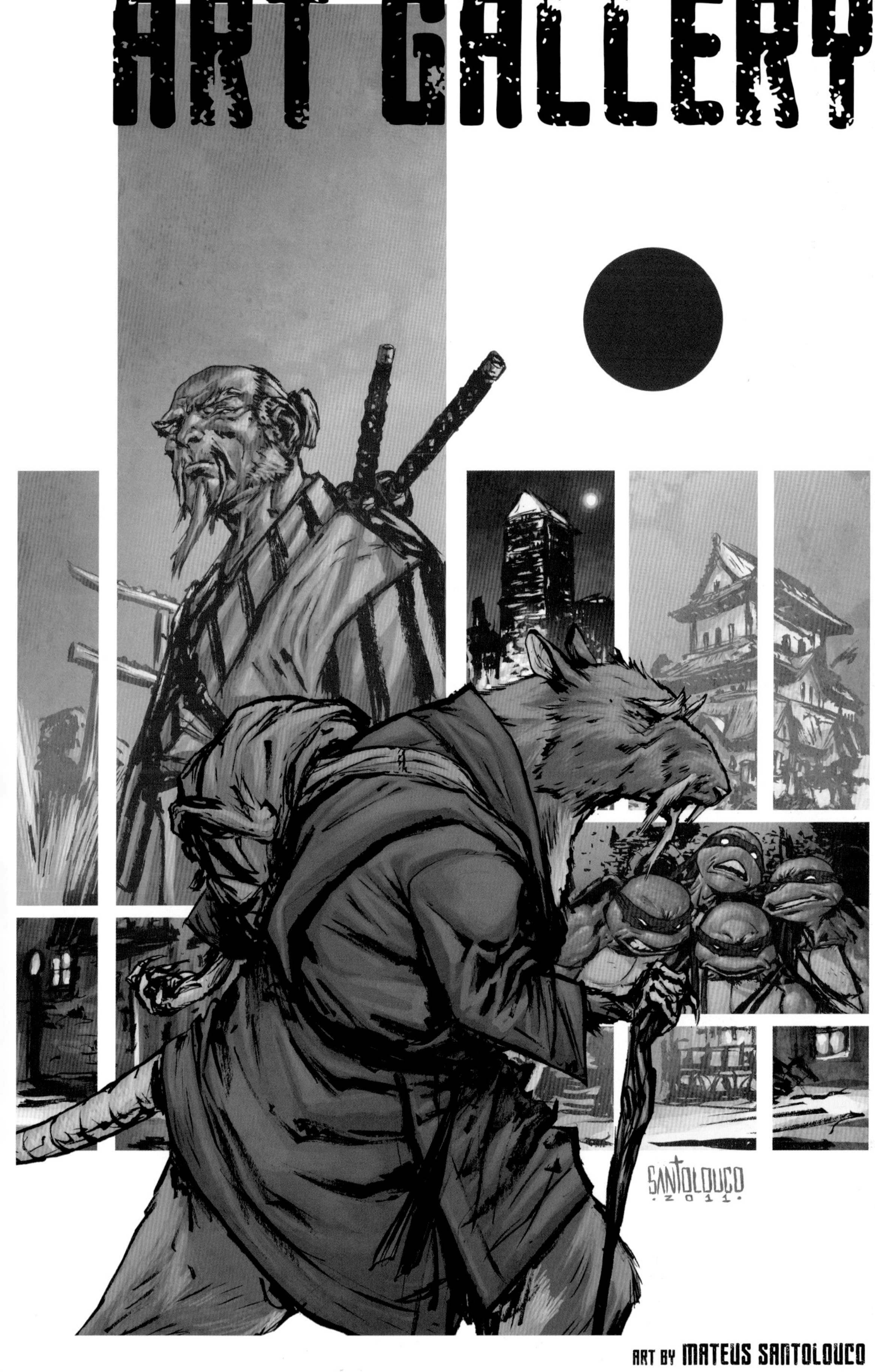
SANTOLOUCO
2011

ART BY MATEUS SANTOLOUCO

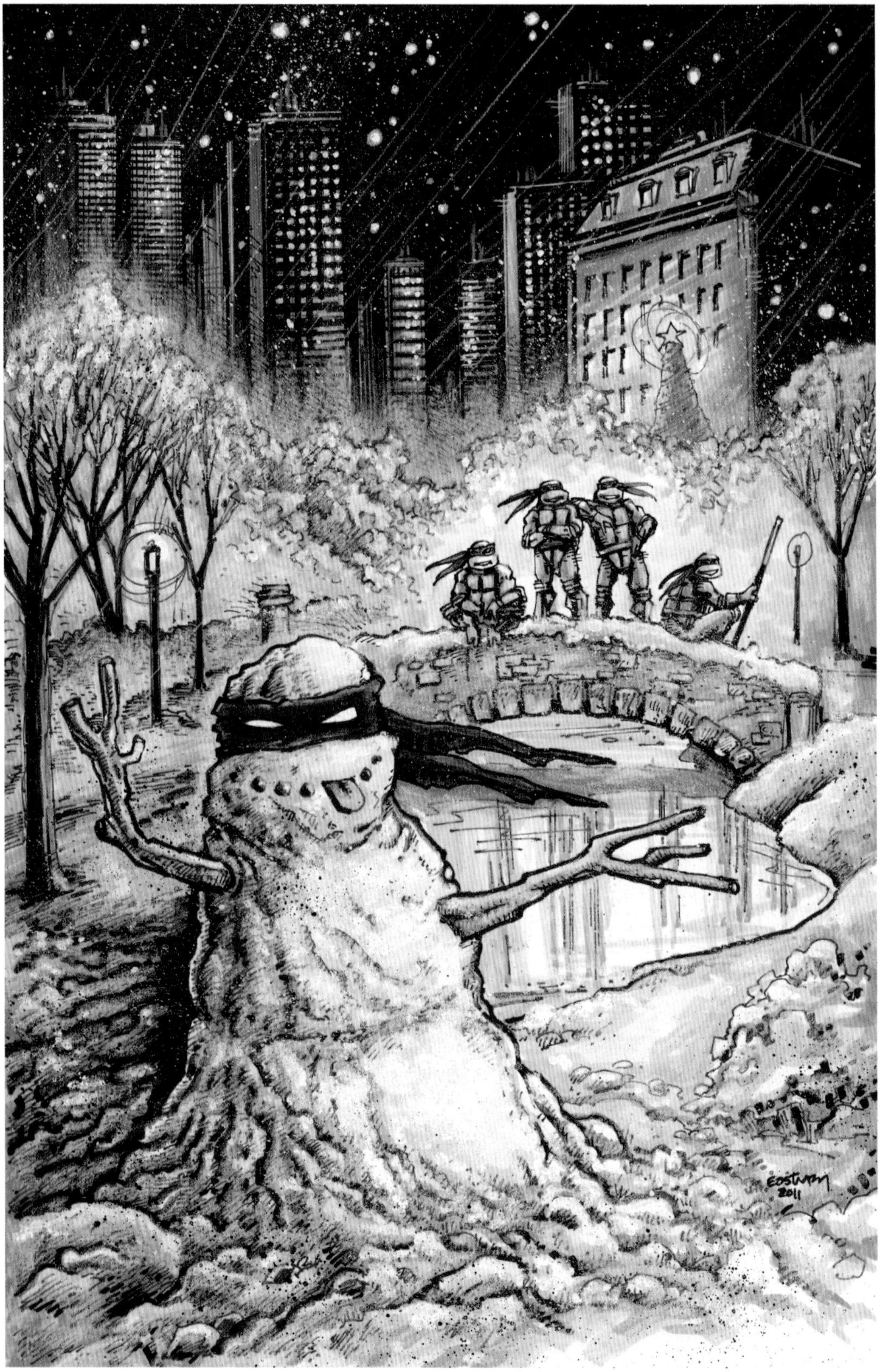
EASTMAN 2011

ART BY KEVIN EASTMAN

OPPOSITE PAGE ART BY KEVIN EASTMAN · COLORS BY RONDA PATTISON

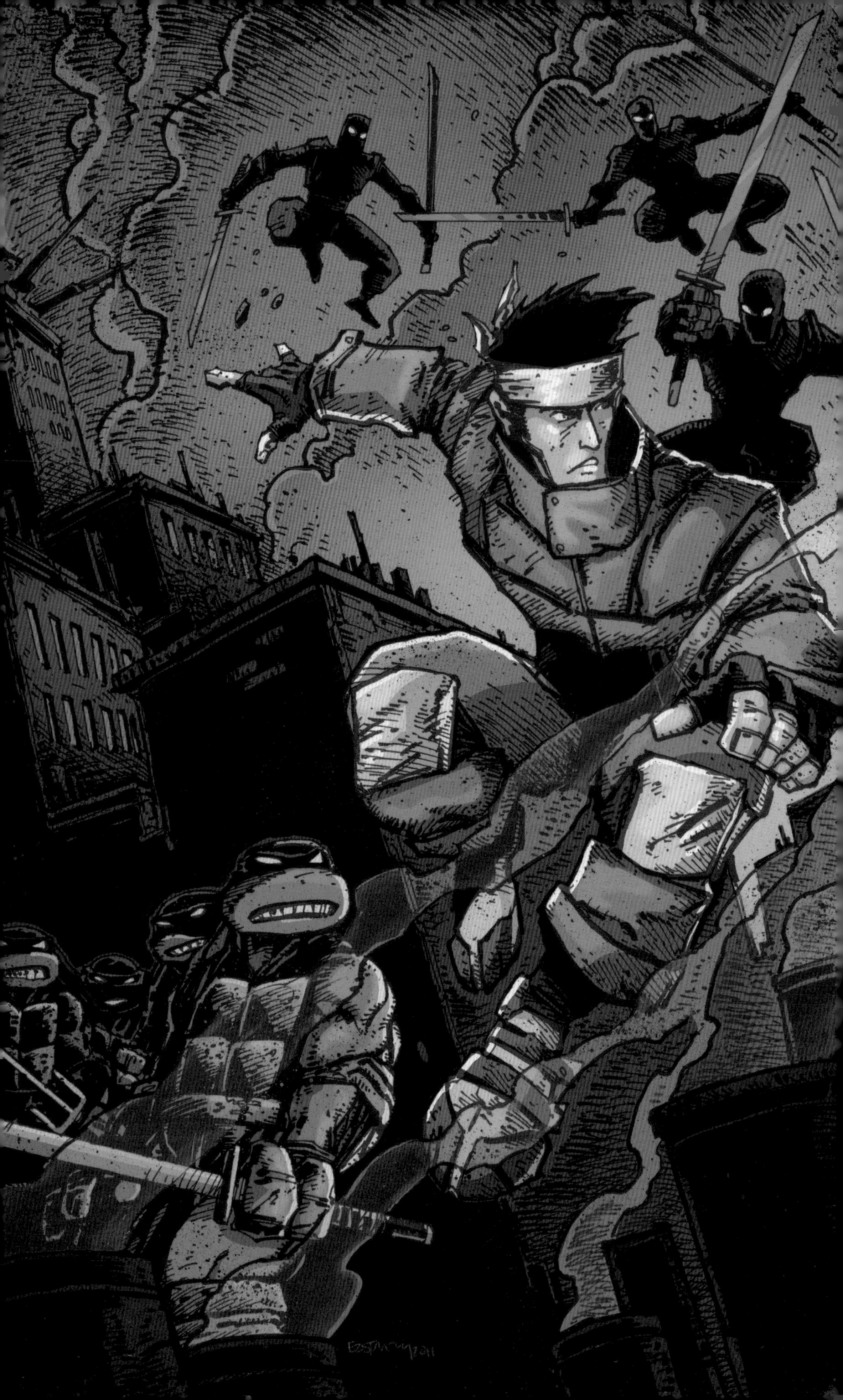

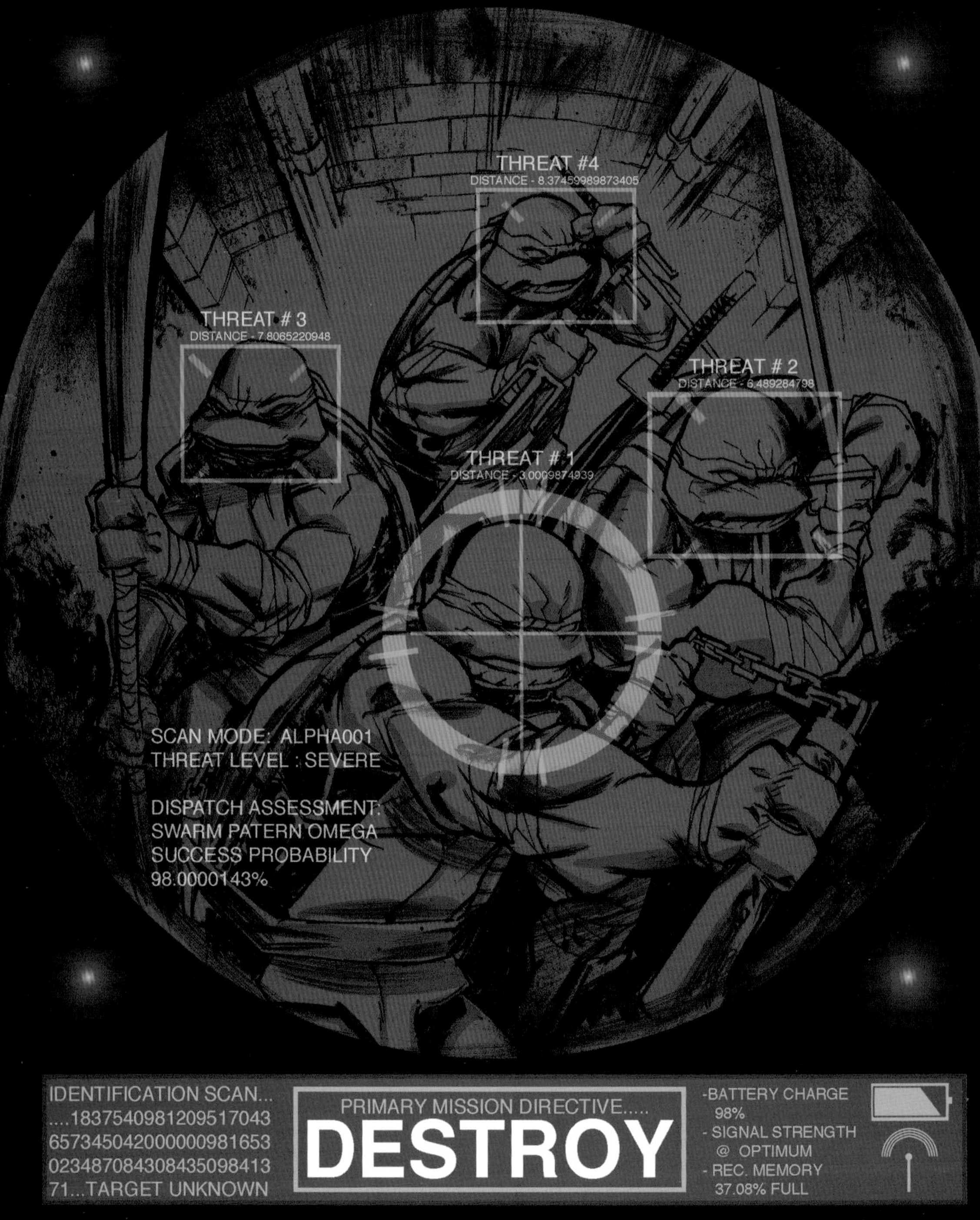
THREAT #4
DISTANCE - 8.37459989873405
THREAT # 3
DISTANCE - 7.8065220948
THREAT # 2
DISTANCE - 6.489284798
THREAT # 1
DISTANCE - 3.0009874939
SCAN MODE: ALPHA001
THREAT LEVEL : SEVERE
DISPATCH ASSESSMENT:
SWARM PATERN OMEGA
SUCCESS PROBABILITY
98.0000143%
IDENTIFICATION SCAN...
....18375409812095170436573450420000009816530234870843084350984137 1...TARGET UNKNOWN
PRIMARY MISSION DIRECTIVE.....
DESTROY
-BATTERY CHARGE
98%
- SIGNAL STRENGTH
@ OPTIMUM
- REC. MEMORY
37.08% FULL

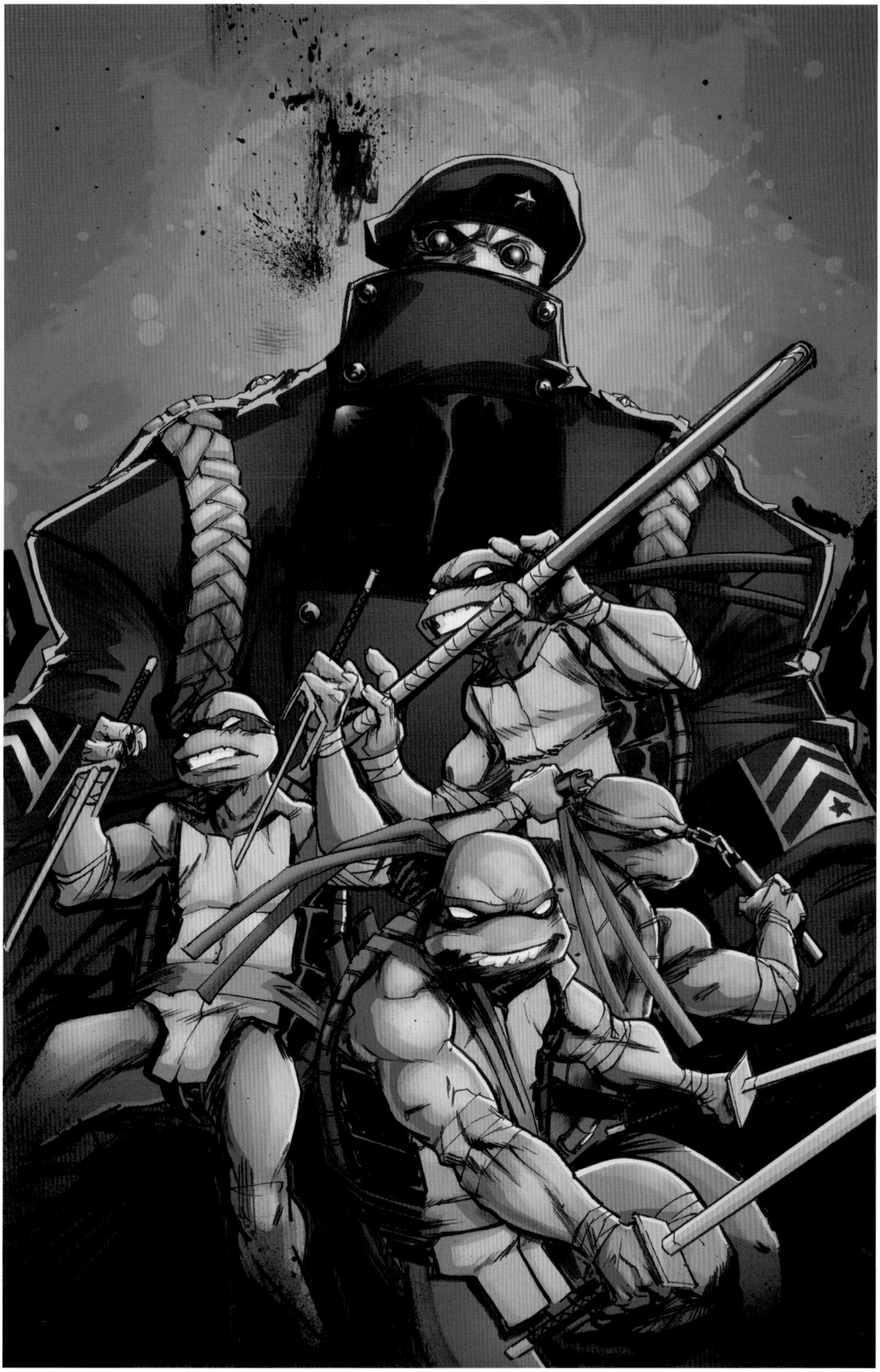

OPPOSITE AND THIS PAGE: ART BY **DAN DUNCAN** · THIS PAGE COLORS BY **RONDA PATTISON**

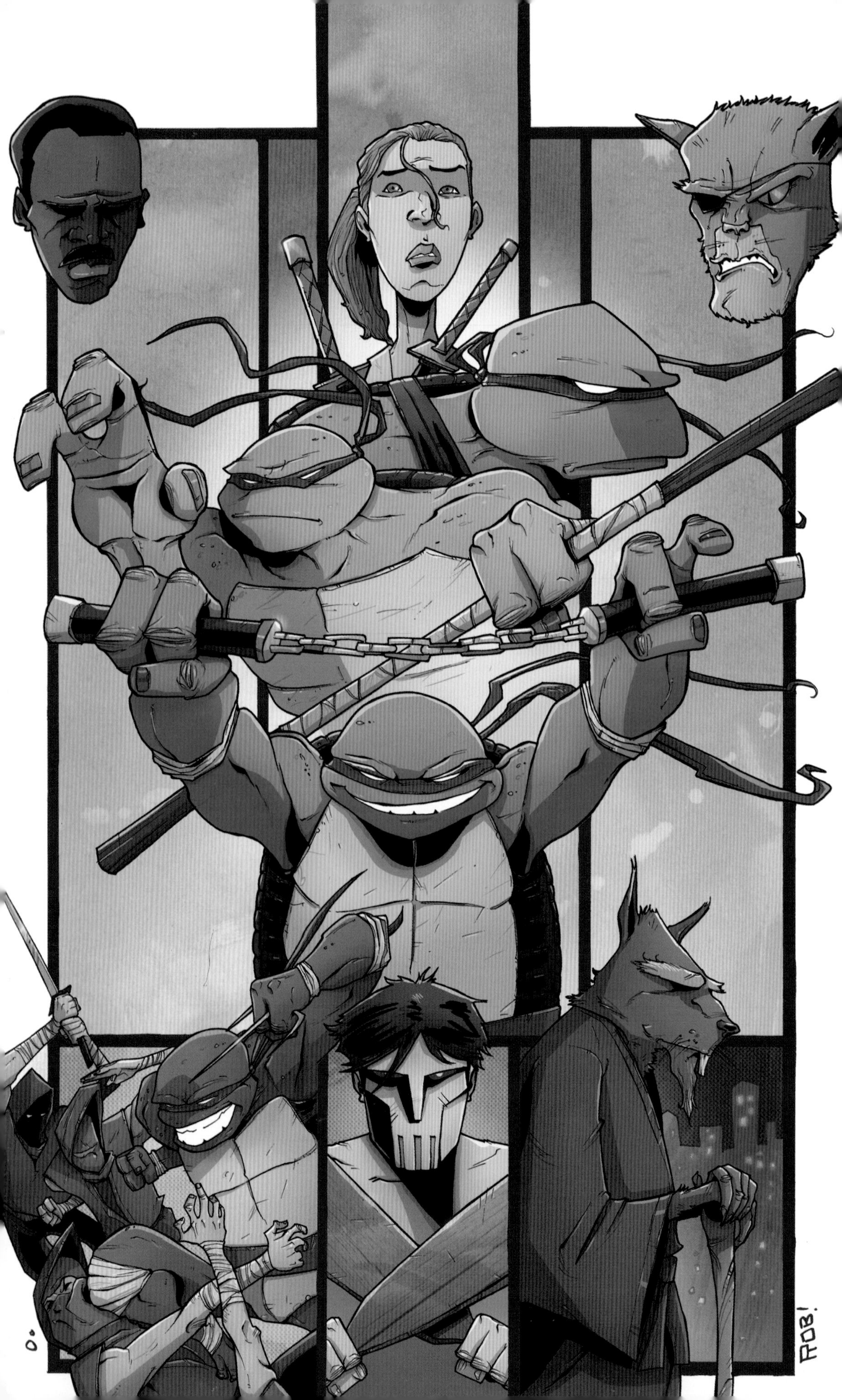
ROB!

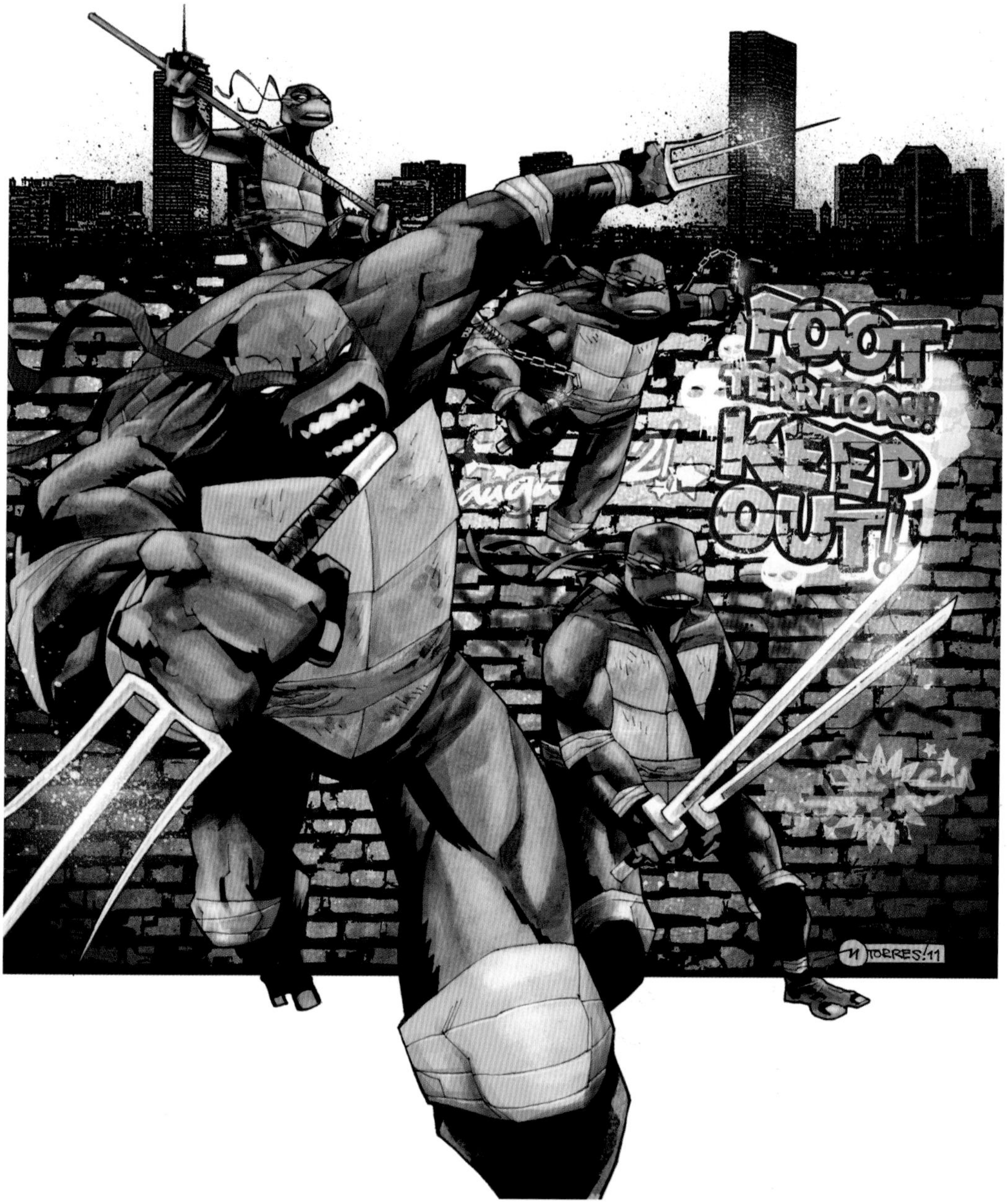
FOOT
TERRITORY!
KEEP
OUT!
M TORRES!11

ART BY MARK TORRES

OPPOSITE PAGE: ART BY ROB GUILLORY

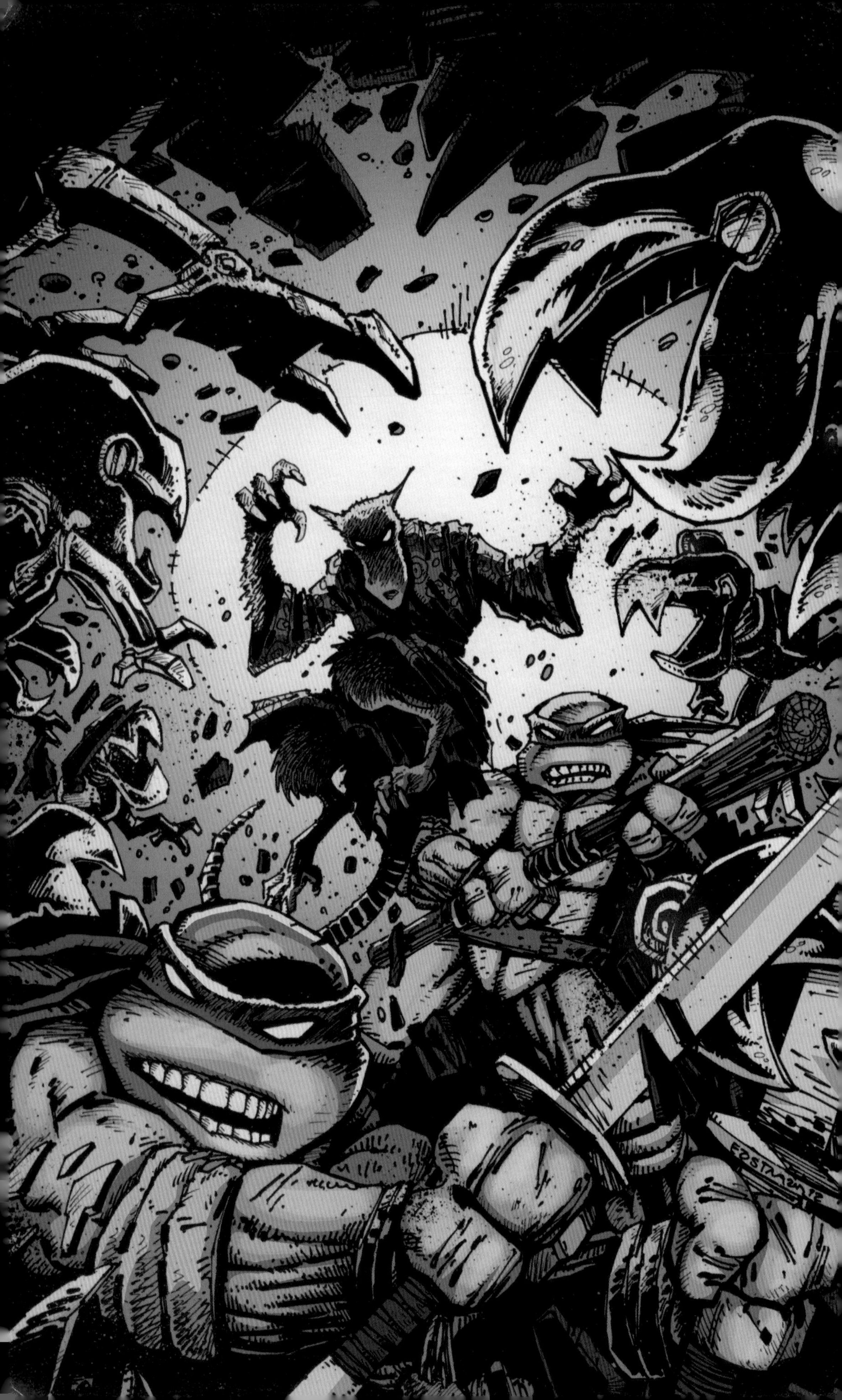

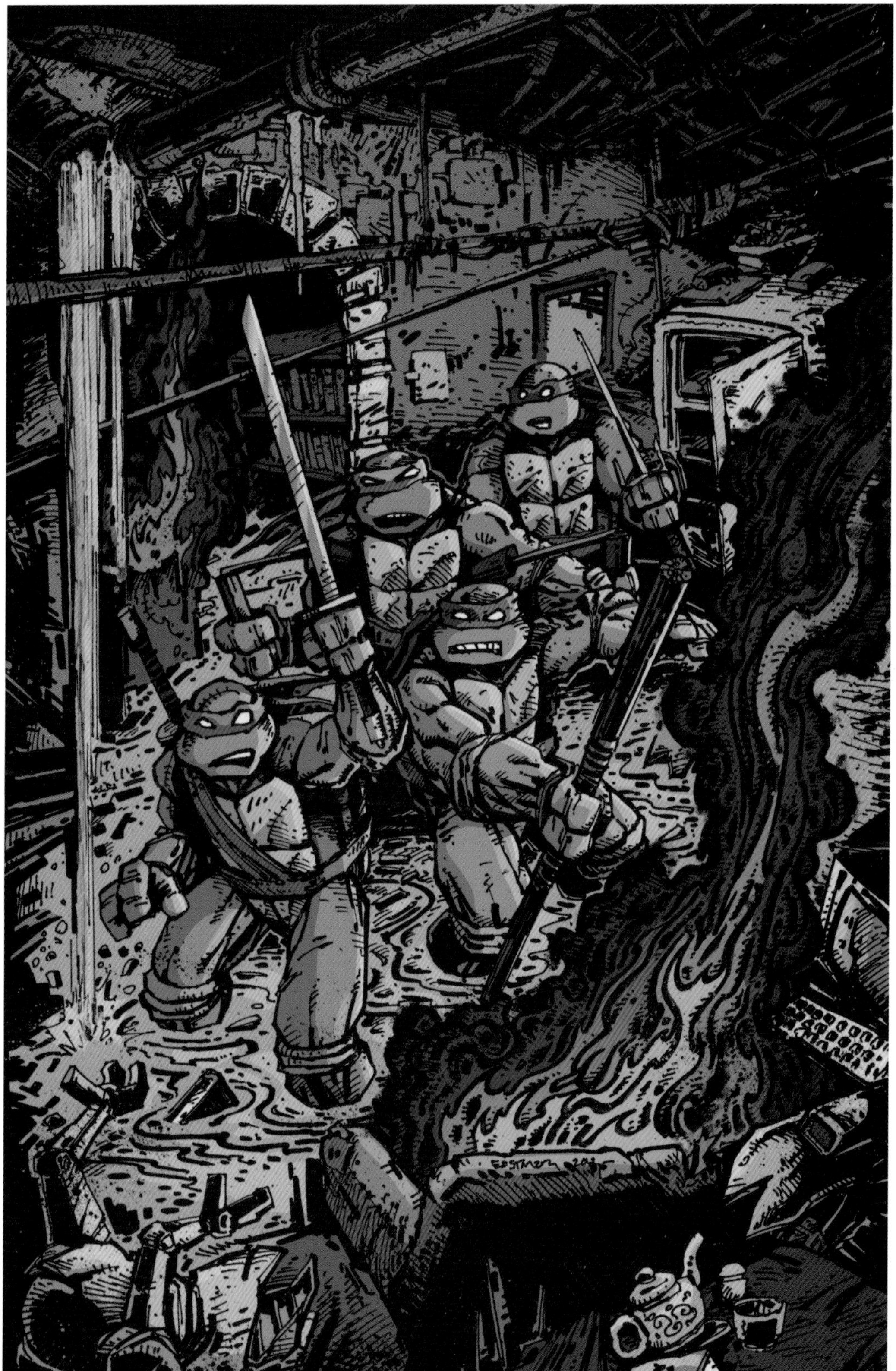

OPPOSITE AND THIS PAGE: ART BY KEVIN EASTMAN · COLORS BY RONDA PATTISON

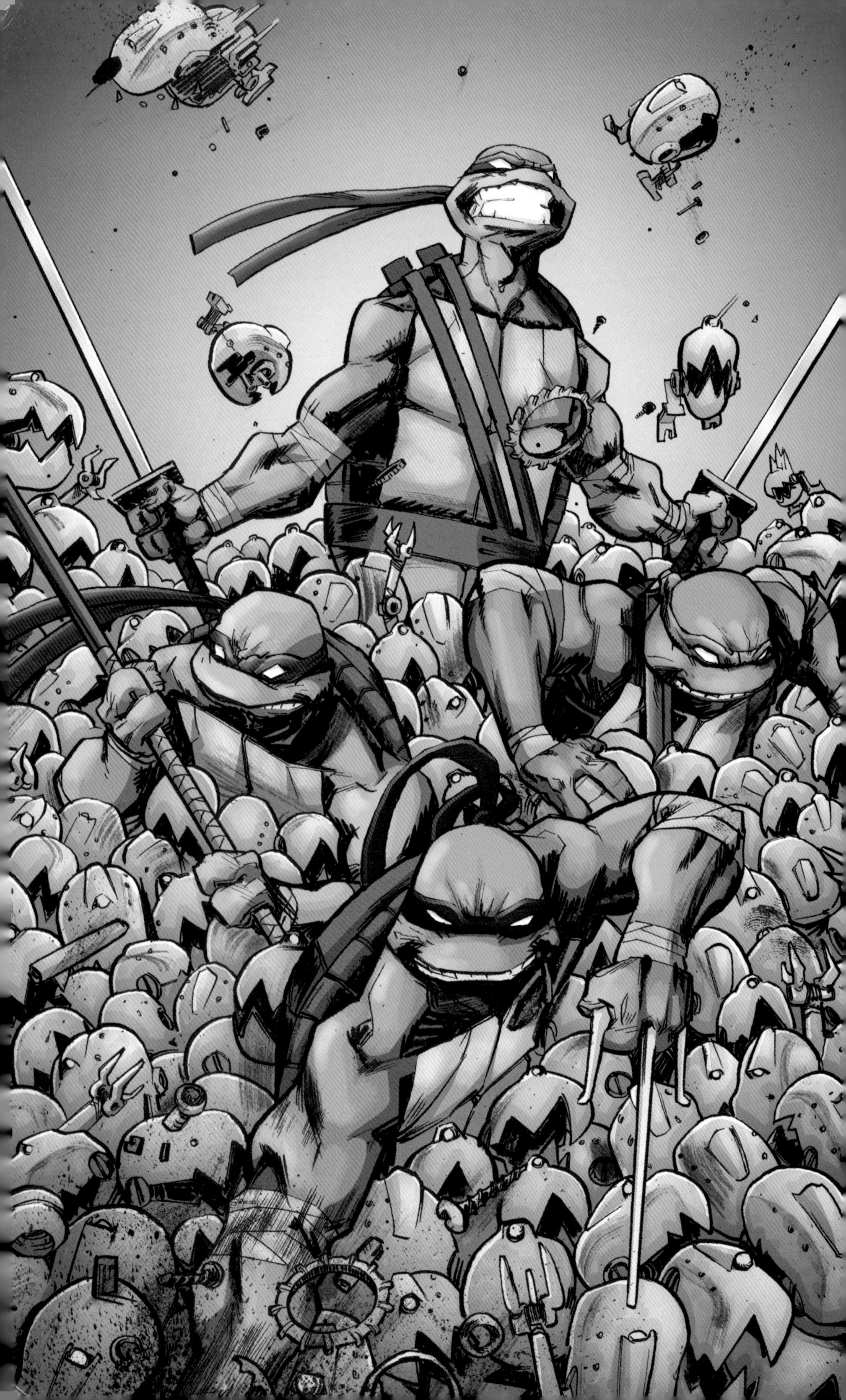

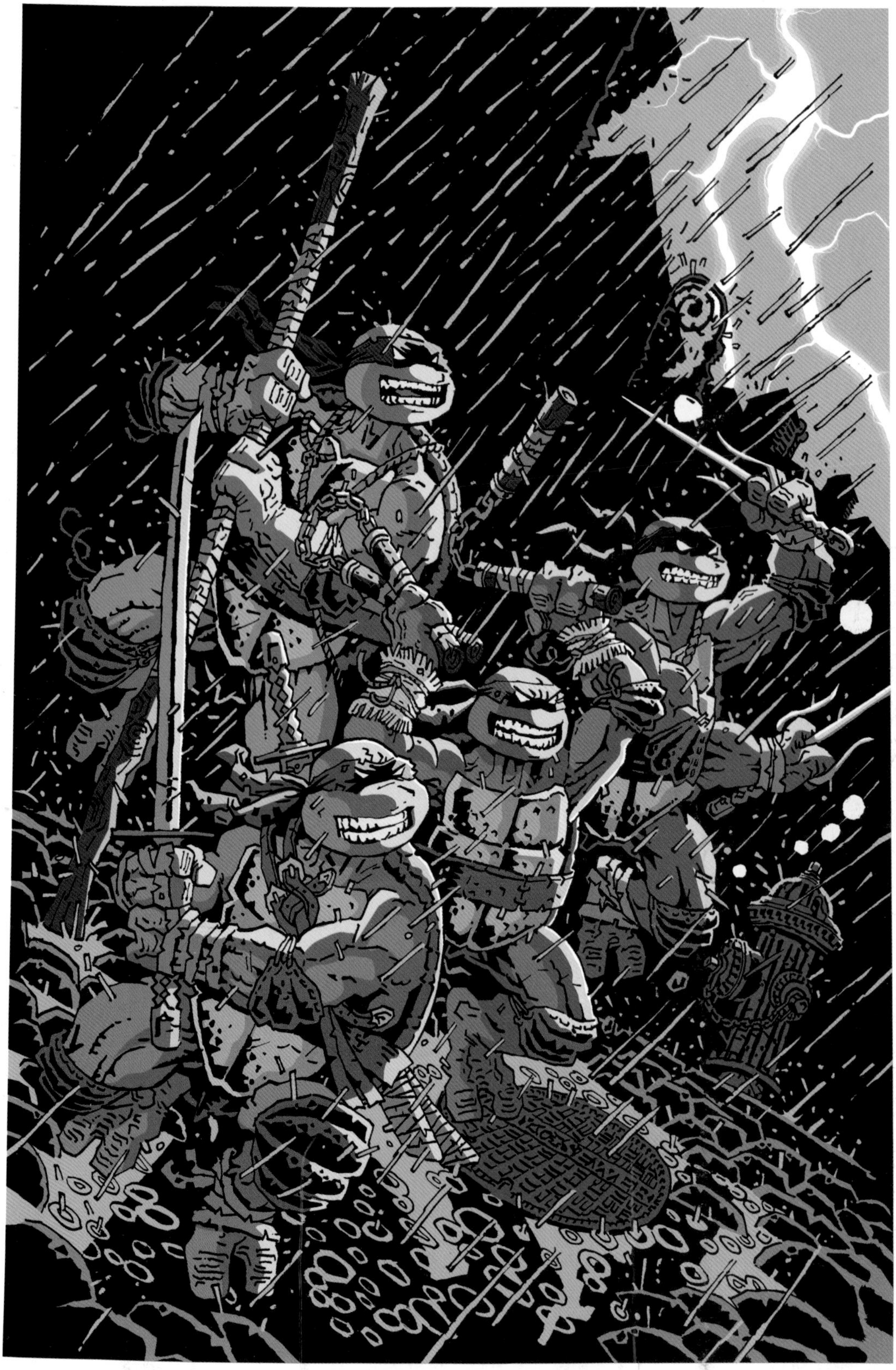

ART BY SIMON GANE · COLORS BY RONDA PATTISON

OPPOSITE PAGE: ART BY DAN DUNCAN · COLORS BY RONDA PATTISON

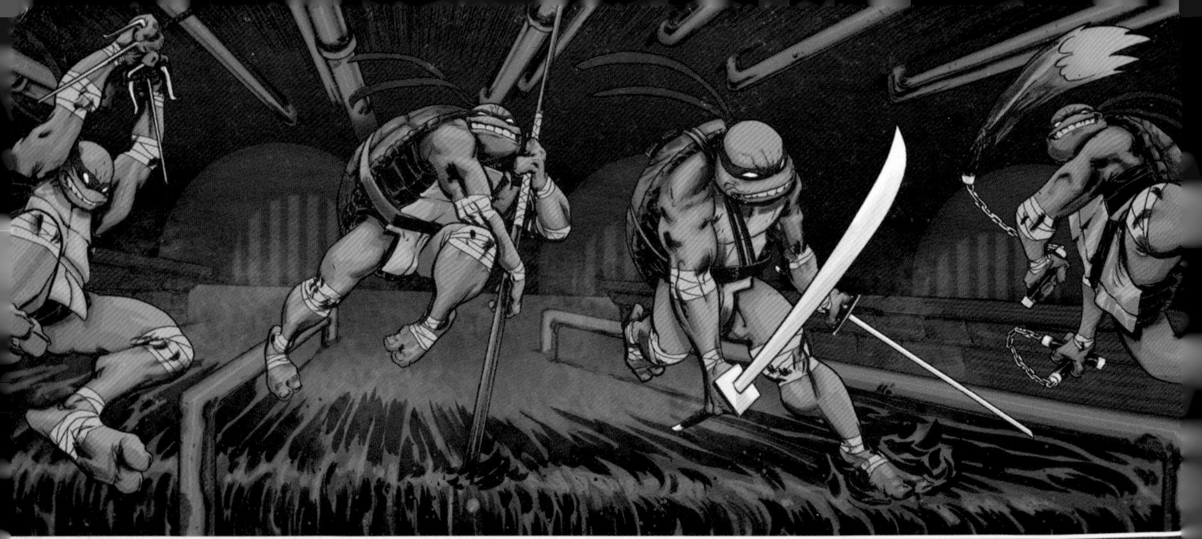

TEENAGE MUTANT NINJA TURTLES

MORE TURTLE ACTION!

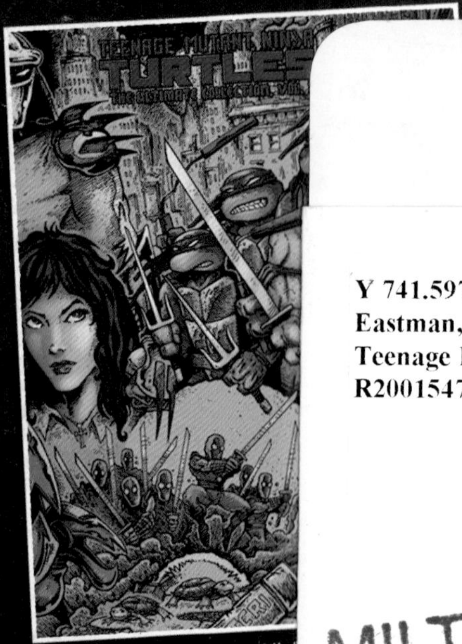

Teenage Mutant Ninj
The Ultimate Collect
ISBN: 978-1-6137

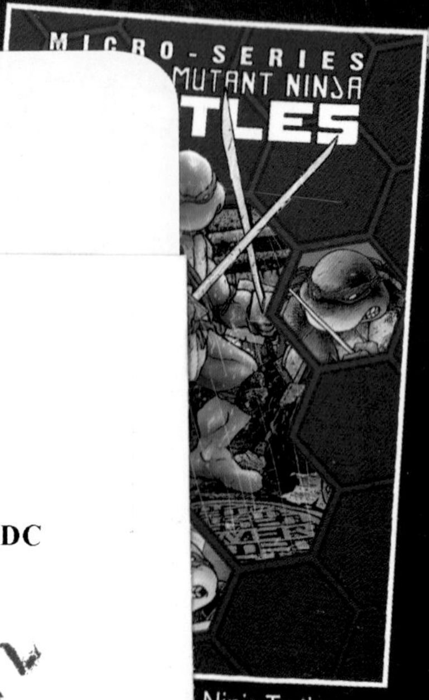

MICRO-SERIES
MUTANT NINJA
TLES

Ninja Turtles:
s, Vol. 1
377-232-4

E NOW
IDW